Studies in Caribbean Languages

Chief Editor: John R. Rickford
Managing Editor: Joseph T. Farquharson

In this series:

1. Irvine-Sobers, G. Alison. The acrolect in Jamaica: The architecture of phonological variation.

The acrolect in Jamaica

The architecture of phonological variation

G. Alison Irvine-Sobers

language science press

G. Alison Irvine-Sobers. 2018. *The acrolect in Jamaica: The architecture of phonological variation* (Studies in Caribbean Languages 1). Berlin: Language Science Press.

This title can be downloaded at:
http://langsci-press.org/catalog/book/203
© 2018, G. Alison Irvine-Sobers
Published under the Creative Commons Attribution 4.0 Licence (CC BY 4.0):
http://creativecommons.org/licenses/by/4.0/
ISBN: 978-3-96110-114-6 (Digital)
        978-3-96110-115-3 (Hardcover)

DOI:10.5281/zenodo.1306618
Source code available from www.github.com/langsci/203
Collaborative reading: paperhive.org/documents/remote?type=langsci&id=203

Cover and concept of design: Ulrike Harbort
Typesetting: Felix Kopecky
Proofreading: Amir Ghorbanpour, Amr Zawawy, Andreas Hölzl, Dietha Koster,
Eitan Grossman, Ezekiel Bolaji, Felix Hoberg, Gerald Delahunty, Ivica Jeđud,
Jean Nitzke, Jeroen van de Weijer & Rosetta Berger
Fonts: Linux Libertine, Libertinus Math, Arimo, DejaVu Sans Mono
Typesetting software: XƎLATEX

Language Science Press
Unter den Linden 6
10099 Berlin, Germany
langsci-press.org

Storage and cataloguing done by FU Berlin

Freie Universität Berlin

Contents

Abbreviations iii

1 Ideologies of the acrolect and English in Jamaica 1
  1.1 The (Jamaican) acrolect 1
  1.2 Sense 1: The acrolect as defined by structure 4
  1.3 Sense 2: The acrolect as the outcome of language acquisition . . 7
  1.4 Sense 3: The acrolect as defined by its speakers 13
  1.5 Sense 4: The acrolect as an idea of Jamaican English 18
  1.6 Aims and methods of the study 23
  1.7 Data collection 24

2 Phonological variation in the Jamaican acrolect 29
  2.1 Why consider phonological variation? 29
  2.2 The phonological variables and their variants 32
  2.3 Features commonly identified in the literature (Group A) 33
    2.3.1 Basic JC and JE phoneme inventories 35
    2.3.2 Word initial glottal fricative /h/ 35
    2.3.3 The interdental fricatives /θ/ and /ð/ 39
    2.3.4 The low back stressed vowel /ɔ/ 41
    2.3.5 Pre-consonantal/pre-rhotic mid tense vowels /e/ and /o/ 43
    2.3.6 The word initial velar stops /k/, /g/ 45
  2.4 Features not widely discussed in the literature (Group B) 47
    2.4.1 The word final unstressed vowel in words that end in -er 47
    2.4.2 The vowel in the final syllable -tion 48
    2.4.3 The alveopalatal affricate 49
    2.4.4 Post-vocalic rhoticity 52
    2.4.5 Word-final clusters 54
  2.5 Discussion 58

3 Sociolinguistic variation in Jamaican English 63
  3.1 Level of education 63
    3.1.1 Group A variables and education 66

Contents

      3.1.2   Group B variables and education   71
3.2   Gender   78
      3.2.1   Group A variables and gender   81
      3.2.2   Group B variables and gender   86
3.3   Parent's background   92
      3.3.1   Group A variables and background   95
      3.3.2   Group B variables and background   98
3.4   Speaker age   101
      3.4.1   Group A variables and age   103
      3.4.2   Group B variables and age   106
3.5   Hypercorrection in the JAMPRO sample   109
3.6   Constructing the acrolect, Standard Jamaican English   114

4 Sociolinguistic Variation in JAMPRO   **121**
4.1   JAMPRO: One site of promoting a SJE ideology   121
      4.1.1   Jamaican institutional discourses on language   122
      4.1.2   The JIDC/JAMPRO: Their construct of the Jamaican lan-
               guage situation   128
4.2   Frontline staff – The public face of JAMPRO   132
      4.2.1   Group A variables in frontline staff   140
      4.2.2   Group B variables in frontline staff   142
4.3   Discussion   144

5 Conclusion   **149**
5.1   The architecture of phonological variation in the Jamaican acrolect   150
5.2   An endonormative definition of SJE phonological features . . .   157

Appendix A: Prepared script for all interviews of JAMPRO informants **161**
A.1   Personal data collected   161
A.2   Data on patterns of workplace interaction   162
A.3   Data on working at JAMPRO   162

Appendix B: Profiles of JAMPRO informants   **163**

Appendix C: Parent's Occupation   **167**

References   **169**

Index   **183**
    Name index   183
    Subject index   187

Abbreviations

AJE	Acrolectal Jamaican English
CXC	Caribbean Examinations Council
EBE	Educated Belizean English
IAE	Internationally Acceptable English
JAMPRO	Jamaica Promotions
JIDC	Jamaica Industrial Development Corporation
JNEC	Jamaica National Export Company
JNIP	Jamaica National Investment Promotions
JSA	JAMPRO Staff Association
JTB	Jamaica Tourist Board
KMA	Kingston Metropolitan Area
MSE	Metropolitan Standard English
PJS	Putative Jamaican Standard
SJE	Standard Jamaican English

1 Ideologies of the acrolect and English in Jamaica

1.1 The (Jamaican) acrolect

The Jamaican language situation was described very early on by linguists such as Le Page (1960) and DeCamp (1961; 1971) as a linguistic continuum, formed primarily from the historical sociolinguistic contact of speakers of various Niger-Congo languages and several dialects of English. Similar continua have also been identified in Guyana, Belize, Trinidad and Barbados (see the discussion in Winford 1997: 233–236). The polar varieties of this theoretical construct, the continuum, are basilectal Creole and "standard" English (discussed below), which have been treated as separate linguistic systems by some linguists (for example Bailey 1971 (Jamaica); Devonish 1978 (Guyana), and more generally Alleyne 1980 and Winford 1997) and which are linked by a seamless range of intermediate lects identified as the mesolect.

These intermediate varieties have been explained in a number of ways. They have been attributed to: decreolization (Bickerton 1973; DeCamp 1971), due to the targeting of English by Creole speakers with varying levels of access to the prestige or high variety; or to basilectalization brought about by increasing numbers of West Africans arriving over time and acquiring approximations of approximations of English (Mufwene 1996; 2001)[1]; or to the social stratification of plantation communities from the earliest stages of language contact (Alleyne 1980). This continuum is depicted as

> ... a continuous spectrum of speech varieties whose extremes are mutually unintelligible, but which also includes all possible intermediate varieties (DeCamp 1971: 28), ranging from the speech of the most backward peasant or labourer to that of the well-educated urban professional (DeCamp 1961: 82).

---

[1]Chaudenson (2001) describes a similar process of basilectalization for French-lexicon Creoles.

It is to this sociolinguistic discussion that W. A. Stewart (1965: 15–16) added the terms *acrolect* and *basilect*, (the label *mesolect* came later). In his description of "Washington Negro speech" he wrote,

> I will refer to this topmost dialect in the local sociolinguistic hierarchy as *acrolect* (from *acro-* "apex" plus *-lect* as in dialect). In most cases what is meant by "Standard English" is either acrolect or something close to it. At the other extreme is a kind of speech which I refer to hereafter as *basilect* (from *basi-* "bottom"). (...) In between basilect and acrolect, there are a number of other dialect strata, and it is in this middle range that the majority of adult Washington Negroes probably belongs.

Acrolect, the focus of this dissertation, is the name for the upper end of the continuum and, while in many cases the term is not explicitly used, it has been defined in the literature in a number of clearly related ways. General descriptions of acrolect speak of,

- the "topmost dialect in the local sociolinguistic hierarchy" (W. A. Stewart 1965: 15);

- the stereotype of the educated standard, focussed by institutions of education, the media, and white collar employment (Le Page 1988: 34–35);

- a "high, prestigious language or variety of a language" in *any* speech community (McArthur 1998: xvii).

Acrolect here is essentially a community of speakers' idea of the speech patterns of those positioned at the top and centre of their social space. It is in particular speakers, in those perceived to be of relatively high social status, that we initially locate the acrolect in a community and idealise their ways of speaking as "good" or necessary. This then makes the acrolect coterminous with "the standard" for members of communities with that type of metalinguistic labelling. This view of the acrolect is also reflected in many of the definitions applied to the Caribbean generally and Jamaica specifically:

- the educated counterpart of the lexifier in the Creole speech community (Chaudenson 2001: xi (n1));

- the English of educated nationals of the Caribbean used in formal social contexts, bound to a common core of morphology and syntax shared with "Internationally Accepted English" (Allsopp 1996: lvi);

- the speech of those with high education, typically urban residence and the higher socio-economic status that comes with certain (non-manual) occupations (DeCamp 1961; 1971 who used the speech of Philip Sherlock and Norman Manley as examples).

Central to these views of the acrolect is the speaker, as it is a particular set of speaker variables that are typically associated with and used to identify the acrolect in specific communities.

In another approach, the acrolect has been defined by its structures or in relation to the structures of other varieties that coexist with it in the community:

- the local standard, similar to other standard Englishes except in "a few phonological details and a handful of lexical items" (Bickerton 1975: 24);

- the variety or varieties used in Jamaica that are structurally farthest removed from the Creole, i.e. basilect (Akers 1981: 73; Bailey 1971: 342 for example).

Finally, the acrolect is seen as the outcome of Creole speakers' acquisition of an idealised superstrate that is (and was) the target in language contact:

- a non-native version, derived from spontaneous or guided learning, of the standard language (Escure 1997: 67).

We can abstract from the above that the acrolect has been defined,

1. in terms of its structure, and this includes not only its relationship to English, say, but also its relationship to the Creole basilect;

2. as a consequence of language acquisition, as it is suggested that the acrolect is the learned English of Caribbean peoples who are not themselves vernacular speakers of English;

3. sociolinguistically, in relation to its speakers and the situational contexts in which these speakers use language, i.e. the formal, public speech of those with high social status;

4. ideologically, an idea of English that is legitimised by institutions that construct norms by their own expectations and practice.

1.2 Sense 1: The acrolect as defined by structure

The focus of research in Caribbean continuum situations has, understandably, been the Creole basilect, the less well-known variety to linguists. This has generally meant that the speaker's central role in the characterization of lects along the continuum has been overshadowed by the search for what Bailey (1971: 341) called "neat, clearly defined patterns of behaviour" and the analysis of idealised basilectal linguistic systems. This process of erasure or selective disattention to "often unruly forms of variation" (Kroskrity 2000: 23) is no doubt driven by the requirements of linguistic description (J. Milroy 1999: 33); but it is also, ironically, a reflection of the way speakers themselves construct language and language use, particularly in the process of social differentiation (J. Irvine & Gal 2000: 38). Jamaicans, for example, tend to see the local language situation in terms of what we Jamaicans call Patwa and English, and to produce speech in a socio-functional relationship that would accurately be described as diglossic (Akers 1981: 8; Winford 1985, Devonish & Harry 2004: 256). This has had consequences for the study of the continuum generally, but in particular the acrolect, because the underlying system that generates acrolectal speech is thought by both the speaker and the linguist to be no different from that of other Englishes. Therefore, much of the literature assumes, but has not verified, the features associated with the acrolect (Akers 1981: 73; Bailey 1971: 342; Mufwene 2001: 209 n6; Patrick 1999, Patrick 2000: 11; Winford 1991) even when making passing reference to "a local standard". With few exceptions (see below), this local standard has not itself been the focus of research as most linguists presumably already know the structural properties of English and are seeking to uncover those of the Creole. In this respect, these studies are following in an earlier ideological tradition, described by J. Irvine & Gal (2000), which in practice meant that

> "once a variety has been declared to belong to the 'same' language as another, already-described variety, there was no reason to investigate it..." (57).

Additionally, and indeed *because* this "local standard" is putatively not so different, metropolitan Standard English (MSE hereafter) has been used not only to compare but to typologize structures found along the continuum[2], particularly the morphology and syntax but also the phonology (J. C. Wells 1982c: 575). As Alleyne pointed out over two decades ago, Creole languages are compared with Standard Written English of the most formal registers (1980: 16).

---

[2]J. Milroy (1999: 33 in particular) discusses the effect of a standard language ideology on the investigation and description of "less well-known languages".

A few examples can be used to illustrate the approach. Firstly, the negative past particle *neva*, in the sentence *Jan neva tiif di moni* 'John did not steal the money', has been analysed syntactically as Creole (Bailey 1966) or as non-acrolectal (Escure 2000: 141; Schneider 1998: 217) even though it is used as a negative preterite marker throughout the Jamaican continuum (as in *John never stole the money* or in the following: Speaker A – *Give Damian back his book*; Speaker B – *What? I never borrowed it*). This type of analysis is not limited to contact situations like Jamaica. As Cheshire (1999: 133) points out, the construction *never* + V-ed when used like this (in MSE) is "...frequently label[led] (...) as 'non-standard', despite the fact that the contexts occur in educated speech and writing".

Secondly, Meade (2001), in his study of phonological acquisition in Jamaican children, uses MSE phonology to determine what he labels acrolectal phonological features. Some of his Jamaican children are said to be acquiring at least one feature either late or at the mesolectal level (162) – in this case the interdental fricative – because they continue to vary them with dental stops up to ages 4-6 in words that would have [ð] or [θ] in MSE. Both explanations of his results are based on an idea of acrolect that reflects both an external model as well as an idealization of that model of English. One must therefore ask what children in Jamaica are likely to actually hear around them from local models of English, and should that English be treated as "falling short", i.e. non-acrolectal, when it does not resemble the external ideal. Meade does compare the children's output with that of their caregivers in his study and concludes that frequency of use by caregivers of a particular feature is crucial to the rate of acquisition of the children (161). However, Meade treats interdental fricatives and their variants as if they pattern as they do in MSE, i.e. he does not distinguish voiced from voiceless when describing the significance of the feature to Jamaican English which, as he puts it, is "ranked very high on the implicational scale of the Creole continuum" (162). It may well be that the local use of interdental fricatives and their variants differs from that of MSE (see §3.6).

Finally, Akers (1981: 8) argues that the speech of British, American and Canadian tourists provides *one* prestige model for Jamaicans. This suggests that for Akers these three phonetically different varieties are idealized as one "English", notwithstanding the distinctiveness the speakers of the varieties seem to claim when labelling even their Standards. Here, arguably, metropolitan varieties of spoken English are also being characterized as "Standard Written English of the most formal registers", notwithstanding the problems of doing so at the phonological level.

Akers's (1981: 73) description of the acrolect as a rhotic variety was based largely on his analysis of the Creole basilect as non-rhotic, and not on the actual production of acrolectal speakers. His pool of informants consisted of 10 relatively young people (the oldest was 33 years old), only one of whom could have been characterized as having the kind of background typically associated with the acrolectal speaker, a female college graduate. As such, his conception of the acrolect is a sort of *anti*-Creole that stands in opposition to the basilect structurally. Patrick's (2000) is too. While he does not explicitly characterize the acrolect in his analysis of variation in Veeton, he also proceeds like Akers, Meade and Wells when he states that,

> ... variables are here counted in their presence or absence so that maximum usage approximates to the acrolectal standard, i.e. absence of (KYA) [kja ~ kʰa] ... testing the assumption that higher status speakers favour acrolectal speech more often. (Patrick 2000: 11)

What seems to have emerged is a kind of circularity in the definition of the polar varieties on the (Jamaican) continuum that, typically, takes this form: a) Since the acrolect is not unlike other standard Englishes, phonologically as in [kʰ] (in a word like *cat*) or morpho-syntactically as in *did not take*; then b) the basilect reflects structures that are maximally divergent from the acrolect – [kj] or *no ben ~ neva tek*; as such, c) acrolectal speech is maximally non-basilectal and can therefore be expected to produce the forms [kʰ] or *did not take*. Moreover, this circularity extends to the identification of so-called basilectal speakers, so that samples of speech collected in the field are rejected when they are "too English" and therefore "noncreole" (Escure 1997: 74 commenting on the general practice of creolists), because the linguist already knows what is *supposed* to be basilectal.

One way of accommodating the above conception of the acrolect, is, on one hand, the catch-all term "upper-mesolectal" (Bickerton 1975: 161–162 for example) for those forms that do not pattern like those of MSE but have features found elsewhere in the continuum. Patrick (2002: 17) tells us that,

> Speaky-spoky is associated with lower mesolectal and basilectal speakers because of their distance from the standard; and it is associated with 'mistakes', failed attempts to speak a metropolitan prestige variety that is not native to these speakers. (*Acrolectal and upper mesolectal speakers are viewed as using Standard Jamaican English appropriately, and not making linguistic errors in its use*, despite the variation in their spoken and written speech) [My emphasis].

In this description "the standard" is MSE, the prestige target variety, and not Standard Jamaican English (SJE hereafter), the variety used appropriately by both acrolectal *and* upper mesolectal speakers. It is therefore not clear why this distinction is being made, though this could be interpreted as defining acrolectal and upper mesolectal as labels of presumed social group.

The irony of this conception of the acrolect is that Jamaican speech is being analysed in terms of a variety that is not actually spoken in the speech community and the structures used by Jamaicans are being defined in terms of norms external to the community of speakers. Moreover, this speech is being analysed more in relation to written metropolitan structures than to those used in spoken MSE. When Lalla & D'Costa (1990: 89) write, for example, that in the 18th century "basilectal features occur in the usage of all classes sampled, though to varying extents", they beg the question of why a feature is labelled "basilectal" if it is also found elsewhere in the continuum of varieties. There would seem to be no *Jamaica*-based structural criteria for singling out as particularly "basilectal" features attested to in all lects.

1.3 Sense 2: The acrolect as the outcome of language acquisition

The acrolect has also been conceived of as the product of decreolization (Escure 1997), the outcome of (post) Creole speakers' acquisition of English as a result of access to education or increased exposure to an external linguistic model (in Belize, British or American Standard English) available in the society. Escure takes issue with the traditional notion of decreolization only because it suggests *replacement of*, rather than *addition to*, Creole varieties. I will use her analysis of acrolect, as it is explicitly discussed by her and includes many of the issues that are relevant to the discussion in this book.

Escure (1997: 67–68) conceives the acrolect to be:

> A non-native version of the standard language, which is acquired through spontaneous or guided learning, functions in formal contexts, and extends its speaker's repertoire without necessarily leading to loss of the speaker's vernacular. The acrolect is not necessarily a dominant or prestigious dialect, although it is usually associated with education. The definition of the term *acrolect* implies that there is an available standard that provides a linguistic model instrumental in the formation of acrolects, even in the absence of any guided learning.

She goes on to add that the label "English" is:

extremely confusing to Belizeans, primarily because English is an external standard, never physically present, although it is officially proclaimed to be the language of Belize. English is not spoken in Belize by any particular group, excepting a handful of immigrants (...) The only direct access to native renderings of a standard English variety appears to be through radio programs, BBC news and American Evangelical broadcasts. Standard English, then, has practically no spoken presence within the country of Belize....

The above quotes suggest the following:

a) Acrolect and standard are not the same – the former is non-native English, the result of speakers targeting the latter.

b) Acrolect is the formal, educated Belizean variety of English (EBE hereafter), but it is not Standard English which is only spoken by immigrants and on foreign radio.

c) What distinguishes Standard English and the acrolect is the issue of being a native speaker and, more particularly, the phonology. In the absence of MSE phonological patterns then no Belizean is a native speaker of (standard) English, though they may write it. Elsewhere in the book (1997: 66) Escure offers a definition of standard that incorporates the ideas of educated and prestige varieties and says that the term English clearly denotes for Belizeans a local standard variety, because they are not motivated to learn the remote (MSE) standard (1997: 73).

As in the discussion above, of Sense 1, the properties of MSE are used as reference for defining Standard English in Belize. Escure, however, goes further by saying that no one who is Belizean speaks Standard English because what they produce, i.e. acrolect, differs from MSE:

...acrolects develop independently because the officially prescribed standard is not present in the country; there is simply no linguistic exposure to a consistent British or American standard of English, either in daily activities or in school contexts (Escure 1997: 73).

Nevertheless, Escure tells us that for Belizeans, what she calls the acrolect *is* standard English as the British or American standards are sociolinguistically remote, and therefore unimportant in the speech community. Moreover, Belizeans feel that they should speak standard English as it is the official language and indexes education (see also Young 1973), and they therefore target what *they* consider it to be, there being no spoken MSE presence in either the school system or the society generally. Escure also suggests that this local EBE is not the superstrate (1997: 74), even as it is the variety that lives in the community of speakers and is the variety of English Belizeans (will) target and/or acquire. In this respect Escure is not unlike Patrick (quoted above), as both suggest that the target (for Belizeans and Jamaicans) is metropolitan English.

In her discussion of acrolects as innovations, Escure questions why, in light of the goals and choices a community or individual might make in the acquisition of a language, "acrolectal speakers would choose, albeit unconsciously, to produce varieties distinct from the official standard" (1997: 66). But EBE is the standard, the spoken variety of educated Belizeans that has its own phonological, lexical and idiomatic forms.

Such an exonormative approach to defining the standard in Caribbean territories like Belize and Jamaica is curious, given the history of English in the Caribbean. It speaks as much to a view of what is "native" English as it does to who is to be called a native speaker of English. It is never suggested, for example, that General American represents the acrolect, imperfect targeting of British English by speakers because of ties of history, even though much of the U.S. population historically were Europeans acquiring/learning a foreign language (Romaine 2001 *passim*). Certainly, the percentage of L_1 English speakers was/is greater in the U.S. than in Jamaica or Belize. However, that suggests that the characterization of a variety as native is a quantitative matter – with an arbitrary decision made as to numbers of L_1 speakers – rather than an issue of acquisition *per se*.

Escure's idea of acrolect necessarily takes into account the historical social context of language contact, but seems to ignore the existence of vernacular speakers of English in continuum situations like Belize. Judd (1998: 148–151) suggests that a vernacular English speaking population in Belize existed since at least the 1900's. And in Jamaica, Lalla & D'Costa (1990: 98) carefully show

> the existence, from the eighteenth century, of extensive variation (among speakers and within individual usage) in features of basilectal and acrolectal models of Jamaican speech [and that] (...) the data also confirm considerable mixing of such features.

The anonymous author of *Marly, A planter's life in Jamaica*, (cited in Lalla & D'Costa 1989: 44) seems to make a distinction, as does Lady Nugent (writing between 1801 and 1805), between white Creoles who have been educated in England

and those wholly "educated" in Jamaica.[3] The latter description applied mostly, but not exclusively, to women. These reports, by speakers of metropolitan varieties, indicate use of (a local variety of) English, with occasional "lapses" into Creole in "moments of excitement" or when "not on guard". The exposure to MSE for some Jamaicans does not negate the vernacular status of English in Jamaica. It only suggests the nature of the variation to be found in Jamaican English. As Lalla & D'Costa (1990) conclude from Long's (1774: 90–91) description of late 18th century Jamaica,

> of the landowning upper class alone (...) we see (1) a British-educated creole élite speaking RP; (2) others of the same socioeconomic class speaking a Jamaican version of RP; (3) others, less educated and less exposed to urban influence, speaking RP "with much difficulty" and creole with ease; and (4) monolingual, rural creole speakers, who were usually women and brought up on plantations. (...) Among blacks (...) (3) creole blacks ("the better sort") acquiring some RP and altering their JC accordingly; (4) locally educated free blacks and coloureds using the Jamaican form of RP in schools such as Francis Williams's; and (5) British educated blacks and coloureds, such as Francis Williams himself, speaking RP.

Moreover, as Michele M. Stewart (2002: 14) notes,

> many [free coloured men] attended Wolmer's, the only secondary school in Kingston, alongside Jews, and some were sent to public schools ... By 1788, free coloureds comprised 12.4% of the population. A few of the English educated men had been admitted to the highest ranks of society by the turn of the century.[4]

In addition Bryan (1996) describes the emergence of the black middle class in 19th century Jamaica, whose institutions included the Jamaica Union of Teachers, the Artisan's Union and the Advocate newspaper.

---

[3]Lalla & D'Costa (1990: 90), citing Long (1774), state that most Creole white women were home tutored if educated. This home tutoring was in many cases carried out by British governesses, though the average governess was "an impoverished and ill-educated female down on her luck" (Brereton 1995: 83, citing Carmichael 1833).

[4]While free coloured men are specifically mentioned here, publications like Mary Seacole's autobiography, *Wonderful Adventures of Mrs. Seacole in Many Lands*, refers to a class of what she called "Creole" and "yellow" women who were also clearly English speakers (Busby 1992).

1.3 Sense 2: The acrolect as the outcome of language acquisition

The acrolect then, as a macrosociolinguistic phenomenon, cannot be learned English alone, as not only were local norms of English identified some two centuries ago, displaying the expected variation that factors such as gender, ethnicity and education would influence, but there was also an idea of Jamaicanness, which for some excluded English born persons and the ascriptive label Englishman (Patterson 1973: 34). Nor can the model for those acquiring English have necessarily been exclusively the metropolitan variety. For most colonies then, contact with the metropole would have been limited to the élite few.

I argue that Jamaican English is not non-native English, as defined by Kachru (1982: 31) (cf. Moag 1982: 270). And I have difficulties with the tacit view of the researchers described above (discussed in §1.1–§1.2) who use an external model to identify the acrolect. The term "non-native" is itself problematic, as it is not at all clear what it means. It is applied to the English of SE Asia, India, the Caribbean and Africa – all of which have different historical contexts of development. It is not, however, applied to the English of North America, Australia or New Zealand. This suggests that ethnicity may be one of the considerations in categorizing regional varieties of English. The distinction seems to be part of what Mufwene (2001: 107) calls the "disfranchising of particular varieties as illegitimate offspring". English in the Caribbean is not really an external colonial language grafted on to indigenous, living languages[5] as it is in Africa or Asia, even if it does not have the continuity that is argued for, say, North America (for example by Fisher 2001, but cf. Görlach 1987, Mufwene 2001). Jamaica was a settlement colony, its primary reliance on the sugar plantations producing a non-European majority. And if non-native means an "institutionalized variety" (Kachru 1982: 38–40), or a "localized form" (Strevens 1982: 24), then English in Jamaica, the acrolect, has nearly always had multiple status for different groups of speakers. It has, however, been the *vernacular* of a section of the population for over three centuries, and can only be called a learned variety for some, maybe even most, speakers.

The guided learning of English in the school system, which would serve to focus and legitimize an educated norm, has, for most Jamaicans with access, been "localized" (Moag Ibid.,278) since the mid 19th century, if not before. Bryan points out that,

> As far as the racial factor is concerned, most of the elementary school teachers were black and coloured … Teachers clearly regarded themselves as an upwardly mobile section of the black population (Bryan 1996: 287–288).

---

[5]I am aware of the indigenous languages of places like Belize and Guyana. I am therefore referring to the general context of language contact between West Africans and Europeans.

And Wilmot's (2002: 317) description of early local government politics in Jamaica notes that

> In order to provide more prestige for this public meeting [in 1854], individual black and coloured teachers from the Beckford's Free School in Spanish Town and the Wolmer's School in Kingston, respectively, addressed the gathering.

For high schools, a "limited number of elementary school children [were] given the opportunity to attend" (E. Miller 1989: 209, citing B. H. Easter, the Director of Education, Jamaica 1946).

These high schools, some of which had been administered by British (trained) teachers, were almost completely localized and feminized by the last decade of the colonial period, the 1950's (E. Miller 1989). This produced what Le Page (1968: 440) called the gap between "what is supposed to be happening in the schools and what is actually happening".

Local educated norms of English were identified in Jamaica at least a century ago, if not before. The acrolect was then being added to or altered, not created, as these norms became generalized for more educated Jamaicans, as fewer and fewer people sent their children to school in England. The speakers of this Jamaican English would have increased the range of stylistic and social variation in the acrolect and perhaps generated different models of acceptable English. The acrolect as an aspect of a linguistic and sociolinguistic continuum, however, must have existed and been contemporary historically with a creole basilect.

The issue here, then, is not the theoretical validity of decreolization. It is that without a clear idea of what the phonology or syntax of the acrolect is, it becomes difficult to discuss what it is speakers are targeting when they acquire or learn English. For example, Rickford (1987: 275) gives instances of the speech of a Guyanese teacher and of a barrister delivering his summation in a Guyanese court. In both cases he identifies aspects of the phonology of these speakers that he labels "non-standard" – [d ~ ð] as in 'them', [fʌŋ] 'found', non retroflexion in words like *culture* or *render*. And as Rickford goes on to caution, "their classification as "non-standard" in the Guyanese context is open to question". I suggest that Guyanese speakers are more likely to target these local features than RP or GenAm. variants.

Discussions of the acrolect, in both Sense 1 and 2, represent English as if it was and is a thing apart, foreign to places like Jamaica and "a more or less well-defined and discrete" layer that has little relation to the continuum (Winford 1997: 241). If English is for its speakers locally defined, then continued analysis of that

English in terms of MSE will result in paradoxical conclusions. Some of these conclusions reflect what Kachru (1982: 50) calls "linguistic schizophrenia ... [an inability] to decide whether to accept a mythical non-native model [MSE], or to recognize the local functioning model [acrolect] instead".

1.4 Sense 3: The acrolect as defined by its speakers

A smaller set of work on the (Jamaican) continuum has looked at the acrolect, in terms of its speakers and the contexts in which they use language. The speaker variables that are generally used are socio-economic class, residence and level of education, particularly the latter. DeCamp's original characterization of the acrolect, for example, was the speech of "the well-educated urban professional" (1961: 82), although the implicational scales he eventually produced were a structurally defined linear spectrum of features. Beckford-Wassink (1999a) also uses education, urban residence and social class to locate acrolect-dominant speakers. The situational context of use is generally described as formal, as a distinction is made between formal speech and the production in relaxed, informal interactions.

Allsopp's (1996: lvi) definition of Caribbean Standard English in the introduction to the *Dictionary of Caribbean English Usage* is typical, focussing on the two variables of education and formality - "the literate English of educated nationals of Caribbean territories and their spoken English such as is considered natural in formal social contexts".

Thaxter (1977), in his study of what he calls Standard Jamaican English, defines it as, "the kind of language which most educated Jamaicans speak on formal occasions in business transactions, legal affairs, in educational institutions and in public life" (2). F. Miller (1987: 48,182) describes Acrolectal Jamaican English (AJE hereafter) as "the actual spoken variety [of English] which the educated élite uses in formal circumstances".

The focus on education may be explained in a number of ways, although, as Pollard (1998: 179) points out, SJE is the "first language of the man at the top of the social ladder". Firstly, it is the case that many, if not most, Jamaicans learn what Allsopp calls Internationally Acceptable English (IAE hereafter) in school and English has been a compulsory exam always required by the school system. Secondly, the school system is one of the means of legitimising and standardizing norms (Lippi-Green 1997: 65). It is in the classroom that, according to Bourdieu (1991: 61–62), "...mastery of the legitimate language may be acquired through familiarization, that is, by more or less prolonged exposure to the legitimate language...".

And of course, education as a defining characteristic of "standard" speech is not peculiar to the Jamaican social context and therefore does not entail external origin of the standard. McArthur (1998: 119–137) cites 52 examples of definitions of Standard English from a variety of sources, and of these 18 mention educatedness of speaker as the important criterion.

The school system then links a sociolinguistic notion of acrolect, the speech of a social group called "the educated", with an ideological one, the construct called "Standard English" legitimated by institutions like itself. By analysing the product of the school system, the researcher can identify the individuals in the speech community who have best adopted the sanctioned linguistic forms and been rewarded for doing so. And this identification of speakers, using language in formal contexts, is important so as to minimize assumptions about the forms to be found in the acrolect.

The other important variable in such studies is formality. Thaxter's study (1977) sees formality as the style used in specific kinds of physical and psychological contexts (after Hymes 1974: 55). He recorded students of a Teacher's College during classroom debates, speech training exercises, election speeches and votes of thanks. F. Miller conducted interviews designed to elicit certain self-conscious styles of speech (after Labov 1972: 79). And the Guyanese data presented by Rickford (1987: 275–276), discussed in the previous section, also illustrates speech in certain formal settings – the courtroom and the classroom – as produced by educated informants.

In all these studies the assumption is that the informant's attention to speech, because of where and when language is being used, is likely to produce greater use of prestige variants and the most appropriate variety for the context (Labov 1966; 1972; Wolfson 1976). This is not unrelated to the issue of education and the idea of a legitimised variety, which is, in part, the focussing of a set of norms (Le Page 1980) and the reduction of variation in the language that is to be used in such circumstances.

In his study of SJE, Thaxter looked at productions by informants as well as their evaluations of speech along a series of dimensions that include perceptions of acceptability, suitability for classroom use, and preferences of identity. Among the phonological variables he examined were – [ð/θ ~ d/t], [ɪŋ ~ ɪn], CC## ~ C##, [ɔ ~ a], [o ~ uo] and [e ~ ie]. One of his conclusions is that,

> The speakers have a wider range of language usage in phonology than in morphology and syntax probably because they spent more time learning more morphological and syntactic than phonological features ... [and]

probably because morphology and syntax decreolize faster than phonology (1977: 215).

What Thaxter explains as an aspect of the rate of decreolization, can be explained in another way. The "standard" that speakers learn in the school system is essentially a written variety of English, with prescriptive rules about "correct grammar", i.e. morpho-syntactic use. Gupta (2001: 370) makes the important observation that,

> The remarkable thing about Standard English, especially the Standard English found in edited, printed documents, is its uniformity across the world (...) Even our areas of uncertainty are shared. Countries with contact varieties of English (such as Jamaica, Nigeria, Singapore) participate in this agreement on what Standard English is like (...). We must not forget that the concept of Standard is very weak in lexis and phonology. There is no Standard accent of English (though there are prestige accents...).

The English of the classroom is pronunciation neutral, based as it is internationally on a literary standard, with few prescriptions on segmental features and fewer, if any on prosody (see Ho & Platt 1993: 7; J. Milroy & L. Milroy 1985: 66–67; Trudgill 1999: 118). Moreover, Cheshire (1999: 147) argues, at least for the curriculum in English schools, that it is stylistically neutral, as typically little distinction is made between formal and informal styles of speaking in the English taught in the classroom.

What distinguishes the English of an educated Jamaican from an educated Australian or Nigerian is most clearly the phonological patterns of the speaker, his or her accent. One can identify features of morphology and syntax that are peculiar to communities, but these are relatively few in the educated speaker of formal English. Rickford's examples from Guyana cited above led him to comment that the Guyanese sociolinguistic continuum is gradient really only with respect to the phonology (Rickford 1987: 278–279). The standard/non-standard use of syntactic forms he found much more sharply distinguished socially.

On the evaluative dimension, Thaxter's informants found the "local" voice preferable to the "foreign" one, that of an RP speaker; and the "librarian's speech" the variety they would most encourage their pupils to use. What distinguished "her" speech from the English person was the phonology, specifically a greater use of initial [d] in words such as "this" and the use of mid-vowel diphthongs in words like [fies] *face* and [buot] *boat*. Following the tradition outlined in the previous sections, Thaxter labelled this phonology "mesolectal" (239).

Miller's study (1987) of AJE described aspects of the phonological and morpho-syntactic use of post-secondary educated, urban (Kingston) dwellers. She selected and stratified her 24 informants based on their socio-economic class (indexed by occupation and income), gender and age (18–35 and 45–65 years old). Her conclusions, summarized in the final section of the dissertation, are confusing at times because Miller tends to use the terms "standard" and "prestige" interchangeably, assuming them to be the same thing. For example, she contends that the typical pattern of female speech, the use of a greater number of prestige forms, is not borne out in her study because they differ from metropolitan forms –

> On the whole, the females in this study use more non-standard phonological forms than the males ... Only UMC/UC [upper middle class/upper class] women exhibit the tendency to produce more prestigious pronunciation ...
>
> (1987: 112–113)

Miller does not present support for her assumptions about the prestige of MSE phonological forms. She does say later that the speech of women and younger informants is possibly "a pattern which is emerging where educated speakers are expressing themselves by using linguistic forms which are not part of a British or American model" (177). We do not, however, know if any forms are *entering* the acrolect, and there is enough historical evidence to suggest that its phonology has displayed variation for some time.

The phonological variables F. Miller studied were i) TH Stopping (θ/ð ~ t/d), ii) [ɪŋ ~ ɪn], iii) Vowel laxing [tek ~ tɛk] or [onli ~ ɔnli], iv) [kj ~ kʰ] and v) [jʊ ~ jə ~ i] in words like *education*. (See Chapter 2 for a more detailed discussion of many of these phonological features).

She found, in general, that

> The high frequency of occurrences of palatal realizations (44.3%), a 30 percent occurrence of TH Stopping, a 50.4 percent realization of the [i] variant of the variable /jʊ/ etc. behoves us to realize that we are indeed dealing with 'inherent variation' (1987: 183–184).

This inherent variation, she suggests, is due to substrate Creole influence and its relationship to the emerging Jamaican norms of English – for Jamaicans see MSE patterns as stilted, pedantic and unnatural even in formal circumstances – where aspects of "popular speech" (178) are used to signal this local English language identity.

In a previous study of acrolectal varieties (A. Irvine 1988; 1994), I was interested in exploring the speech of informants who lived in two neighbouring affluent suburbs of Kingston, one characterized by its high level of ethnic minority residents (Whites, Syrians, Chinese for example). My 32 informants were all educated (post-secondary) and were born into households of relative affluence (indexed by father's occupation). The segmental phonological features looked at were post vocalic rhoticity and [kʰa ~ kja], in addition to aspects of intonation and vowel quality. It was found, for example, that the informants from the community with the greater number of ethnic minority residents were much more likely to produce [kja] than [kʰa], and women generally also followed this pattern. The other community, with a predominantly black educated population, tended to use the [kʰa] variant more frequently, particularly the men. It was not at all clear, however, whether this finding was to be explained by the influence/ avoidance of the "Creole" [kja] or by a distancing from the patterns of the other community.

One could take the extreme position that MSE, and certainly the phonology, is not especially relevant to any synchronic discussion of acrolectal speech or variation in the continuum generally; indeed, its relevance diachronically is also somewhat problematic. Winford (1997), in his discussion of Caribbean English continua, suggests that "synchronic style shifting from creole vernacular to more formal standard usage has much in common with historical language shift from creole to more 'standard' or 'acrolectal' targets" (271). But terms like "standard-like" to discuss the production of EBE speakers (268) do, in a sense, presuppose what is standard in the particular social context and therefore what is being targetted.

It is necessary at this point therefore to try and distinguish use of the terms acrolect, Jamaican English and Standard Jamaican English. The first label, acrolect, is more typical of studies that seek to describe formal properties of systems along the continuum (as in the previous sections). In doing so an idealization of the speech at the apex of the continuum is assumed, while variation is explicitly acknowledged and disregarded in the analysis. Beckford-Wassink uses the term *acrolect-dominant* to describe the linguistic characteristics of certain types of speakers, i.e. urban, well educated and of relatively high income. She does analyse variation and argues that no such speaker produces the acrolect all the time, but it does represent the dominant lect in their repertoires. Implicit in the label, however, is the assumption that forms which deviate from MSE represent shift away from the acrolect in speakers, even when produced in formal/self-conscious contexts. Moreover, her later discussion of the changing indexicality of a form like [kja] as in *cat* for example, which she suggests is "now welcome" (Dyer &

Beckford-Wassink 2001: 31) in the speech of the upwardly mobile, speaks to a presumption that non-MSE forms are somehow *becoming* part of the acrolect. Lalla and D'Costa's comments cited earlier would suggest otherwise.

If acrolect is meant to be the idealized variety at one extreme of the Jamaican continuum, essentially a device to describe a basilect, then it cannot be coterminous with "the local standard", as used in the discussions of some Creolists (see §1.1, 5). The latter label suggests forms that are or have been normalised by speakers in the community as "correct", notwithstanding the lack of corroboration for this process in many of the discussions. A shift then "from Creole to more 'standard' or 'acrolectal' targets" as Winford states above is problematic if, for example, a form is used along the continuum or if the discussion centres on, say, phonology. The latter, acrolect, suggests the linguists' construct of Jamaican English, informed as it is by the linguist's knowledge of formal written English; the former, local standard, is an idea held by speakers of what that English should be like, particularly, but not exclusively, when spoken.

I argue that the two should be the same. Any discussion of language change, or targetting of forms, or prestige of forms must incorporate the speakers' ideas of what is English or Creole in their social context. As Shields (1987: 119–120) points out,

> though some phonological features are shared by mainstream RP and Jamaican Creole these are often eliminated from the speech of [English speaking] informants because of their obvious associations with Creole.

1.5 Sense 4: The acrolect as an idea of Jamaican English

Two examples can be used to reinforce why it seems necessary to resituate the idea of acrolect in the speaker and in the (Jamaican) social context. Firstly, in Jamaica, the *Revised primary curriculum* 1999 (Ministry of Education and Culture 1999: 14) states:

> The language programme seeks to sensitize pupils to the richness and variety of language. A major objective is to assist them to acquire the target language *Standard Jamaican English*. [My emphasis]

For the Jamaican government, and specifically the Ministry of Education, there is such a thing as a SJE, the official and prescribed target for Jamaicans in the school system. The current phonics text selected for use in primary/preparatory education in Jamaica contains the following lesson:

> The words which describe the pictures below have vowel pairs (sic) which make the same sound - *bowl* cow towel out couch round mouth (Gbedemah 1995: 14). [My emphasis]

This is the 7th edition of the textbook, and it is normalizing or has normalized the above pronunciation of bowl (on the model of other [aʊ] words) as SJE. An informal survey of most of my own students at the University of the West Indies (Mona, Jamaica) suggests that they do distinguish 'bowl' [baʊl] 'a ceramic dish' from 'bowl' [bol] 'the delivery of the ball in cricket'.

Secondly, the teachers at one preparatory (and therefore private) school in Kingston consistently instruct children to say [brekfaːstʰ] *breakfast* and [lItʰəl] *little*, but seldom ever comment on the structure never + V-ed (for the negative preterite, as in *never borrowed*) unless children say *neva borrow*. The teacher's preoccupation with passing on [lItʰəl] and [brekfaːstʰ] to her students cannot be explained as the targeting of MSE, but is a response to an idea that Creole speakers say [lIkl] and "leave off word endings". Moreover, her actions provide us with insights into her idea of SJE, one obviously connected to her idea of "Creole".

As such, it is the sociolinguistic patterns within communities, fuelled by the ideas speakers hold about language and language users in their community, that explain linguistic behaviour (over time). In that respect, language situations like that found in Jamaica are not likely to be different from other communities of speakers, where it is generally assumed that foreign norms are peripheral.

Le Page & Tabouret-Keller (1985: 191) believe standard, as applied to language, to have two, sometimes indistinguishable, meanings,

> that of *norm*, (...) and that of a prescriptive yardstick against which people and things are measured ... norm often becomes converted into a prescriptive standard used as a yardstick; through the education and examination systems as a test for admission to various occupational elites, and through social convention as a test for admission to social elites.

Le Page mentions, in particular, the emergence of the Caribbean Examinations Council (CXC), the Caribbean Lexicography Project (realized in Allsopp's *Dictionary of Caribbean English Usage*), the civil service and educational institutions that operate as "focussing agencies" (Le Page 1988: 34–35) for these norms, thus converting them into yardsticks. Institutions such as the electronic media or the education system, their effect on the requirements for employment, and the stereotypes that they reinforce do inform speakers' judgements of standard usage.

In media, for example, the British Broadcasting Corporation (BBC) has tended to choose a certain type of voice/broadcaster to sell a particular idea of Britain and the British, particularly in its historical role as *the* model for the English language community. Lippi-Green (1997) cites the then (1924) Managing Director of the BBC as explicitly supporting the prescriptive role of media:

> One hears the most appalling travesties of vowel pronunciation. This is a matter in which broadcasting may be of immense assistance ... We have made a special effort to secure in our stations men who ... can be relied upon to employ the correct pronunciation of the English tongue (1997: 137).

She provides similar documentation from National Broadcasting Corporation (NBC) urging use of General American, as it is "most readily understood" (Lippi-Green 1997: 138). Pronunciation is the salient feature of language mentioned in directives from media like the BBC or NBC, not only for the hiring of staff, but also because broadcasters are expected to provide a model of "good" English diction for the public.

According to McArthur (1992), the BBC policy on language use in broadcasting continued to favour RP up to the 1950's, using non-RP speakers typically for weather, entertainment (gardening, sport, drama) and less serious topics. The implicit message is clear – regional voices do not have the authority of the RP Standard. The more inclusive language policy of the 1960's did not extend to the World Service, the branch of the corporation aimed at external markets, which continued to prefer RP speaking broadcasters (at least until 1990). The British English heard by outsiders, as reflected in this distinction between local and foreign broadcast requirements, is still, to a great extent, RP. And Sharwood-Smith (1999: 59) notes that this is itself the wish of the World Service target audience, who, like the bosses of NBC in relation to American English, hold to an ideology that RP is the English "everyone understands".

In education, Lippi-Green (1997: 109) cites documents published by the National Council of Teachers of English (USA), and Cheshire (1999: 147) the National Curriculum for English (England and Wales), which suggest that language education policy is also founded on the belief that the school system can and does (re)direct pupils' language in the appropriate way. And appropriate means the legitimised "standard", the variety

> at the neutral (hegemonic) top and center of stratified society; any deviations can only be interpreted as marked variants that index (...) the producer as also being a correspondingly removed one (Silverstein 1998: 412).

Jamaican teachers and pupils are told in the curriculum that there is such a standard locally – SJE – the target language for all Jamaicans in the education system. However, examination of the material in the curriculum suggests that SJE is, at least in morphology and syntax, little different from the IAE in use in the school system of countries in which English is in general use. There are, of course, Jamaicanisms that occur, even in formal written Jamaican English (Christie 1989; 1998b; Craig 1982; Shields-Brodber 1997) but these are not generally accepted in exams.[6] SJE in texts is little different from MSE, though students are drilled in the specific aspects of structure that are deemed to be problematic because of Creole. The syllabus for secondary schools is designed to equip the student with (among other things) "the ability to use the language with precision, clarity and grammatical correctness". As Christie (1989: 256) notes, however, "it is not usually the case (...) that conscious attempts are made to depart from the traditional model, British Standard English".

The examples of teaching practice given at the start of this section, and the data from sociolinguistic studies of Jamaican English, suggest that phonology is therefore going to be the locus of any construct of a Jamaican norm of Standard English. It is the phonology of standard English that is simultaneously the carrier of national identity - transforming members of the English language community into participants in a speech community (Silverstein 1998: 407) – and one of the indices of what Bourdieu (1984: 228) called "cultural capital", aspects of behaviour that reproduce the local social structure and privilege the holders of the legitimised patterns of these behaviours. Thaxter's and Escure's works (cited above) show that foreign models of spoken English are not used or targetted in either Belize or Jamaica. Arguably, they can tell the listener only that the speaker is foreign or pretentious. But when a speaker of SJE has options such as, *standard* [standa:rd], [standʌd] or [standəd]; or *only* [onlɪ], [ʌnlɪ] and [ondlɪ] in the social context, each will be associated with particular groups, length and type of schooling, and other such factors that can locate the speaker socially in the speech community for the hearer.

---

[6]Christie cites as examples *Today, when the eyes of the world is on us* . . . or *The water entering the reservoirs were extremely muddy.* Additionally, in formal Jamaican English (written and spoken) sentences such as *Here we have yet another of the anti-drug rally being held* or *A suspect charged with possession of firearm* are more and more common. In both cases, speakers seem to be assigning number based on a logic that a) another = one = rally (SINGULAR) and b) the suspect had one, therefore SINGULAR, firearm. In addition, the use of prepositions (as in *I've been in school from I was six*) needs further investigation. She points out, however, that many of these forms are not necessarily peculiar to Jamaica, but occur in MSE also (Christie 2003: 17–18).

Notions of standard, then, are fundamentally informed by perceptions of *who* is using the language in the speech community. Thakerar et al. (1982: 235) report that listeners presume "standard" forms in speakers they *expect* to use them. They suggest in their discussion that, "it may well be that speech stereotypes exist such that high status speakers are expected to talk with a standard accent (...) low status speakers are expected to talk with a more non-standard accent". Informants in a previous study (they cite Thakerar & Giles 1981) heard more standard phonological forms in the speech of a voice they were told belonged to a man who was doing well in his university exams; the group who was told he was doing poorly, heard more non-standard forms in the same voice (236). Accent is the term used to define the supposed difference in speakers, with an assumption that success in education is naturally associated with "proper" use of English.

Dyer & Beckford-Wassink's (2001) study shows how problematic the issue is in their discussion of Jamaican respondent's judgements of other Jamaican's speech. 19 informants were asked to listen to three guises of Jamaican speech and judge who spoke better English or used more Patois. To summarize the data (25), the particular structures that occurred (usually once or twice) in two of the guises were as in Table 1.1.

Table 1.1: Features in two Jamaican guises (from Dyer & Beckford-Wassink 2001: 25)

	Speaker 1	Speaker 2
[kja]	yes	yes
[kʰa]	no	yes
[tʌn] (turned)	yes	yes
tur[nd] (turned)	no	yes
fi im (his)	no	yes
his	yes	no
copula (attr.)	yes	no
noun + dem	yes	yes
noun + s	yes	no

Speaker 1 cannot be said to use fewer Creole forms than speaker 2, but she was judged to be a Patois speaker by more listeners than Speaker 2. Speaker 2 was also the only voice considered to be possibly someone from Kingston, "stoosh" and "mixing" English and Patois. Speaker 2, for example, was presumed by listeners to be the younger guise and therefore her use of Creole forms did not suggest rural origin as it would in older speakers. Moreover, Speaker 2 was the only one perceived to be a speaker of proper English by any of Beckford-Wassink's informants. It is, however, not clear if informants were interpreting the question, who "uses" Patois or English, as meaning a) "is likely to be a user of" or b) "is here using". The single instance of "turned" in Speaker 2 might have been enough to index the former in relation to English, notwithstanding whatever else the speakers said. What may be important then is not how many English forms the speakers uses, but which English forms and which Creole forms.[7] Additionally, given a particular social profile in the listener's judgement, here in Beckford-Wassink's data being perceived as young and urban, occasional use of a particular variant like [tʌn] *turned* or [fɪ ɪm] *his* may not index the same things as if those same variants are used by another type of speaker.

What seems to be at issue here is that the expectation of a particular phonological pattern, informed in large part by the idea of the speaker held by the hearer, affects judgements of speech. And these judgements, of standardness or intelligibility or group membership, are not necessarily altered by what is actually produced. Indeed they colour perceptions in spite of it. So one identifiable influence on a speaker's construct of standard speech is the forms they perceive to be used by successful or high status persons in the community, notwithstanding the circularity inherent in the idea that standard pronunciation is more likely to be heard in speakers we expect to produce it.

1.6 Aims and methods of the study

I wish to explore aspects of the phonology of educated Jamaicans, speaking in formal circumstances in the workplace, as I argue that SJE is essentially going to be distinctive for its phonology. The study will have two main sections. In the first (Chapters 2–3), the phonological characteristics of the staff of a government agency, called JAMPRO, will be described and subject to a number of sociolinguistic correlations. The aim of this first section is to provide a description of the use of select linguistic variables and their variants by a sample of educated Jamaicans. I am especially interested in providing data on the extent to which these features are in use in actual spoken formal Jamaican English. In the second section (Chapter 4), the agency in question will be explored as an example

---

[7]Mühleisen (2002) reports that for young black Londoners "the actual competence is of secondary importance, it is the symbol that matters. (...) phatic uses of Creole like the greeting "wha'appen" is often enough to stake one's claim of "talking black" and belonging to a certain group" (169). In much the same way, interviews on Jamaican television often start out in English (thus establishing the speaker's competence) and then move into more Creole varieties.

of one of the mechanisms for normalizing SJE phonology, as it functions in the Jamaican social context as a government marketing agency set up to promote Jamaica to both local and international investors.

I take acrolect to be the following:

- The acrolect is the English normalized in Jamaica through public/formal use by speakers at the top of the sociolinguistic spectrum, which evolves with reference to that local sociolinguistic context. The evolution of course is more constrained by the prescriptions of written English and the greater access to education.

- The acrolect, SJE, is therefore typically going to be phonologically distinctive from other varieties of Standard English. Moreover, the patterns that occur in the acrolect or SJE must be informed by those that occur in the speech perceived to be Creole. This is why some forms that occur in MSE are avoided by SJE speakers when they are also aspects of Creole.

- While some speakers in the Jamaican speech community are vernacular speakers of a variety of JE, and many more are vernacular speakers of a variety of JC or both, SJE represents a situationally defined and defining variety that is sanctioned and reinforced by institutions and agencies of the state for formal/public discourse.

1.7 Data collection

Data was collected in 1994 at Jamaica Promotions (JAMPRO). JAMPRO has a total staff complement of 188, in various offices in both urban and rural Jamaica. The principal JAMPRO building, from which all data was collected, is a five storey structure located in New Kingston – the financial\business district in the Kingston Metropolitan Area (KMA hereafter). It housed 153 members of staff at the time data was collected. The layout of the building is depicted in Figure 1.1.

Of the 153 staff members in the Head Office, 104 were interviewed. Of this 104, 82 had their interviews recorded. The results presented here reflect the organization as it was at the time of data collection. This sample of the JAMPRO population was then grouped in a number of ways, based on information gathered from the questions asked of each of the 104 informants.

All interviews were done in an office on location loaned to me by the company. All informants were given appointments, usually a day before the actual recording session, and told that I was conducting research on the company itself

FLOOR 5 – President's Office, Legal Services, Corporate Services No. of staff, 12 President (Female) Vice Presidents (1 Female, 1 Male) Group Director (1 Male) Directors (2 Female) Officers (3 Female) Secretaries (2 Female) President's Driver (1 Male)
FLOOR 4 – Research, Documentation Centre, Library, Market Development, Policy & Projects No. of staff, 26 Group Directors (2 Female) Directors (5 Female) Officers (8 Female, 2 Male) Secretaries (9 Female)
FLOOR 3 – Manufacture, Tourism/Film, Productivity Centre No. of staff, 29 Group Directors (2 Female) Directors (3 Female, 1 Male) Officers (10 Female, 6 Male) Secretaries (7 Female)
FLOOR 2 – Agriculture/Agribusiness, Public Relations No. of staff, 28 Group Directors (1 Female, 1 Male) Graff Directors (3 Female, 2 Male) Officers (10 Female, 1 Male) Secretaries (9 Female) Ancillary Staff (1 Male)
FLOOR 1 – Human Resources, Office Administration, Registry, Intl. Trade No. of staff, 53 Group Directors, (1 Female, 3 Male) Directors (2 Female) Officers (9 Female, 7 Male) Secretaries (13 Female) Ancillary Staff (9 Female, 9 Male)
LOBBY/RECEPTION No. of staff, 5 Secretaries/Receptionists (4 Female) Security (1 Male)

Figure 1.1: JAMPRO, Layout of Company by Sex, Rank and Floor

and the morale of staff. All were tape recorded with a notebook in plain sight in which I would, from time to time, make jottings.

Wolfson (1976) and Bell (1984) both discuss the effect of the audience on speaker style. Both advance a notion that speakers design their speech style in response both to the situational context and to their audience. Wolfson focusses more narrowly on the interviewer's effect on the subject, particularly when background, variety and/or gender are seen to be different. In addition, she argues that interviews, of the type conducted here with a question and answer format, constitute a specific speech event with its own norms of interaction and language use. This is, however, precisely the situation that an employee of JAMPRO is likely to face when dealing with clients – providing answers to questions about doing business in Jamaica. These interviews were all conducted by me, a female, a stranger and one expressly from the local University. Moreover, all informants knew they were part of a study and that they were being recorded. The audience in these interactions is therefore a local one which includes not only me, the interviewer, but, potentially, others at the University. I was interested in eliciting formal speech, and was attempting to set up a situational and interactional context that would discourage informality.

An informant can, of course, in contexts like this, "exploit available linguistic resources to construct for herself a particular persona or to construct an encounter as intimate, distant, friendly or otherwise" (L. Milroy & M. Gordon 2003: 206). The informant, like all speakers, is an active initiator of use of particular styles of speech (Rickford & McNair-Knox 1994), and might choose to depart from the SJE that would be considered, certainly among educated Jamaicans, unmarked in a formal, taped interaction with a stranger. As such, this study of speech at JAMPRO rests on the assumption that for most, if not all, informants, the speech produced during the interviews reflects their use of this unmarked variety.

Each interview lasted, on average, 20–25 minutes. Each interview was transcribed phonetically for subsequent analysis. These are, of course, relatively short interviews, as I did not wish to give informants time to relax, but still wanted to record a reasonable sample of each speaker's production.[8] This, of course, means that for some variables the number of tokens recorded per speaker was small. For many commonly occurring forms like the interdental fricatives or the vowel /e/ I was able to collect adequate data. For example, on average each informant

---

[8]Young (1973: 188, 191) shows that speakers in Belize used different frequencies of variants of the same variable in earlier and later parts of interviews. Speakers who started with high frequencies of "Standard English" variants, used fewer later on.

produced roughly 50 tokens of the voiced interdental fricative variable; or 27 to-kens of the mid-vowel variable. However, for other variables the data set is small, and below the minimum recommended amount (10) for sociolinguistic analysis (L. Milroy & M. Gordon 2003: 164, for example).

The collection of this data was therefore affected by two competing necessities. The first, getting enough data for good statistical analysis, requires a fairly long interview with each subject. The second, eliciting formal speech from an infor-mant who is neither relaxed nor becoming more accustomed to the interaction with me, required that interviews be kept short and business-like. In my favour methodologically, the literature shows that judgements about the social place of a speaker in the speech community, informed by their language use, are likely to be based on the occurrence of a few forms rather than how many times that form occurs (see results in Graff et al. 1986: 57; and other matched-guise studies such as Dyer & Beckford-Wassink 2001). Indeed, the use of a single token, which has significance to others in the speech community, can be enough to signal a claim to a particular identity (Bell 2001: 167).

It is not unreasonable for me to assume that in cases where a few tokens of a particular variable were collected from an informant, these not only reflect appropriate use for the context of interaction but are also the basis on which other Jamaicans can and do make judgements about the speaker.

All informants, whether recorded or not, were interviewed using the same set of questions. None were required to fill out a questionnaire, nor were they shown the questions. However, I asked all informants questions from a prepared script (Appendix A).

The issues that I wish to explore, through use of this social and linguistic data, are therefore:

- What is the construct that is SJE, as reflected in the patterns of phonologi-cal use found in this sample of educated Jamaican speakers when in formal interaction?

- How do the various groups identified differ in their use of these phonolog-ical variables?

- Does JAMPRO select speakers of a particular sociolinguistic type for high status positions?

- Do speakers with mobility aspirations pattern the phonology of their suc-cessful colleagues?

- Is JAMPRO, in its practice and expectation, legitimizing certain speech patterns?

- What is JAMPRO's role in reflecting or promoting a Jamaican Standard English?

2 Phonological variation in the Jamaican acrolect

2.1 Why consider phonological variation?

This study is concerned with the formal, spoken language of a sample of educated Jamaicans, the Jamaican acrolect as explained in Chapter 1. The informants used in this study all work for JAMPRO, an agency that has explicit language requirements for staff, and this is reflected in the various language qualifications prospective employees are expected to have. This agency, as outlined in Chapter 4, also describes in its publications a construct of the language situation and of the socio-cultural milieu in which it operates in Jamaica. In both descriptions, the use of Standard English is stated to be an imperative. As such, there are a number of reasons why the analysis of language variation in the speech of JAMPRO informants is necessarily going to focus on phonology, the essential concern of this book.

In general, qualifications in English are required for non-manual employment in Jamaica. Certainly, nearly all advertisements for white-collar jobs require applicants to have "a good command of the English language" or "excellent written and oral skills" (in English, by implication, since JC is not normally written) or "proficiency in English". Additionally, announcements of these positions are accompanied by phrases such as "the ideal candidate should have..." – typically a university degree, a credit in CXC English, or other such stipulations about educational qualifications. These qualifications are, for the most part, locally or regionally attained and success is judged through these examinations.

The CXC (and the national) exams, designed to assess proficiency in English, have no equivalent test of *oral* communication on leaving the school system.[1] Employers, therefore, rely on interviews, particularly, but not exclusively, for those candidates to supervisory or management positions.

A number of comments by senior management at JAMPRO can be used to reveal this focus on the interview and its importance in selecting staff.

---

[1] The Caribbean Advanced Proficiency Examinations did introduce an oral English examination in 1995, for students at the sixth form level.

...there was the question of why is it that we could not find any [men] at the interview and selection. We always came up with women and we were doing it strictly on the criteria that we set for recruitment...one of the first criterion (sic) for employment is a first degree from CAST [now the University of Technology] and any other tertiary institution. I think they were so much better at the interview. The women are qualified...am...I wouldn't say better qualified, wouldn't say better qualified, in fact...at the stage of the interview I ask is this person somebody I could send away next week to go and talk to an investor or to go and sell Jamaica. (F55).[2]

...the women did better, they were more reliable, more conscientious in their work. And even in interviews the women seem to shine more than the men, so invariably they ended up employing more women than men (F87).

It seems to me that they [women] seem to do better at the interviews...(F56)

These comments clearly demonstrate the perceptions held by senior management about male and female suitability for JAMPRO employment (see §3.2). But they also reveal that the interview, face to face and spoken interaction with the would-be employee, is crucial. Candidates for JAMPRO jobs are short-listed based on their paper qualifications; but it is in the interview that the selection is made, other qualifications notwithstanding.

In the interview, and in other contexts of spoken interaction, attention usually focusses on phonology and lexis when standards (in both the linguistic and denotative sense) are being assessed. Hudson (1980: 44–45) proposes that within communities alternatives in phonology are more likely to mark social differentiation than those in syntax or morphology, particularly as mass education has increased the spread of a (written) standard (see also Lippi-Green 1997; Sahgal & Agnihotri 1985). It is true that broadly speaking in communities like Jamaica, differences in morphology and syntax will sharply distinguish social groups across the continuum, as in *im ben a sliip ~ shi did a sleep ~ she was sleeping*. However, Hudson's proposition would apply in the context of a formal interview, particularly for a white-collar position, where the expected variety is SJE.

Salikoko Mufwene (pers. comm.) relates an example in support of this. Students were asked to listen to two speakers, one an elderly woman and the other a middle-aged man, both of them comedians, and to judge which seemed more non-standard. There was general agreement that the man was the more non-standard

---

[2] The code here is to be interpreted as M = male, F = female; the numbers represent the sequence of interviews. This was then the 55th interview. Appendix B has profiles of all informants.

of the two, even though he used a more standard morphology and syntax. His phonology (especially the prosody), however, seemed to inform the listener's judgement of his standardness, as little attention was paid to his grammar until it was brought to the students' attention.

Further, Rickford's (1987: 275) examples of Guyanese English related in the previous chapter, involving the speech of a teacher and of a barrister, are distinctive only for the phonology. The informants used in this book are Jamaicans who have mastered this written standard English well enough, as all but four have completed at least a secondary level of education, and many have a tertiary or graduate level education. JAMPRO would not have otherwise considered them for employment.

As suggested above by Gupta (2001: 370), and as already shown in sociolinguistic research, particularly for English speaking communities (Hewitt 1986; Labov 1972; Mugglestone 1995; Trudgill 1978), there are some accents that are considered prestigious, as markers of identity, or social class membership or level of education. While certain accents, such as RP, may have historically been given high status socially, it is not clear that they still universally carry such associations. L. Milroy (2002) suggests, for example, that in the UK it is apparent that RP "does not constitute the general model of careful or educated speech" (9) for many regions whose populations favour local patterns. Outside of the UK, as shown in Thaxter's (1977) Jamaican study, speakers also favour the local voice, the RP accent assessed as foreign and/or pretentious (239). And Nair-Venugopal (2001: 47) reports that in Malaysia exonormative models of English might be viewed as nonconventional or unexpected in corporate business contexts.

The idea of prestige accent(s) is therefore locally developed and particular to the specific speech community in which speakers operate. It is within the speech community that the shared indexicality underlying communicative acts of identity and groupness evolves (Silverstein 1998: 407). This would necessarily seem to be most focussed around the phonology, especially for speakers who pass through institutions that disseminate a near universal literary standard of English.

There is evidence that Jamaicans perceive accent and vocabulary also to be the primary difference between Creole and English, at least as suggested by Beckford-Wassink's data (1999b: 66). Of 51 informants in her study, only 9 (18%) identified any aspect of morphosyntax as distinguishing Creole and English, while 42 (82%) mentioned either accent ("how they sound their words") or accent and vocabulary. And, Beckford-Wassink adds,

All the professional domains about which they were questioned (those where the auditor might be a non-familiar or subordinate, as when answering the telephone, addressing an employer, or teaching) were deemed inappropriate for Patois usage. (Beckford-Wassink 1999b: 72)

Mühleisen (2002) reports a similar functional distribution of language use among Trinidadians. What respondents referred to as "Standard" (Trinidadian English) was mostly used in formal contexts (classroom, workplace, church) and with strangers (40). The speakers I recorded at JAMPRO did find themselves in such a context, interacting with a stranger in a formal interview at their workplace. There is every reason to expect them to be using the appropriately formal style, with the focussed morphosyntactic norms typical of the acrolect. It is their phonology, therefore, that is of primary interest here.

2.2 The phonological variables and their variants

This study, which takes an endonormative approach to defining the acrolect in Jamaica, will therefore analyse use of a set of segmental phonological features in the JAMPRO sample. The phonological features are as follows:

a) the word initial glottal fricative [h]

b) the voiced and voiceless interdental fricative, in word initial, middle and final environments.

c) the low back stressed vowel, in words like *not* and *possible*.

d) the mid tense vowels [e] and [o] as they occur pre-consonantally, in items like *face* and *goat,* and before [r] in *beer* and *poor* type words.

e) the word initial velar stop [k] before the low central vowel [a].

f) post vocalic rhoticity, before [+coronal] consonants in words like *party* and *forty.*

g) two word final phonological stop clusters, specifically [st] and [nt].

h) two word final morphophonemic clusters, -n't when used as not (*can't, won't, don't*); and past tense marking.

i) the word final unstressed vowel in words that end in -er (*butter, teacher*).

j) the vowel in the final syllable -tion, as in *education* type words.

k) the voiced and voiceless alveopalatal affricate, in words like *culture* and *soldier.*

I attempted to include all features that showed phonological variation in my data. Most of these features were present in my data in adequate frequencies. Where they were not, the data that can be discussed is presented. For example, rhoticity is analysed before certain kinds of consonants, [+ coronal], because there was, in part, better data in that phonetic environment than before [−coronal] consonants.

The literature on Jamaican language varieties has identified some of these phonological features as having variants that are described as either typically, if not unequivocally, basilectal or mesolectal and has not included them as part of the acrolect. These are presented in Group A, i.e. features a–e above. Additionally, there were some features that I was interested in exploring, and which I have not seen specifically discussed elsewhere in the literature. These are categorized as Group B, i.e. f–k above. They might prove interesting in this sociolinguistic analysis. As a Jamaican, and as someone who considers herself a vernacular speaker of Jamaican English, I recognize all of these features in my speech community. While phenomena like h-dropping and voiceless TH stopping are possibly now stereotypes (in the sense used by Labov 1972: 248) in Jamaica, pronunciations such as [kʌltjʌ] *culture* are perhaps less in the consciousness of speakers. I wish to explore how widely they are in use, particularly in the formal speech of educated Jamaicans. The middle three features, in particular (f–h), have been described elsewhere for Jamaica. However, there has been little focus on their use by acrolectal speakers (but see Shields's 1987; 1984 study of consonant clusters in JE).

The results for the total JAMPRO sample, all 82 informants, will therefore be presented for each feature discussed, so that some comparison can be made with the descriptions in the literature and generally.

2.3 Features commonly identified in the literature (Group A)

Generally, the discussion of these features across the Jamaican continuum is typified by the following description by J. C. Wells:

> At the upper (acrolectal) end of the social and linguistic scale, Jamaican consonants are phonetically much as in the standard accents (. . .) Further down the scale, in the mesolect and basilect, the characteristics emerge: TH stopping, Cluster reduction, avoidance of [ʒ] and some [v], H Dropping, semivowels in words such as /kjat/ *cat* (. . .) *face* acrolectally [fes] and basilectally [fiɛs]...
>
> (1982c: 575–576)

Acrolectal varieties in this description are characterized by very low frequencies, if not an absence, of certain variants; it is, in fact, this absence that distinguishes them from mesolectal and basilectal varieties. Interestingly, Wells says that the *phonetic* properties of acrolectal varieties are much as in other standard accents. Clearly, an American, Canadian and British speaker (or an Indian, an Australian and a Jamaican) will not sound the same. This analysis suggests, therefore, that Wells is either speaking of an idealization of Standard English that disregards even regional variation in spoken norms or is locating much of the distinctiveness of the acrolect in prosody. As discussed above, there is no standard English accent. Spoken English is generally outside the normative pressure exerted by the literary standard and it is typically the phonetic characteristics of the educated speaker that distinguish varieties from different speech communities. My concern here is then phonetic, the distribution of the variants of these variables in formal spoken JE. As was pointed out in the previous chapter, very little investigation of what has been called "the local standard" or acrolect, as used by speakers, has been done. I will therefore use the term Putative Jamaican Standard (PJS) to label an unverified but presumed local standard in order to distinguish it from the SJE which is the subject of the research in this book.

As point of reference I include the following phonemic inventory of JC and JE in Tables 2.3–2.4. The JC vowel inventory is based on Meade (2001: 35–42). Meade's inventory discusses a number of previous texts[3] and his own work done on language acquisition in Jamaica. The JE vowel inventory is based on Beckford-Wassink's data (2001: 150–151), which discusses earlier work by J. Wells (1973). The consonants of both systems are taken from Meade's work. As such these inventories can provide some indication of what phonological variation may occur in this JAMPRO sample as well as an example of what is idealized at the polar ends of the Jamaican continuum. While both Meade and Beckford-Wassink use similar symbols for most of the phonetic representations of phonemes, one or two differences did occur. Meade, for example distinguishes [a] and [ɐ] in

---

[3]Meade's work discusses, for example, Akers (1981); Alleyne (1980); Cassidy & Le Page (1967); Beckford-Wassink (1999a); Devonish & Seiler (1991).

JC, which is more typically presented as [a] in the literature and by Beckford-Wassink. I have therefore taken the common symbols from both accounts in order to facilitate comparison.

2.3.1 Basic JC and JE phoneme inventories

Table 2.1: JC and JE vowel inventory

Item	JC	JE
bit	/ɪ/: [ɪ]	/ɪ/: [ɪ]
beat	/i/: [i]	/i/: [i]
bet	/ɛ/: [ɛ]	/ɛ/: [ɛ]
bait	/ɪɛ/: [ɪɛ], [ie]	/e/: [e]
bat	/a/: [a], [ɐ]	/a/: [a]
bath	/aː/ [aː]	/aː/ [aː]
Bob	/a/: [a]	/ɔ/: [ɔ]
but	/ʌ/: [ʌ]	/ʌ/: [ʌ]
boat	/ʊʌ/: [ʊʌ], [uo]	/o/: [o]
book	/ʊ/: [ʊ]	/ʊ/: [ʊ]
boot	/u/: [u]	/u/: [u]
bout	/ʌʊ/: [ʌʊ], [au]	/aʊ/: [aʊ]
bite	/aɪ/: [ɐɪ]	/aɪ/: [aɪ]
noise	/aɪ/: [ɐɪ]	/ɔɪ/: [ɔɪ]

Essentially, we can identify the mid-vowels and the low back vowels as areas of difference between the two systems. JC typically does not distinguish /a/ and /ɔ/; and the JE mid vowels /e/ and /o/ are diphthongs in JC.

Most of these consonant features are discussed below in more detail. Briefly, JE is typically described as having interdental fricatives, the voiced alveopalatal fricative and the glottal fricative while these features are not usually identified for JC. Additionally, JC has contrastive palatalization of the velar stop in some environments.

2.3.2 Word initial glottal fricative /h/

/h/ is not phonemic in many varieties of Jamaican Creole (Akers 1981: 32; Devonish & Seiler 1991: 7; Meade 2001: 40), though there is evidence that in Western Jamaican varieties (e.g. Trelawny, St. Elizabeth) it is (J. Wells 1973: 12). Hypercorrect use of the fricative is common in Jamaica (Cassidy & Le Page 1967: lxii),

Table 2.2: JC and JE consonant inventory

Item	JC	JE	Item	JC	JE
bat	/b/: [b]	/b/: [b]	fat	/f/: [f]	/f/: [f]
pat	/p/: [pʰ]	/p/: [pʰ]	zap	/z/: [z]	/z/: [z]
dab	/d/: [d]	/d/: [d]	sat	/s/: [s]	/s/: [s]
tap	/t/: [tʰ]	/t/: [tʰ]	shat	/ʃ/: [ʃ]	/ʃ/: [ʃ]
that	/d/: [d]	/ð/: [ð]	rouge	/ʤ/: [ʤ]	/ʒ/: [ʒ]
thing	/t/: [tʰ]	/θ/: [θ]	jack	/ʤ/: [ʤ]	/ʤ/: [ʤ]
kit	/k/: [kʰ]	/k/: [kʰ]	chat	/ʧ/: [ʧ]	/ʧ/: [ʧ]
give	/g/: [g]	/g/: [g]	lap	/l/: [l]	/l/: [l]
cat	/kj/: [kj]	/k/: [kʰ]	wag	/w/: [w]	/w/: [w]
gab	/gj/: [gj]	/g/: [g]	rat	/r/: [r]	/r/: [r]
mat	/m/: [m]	/m/: [m]	yak	/j/: [j]	/j/: [j]
nab	/n/: [n]	/n/: [n]	hat		/h/: [h]
ing	/ŋ/: [ŋ]	/ŋ/: [ŋ]			
vat	/v/: [v], [b]	/v/: [v]			

particularly in Kingston where my sample was recorded. In local theatre, for example, this hypercorrect use is often played for comic effect in characters understood as "speaky-spoky". According to Patrick (1997) this style of Jamaican speech "is clearly recognised and labelled by Jamaicans, and is realized regularly by hypercorrect [h] and [ɔ]" (48). He gives examples like [hɔlon] *alone* and jokes such as "*hemphasize your haitch you hignorant hass*" which are heard locally.

In my total sample of speakers, eleven informants produced this hypercorrect pattern, as in F52 [honiŋ] *owning* or M27 [haʊt] *out,* and typically with single attestations. The more general pattern was h-dropping, a term that clearly assumes that speakers are using an English phonological system, which does have /h/. Evidence for this is furnished in the pattern of use of aitch in the texts collected. Except for the 11 whose usage suggests non-contrastive [h], as in [haʊt ~ aʊt] *out,* most informants produced /h/ in the same way as in IAE, distinguishing lexical items like 'hand' and 'and', without inserting [h] where it is not lexically specified in IAE. It is entirely possible that some speakers have idiolects that have neither /h/ nor a hypercorrect usage of [h], while having other English phonological features. I did not find such a speaker in my sample.

Outside of Jamaica, [h]

> ...has become one of the principal signals of social identity, its presence in
> initial positions associated almost inevitably with the 'educated' and 'polite',
> while its loss commonly triggers popular connotations of the 'vulgar', the
> 'ignorant' and the 'lower class' (Mugglestone 1995: 107).

For some Jamaicans, h-dropping is also overtly stigmatized, though it is not at
all clear that this is universally the case or that h-lessness is even perceived by the
hearer. It is a stereotype held by others in the Caribbean of bad Jamaican speech
(J. C. Wells 1982c: 569). This stereotype is confirmed in Roberts (1988: 90) and in
Allsopp's dictionary. As Allsopp points out, "/h/, especially in initial position, is
lost noticeably in Jamaica, even in the speech of educated persons" (1996: xlvii).

Historically, variable use of [h] was a feature of some of the varieties of English that came to and were used in Jamaica during the early years of British
settlement in the mid to late 17th century. H-dropping became salient and the
shibboleth of vulgar speech in the metropole by the 18th century (Beal 2002: 103).
The more consistent pronunciation of [h], largely due to its presence in the orthography, indexed literacy; and therefore it was the "illiterate speaker" of the
1850's in Britain who was perceived to drop [h]. Mugglestone (1995) documents
that:

> While 'literate speakers', at least in terms of the prevailing prescriptive ide-
> ology, thus made plain the facts of their superior education by matching
> grapheme with appropriate sound, or <h> with [h] in their speech, so there-
> fore did the non-appearance of [h] take on the values (. . .) of the 'lower
> class' (117).

As such, hypercorrect use of [h], due to the stigma attached to [h] dropping,
developed as a stable feature in sections of the British population over two centuries ago, a function of the changing prescriptions on [h] articulation and the
focussing of attitudes to "h-less" speakers. Mugglestone (1995) cites a number
of examples, one of which is from Poor Letter H (1866): "...he would persist in
saying that the habbey was his 'obby" (124).

However, J. C. Wells (1982b: 432) tells us that h-drop is not a feature of Irish
English; moreover /h/ is more widely distributed in Irish than it is in English.
This suggests that variable (but not yet hypercorrect) use of [h] would probably have been more typical of founder English varieties (Cassidy & Le Page 1967:
lxii) than an aspect of the speech of the Irish indentured servants who were also a

presence in Jamaica at the time (see for example Beckles 2000: 228). Moreover, it is possible that given the regional associations in Jamaican Creole with variable use of [h] (Eastern Jamaica and Kingston), and the early history of English settlement in Eastern Jamaica (Sherlock & Bennett 1998: 85) particularly in urban areas like Port Royal and Kingston, the pattern of aitch distribution in Jamaica reflects to some extent the pattern of white settlement in the early years of the colony. In that respect, the linguistic data may, as Devonish argues (2002: 180), provide historians with information that points to particular demographic patterns that require exploration.

Lalla & D'Costa (1990) cite the example from the early 19th century of a Jamaican planter who is reported as saying "hedicating the negroes is the only way to make them 'appy (...) hedication is hall in hall" (142). This suggests that hypercorrect use of [h], specifically h-insertion, has also been a feature in some Jamaican varieties for at least the past two centuries, no doubt also influenced by varieties of Creole coexisting in the speech community. It is interesting that neither h-drop nor h-insertion has been identified in US varieties, though occasionally "an" occurs before words beginning in aitch, suggesting possible absence (Krapp 1925: 206 gives the example *an halfe* from 1653). It has been described in some Canadian (Newfoundland) varieties of English (Kirwin 2001: 447). It appears, therefore, that some ecologies were more favourable to the persistence of variable/hypercorrect [h] than others. Certainly, speakers acquiring or learning English in Jamaica would have been exposed to and selected these hypercorrect forms, options existing in the Jamaican "feature pool" (Mufwene 2001: 4), especially if such forms were used by some speakers at the top of the society.

The JAMPRO data show the pattern in Table 2.3 for h-dropping word initially[4].

Table 2.3: h-drop in the total sample

h-drop	h
184 (10.4%)	1592 (89.6%)

The data here points to a fairly low incidence of h-drop in these speakers, with many not doing it at all. The hypercorrection discussed above does suggest a sensitivity to use of this variable as marking a speaker of "good" English. Of the total sample, 15 of the 82 informants account for the majority of cases of h-drop

---

[4]This data does not include occurrences of typically unstressed items like *has*, as when the auxiliary of a participle (he [həz] gone) or *have* (we [həv] seen).

(111 of the 184 or 60%), the more typical pattern being one or two instances of the feature in speakers' recordings. Of those 15 informants, 8 – two men and six women – had no productions of hypercorrect h-insertion. A fuller discussion of hypercorrection in this sample is presented in §2.4 of this Chapter, and Chapter 3 and 4 present the results of a number of sociolinguistic correlations.

2.3.3 The interdental fricatives /θ/ and /ð/

The interdental fricatives [θ] and [ð] vary with the alveolar stops [t] and [d] in Jamaica, as in [θɪk ~ tʰɪk] *thick* and [ðat ~ dat] *that*. The alveolar stop variants are identified as a Creole feature in this social context, though it is found in varieties of non-standard English such as Irish or some US varieties. The literature on Jamaica has generally suggested that the stop variants are not part of the acrolect (Akers 1981: 33; Meade 2001: 23; Thaxter 1977: 239) or the speech of the highly educated (J. C. Wells 1982c: 575). However, Allsopp (1996: xlvi) sees this as a general feature of Caribbean speech; and Young (1973: 188) found relatively low frequencies of the fricative variants in even formal Belizean speech. Similarly, F. Miller (1987) in her study of AJE found that her speakers, in formal contexts, used the alveolar stop variants about 30% of the time (183).

Miller's analysis does not distinguish patterns of use for the voiced and voiceless stop, though the tables she presents suggest that the voiced stop is produced more frequently by speakers (57). In Thaxter's (1977) study, the "librarian's speech", identified by his sample of Jamaican teachers as the type of speech they would pass on to their students (249), was characterized by no voiceless TH stopping, slightly more use of [d ~ ð]. It seems necessary then to distinguish the patterns for the voiced and voiceless variables in our analysis. Certainly, I have heard the use of [θ] where most speakers would have [t] in items like [θrut] *truth* and [θɛrərɪzm] *terrorism* in some Jamaican speech, including the JAMPRO sample (F76 [θʌg] *tug*). This suggests that contrastive /θ/ is an aspect of the acrolect and that some informants perceive the interdental fricative to be "correct". A parallel use of [ð] did not occur in my sample and is rare, even though J. C. Wells (1982c: 565) says that [bɛð] *bed* is possible. It is not clear from his text, however, whether he is suggesting a theoretical possibility, as his analysis does not differentiate patterns for the voiced and voiceless stop either.

TH stopping is a general feature of most dialects of British English (Cassidy & Le Page 1967: lviii), and in some with an additional variant [f]. This latter variant is also found in AAVE and Bajan but not in Jamaica. The pronunciation of the interdental fricative, influenced by spelling changes prior to the 15th century (Pyles & Algeo 1993: 168), was normalised at the time of language contact in

Jamaica. I find no references to hypercorrect use except in varieties of Hiberno-English. Baugh & Cable (1993: 313) cite 19th century forms such as [θru] *true* and [bʌtθər] *butter*, pronunciations that occur today in southern Irish English (Trudgill & Hannah 1994: 105). There is evidence of an Irish population in early Jamaica, particularly in the early colonial period before the 18th century. According to Cassidy & Le Page

> Thus, whilst it is almost certain that [interdental fricatives tended to be produced as alveolar stops] due to the lack of /ð/ and /θ/ in many West African languages, the possibility remains that in the speech of [early white settlers] these processes had already begun without African influence (lvii).

I find no reference to hypercorrect use of interdental fricatives in early Jamaica. It is possible that the forms came from the speech of Irish indentured servants, but the citations I can find are all from the 1960's, when there was more widespread access to education and greater exposure to the standard usage for speakers. Moreover, hypercorrect [θ] is not identified in American varieties, notwithstanding the Irish influence in some regions.

I will analyse use of these two variables in different positions in the word. For one, it is possible that the most common occurrences of word initial /ð/ (words like *the*, *them*, *that*) are less consciously monitored by speakers, even in formal contexts, because they are typically unaccented and weak in discourse (see Gimson 1980: 185). In addition, the type of word that will have a middle TH is, at the very least, disyllabic and the variant use here may better reflect the patterns of formal speech, with its greater proportion of longer and more erudite words.

The data show the pattern in Table 2.4 for the interdental fricatives and variants in all speakers.

Table 2.4: TH stopping in the total sample

	d	ð	t	θ
Word Initial	2290 (54.3%)	1924 (45.7%)	117 (14.4%)	693 (85.6%)
Word Middle	76 (25.0%)	228 (75.0%)	22 (18.8%)	95 (81.2%)
Word Final	33 (27.0%)	89 (73.0%)	20 (24.0%)	63 (76.0%)

The data reveal two things. Firstly, the pattern for the word initial voiced fricative is noticeably different from all the others in the table. It could be that contrastive /ð/ is not a feature of some idiolects in my sample, while /θ/ is; however, as I have no instances of forms like [ðɔg] *dog*, it is more probable that it is and that its phonetic realizations are less focussed in word initial contexts. Crucially, in the same context, speakers produce significantly fewer voiceless stops – and the hypercorrection mentioned above again indicates that use of [0] particularly is a salient feature of "correct" speech. The relatively low incidence of TH stopping in all other environments also suggests that use of fricatives is the more general pattern for these speakers in formal contexts, with some variation with the alveolar stop.

2.3.4 The low back stressed vowel /ɔ/

In "not" words the possible variants are [nat ~ nʌt ~ nɔt]. The "Creole" variant in this set is the low central vowel [a], as Jamaican Creole has one low vowel phoneme /a/, with [at] produced for both *hat* and *hot*. J. C. Wells (1982c) says that, "block is acrolectally [blɒk] (or sometimes with an unrounded back vowel [blɑk], but basilectally homophonous with black [blak]" (576).[5] Similar analyses of the basilect can be found in Akers (1981: 25) and Devonish & Seiler (1991: 5).

Hypercorrect use of [ɔ] is the other feature that Patrick (1997) associates with "speaky-spoky". Forms like [sɔlɛrɪ] *salary* (M47), [rɪlɔks] *relax* (F53) and [fɔːmʌ] *farmer* (F80) produced by some of my informants would suggest the kind of sensitivity to the feature discussed by Patrick and a belief that [ɔ] is the "correct" reflex of [a]. Like Wells, Beckford-Wassink (2001: 151) and Meade (2001: 42) describe acrolect (dominant) speech as clearly distinguishing /a/ and /ɔ/ in "not" words. However, words like *mother, government* and *colour* can be, and often are, pronounced as [mʌðʌ ~ mɔðʌ], [gʌvəmɛnt ~ gɔvəmɛnt] and [kʌlʌ ~ kɔlʌ] in Jamaican English. This suggests that the relationship between /a, ʌ, ɔ/ is a complex one at the upper end of the construct called the continuum and that, for some speakers, [ɔ] is a reflex of /ʌ/ as well. In Beckford-Wassink's (2001) analysis, her sample of speakers from rural St. Thomas in Jamaica did not have a distinct /ɔ/, though they did distinguish the other two sounds (150).

Prescriptive texts for British English from 1673 are cited by Freeborn (1998: 356) as listing the following as homophones: *chaps* and *chops*; *band* and *bond*; *knots* and *gnats*. By the end of the 17th century there is evidence of variation between [a] and [ɔ] – in words such as *quality, watch, what* – the latter variant initially regarded as vulgar but becoming more standard by the 19th century (Beal 2002: 128). Mugglestone (1995) gives an example from 1697 of an "affected" literary

---

[5]Wells uses the symbols [ɑ] and [ɒ] to depict what I will identify as the [ɔ] sound. I find the Jamaican vowel to be higher and rounder than he suggests (see also Beckford-Wassink 2001: 142).

character, Lord Foppington, who is depicted as speaking in this way: "Now it is nat passible far me to penetrate what species of fally it is thau art driving at (...) I must confess, I am nat altogether so fand of" (216). The rounding of the vowel seems to have spread from pre-rhotic environments (*warm, quart*), gradually becoming the prestige variant generally (Beal 2002: 128). Essentially, the varieties of English that came into Jamaica would have had this variation between [a ~ ɔ], and, like the "problem" with [h], it persisted for some time.

A number of commentators on Jamaica remark on the language of white Creoles, in particular women's speech. Lady Nugent writing in the early 1800s remarked that "...many of the ladies, who have not been educated in England, speak a sort of broken English" (Wright 2002: 98), a complaint echoed by Marly, Moreton and other contemporary writers (Lalla & D'Costa 1989: 131). They cite the forms "haut" (*heart*) and "knaum" (*nyam*) in a 1793 publication, which I interpret as [hɔːt] and [njɔːm], both of which would be called hypercorrect in current JE. It is not clear whether they should be so labelled in the cited female speaker, but the forms have therefore been in the Jamaican speech community at least since then. Crucially, the speaker has taken a clearly African lexical item ([njam] *eat*) and adapted the phonology to what she considers a prestige pronunciation. Jamaican ideas of correct pronunciation must have been informed by a Creole that did not have the /ɔ/ vowel, and it is even possible that its selection as prestigious was an autonomous Jamaican occurrence, and not one that *necessarily* followed from metropolitan norms of use. Table 2.5 presents the JAMPRO data.

Table 2.5: The low back vowel and variants in the total sample

nat	nʌt	nɔt
385 (19.8%)	325 (16.8%)	1230 (63.4%)

In these speakers there is a low incidence of the "Creole" variant, in contrast to the relatively high incidence of [ɔ]. There is also a low occurrence of the [ʌ] variant. However, close to a third of the time the [ɔ] variant is not produced. Again, this is one of the variables for which we find speakers producing hypercorrect forms, which may indicate what is perceived to be correct and to be stigmatized in the general speech community. For some speakers at least, [a] is to be avoided, even where an item is lexically specified in IAE to have this phoneme.

2.3.5 Pre-consonantal/pre-rhotic mid tense vowels /e/ and /o/

In words like *boat* [buot ~ bot] and *face* [fies ~ fes], speakers vary the mid tense vowels with a diphthong (described by Devonish & Seiler 1991: 8 as a syllable nucleus preceded by either a palatalized onset in the case of [fjes] or a rounded one in the case of [gwot]). Beckford-Wassink (2001) found that in her acrolect-dominant speakers, production of this pair of features was related to factors like variation in style (more informal) and gender (male speakers). Generally, she found that all acrolect-dominant speakers showed a predominance of monoph-thongal forms in all test contexts, but particularly when called on to produce care-ful speech in a word list (153). However, her informants did not use the diphthong variants with the same frequency, [uo] being less likely to occur than [ie], specif-ically for men (154). Alleyne (1980) also suggests that [ie] is a more widespread feature in Jamaica (41). Meade (2001: 113) identifies the diphthongs as "variants in most Jamaican varieties, but to different degrees". Use of the diphthongs is de-scribed as mesolectal in Thaxter's study (1977: 239) and basilectal by Akers (1981: 25) and J. C. Wells (1982c: 576).

In my analysis, I make the distinction between the mid-tense vowels as they are produced in a pre-rhotic environment and when occurring before other con-sonants. For some Jamaicans sets of words like *beer*, *bare* and *bear* or *where* and *wear* are homophonous either as [be:r]/[we:r] or [bi^{e}r] / [wi^{e}r]; and this even in speakers who vary for example [e ~ ie] elsewhere before other consonants. Christie (2003: 19) describes the former pronunciations as "hypercorrect", an overuse of the [e] vowel in order to avoid the Creole diphthong, as a distinction between words like *beer* and *bear* is the pattern in MSE.

Historically, the diphthongs (both before other consonants and [r]) were as-pects of some of the varieties of English that came to Jamaica (Cassidy & Le Page 1967: xlvi). In addition, Freeborn (1998: 356) cites late 17th century prescriptions that indicate that *bare* and *bear* or *chair* and *cheer* are to be homophones. To la-bel similar contemporary Jamaican pronunciations "hypercorrect" is, of course, to stipulate that the changes in the Standard in Britain are necessarily to be re-flected in Jamaica.

With the back vowel, speakers can be distinguished by the surface vowel of an underlying /o/ in *poor* type words – having either the vowels [o] or [ɔ]. For some speakers the /o/ can become phonetically [o], [u^o] or [^{u}o]; for others the /o/ is realized as [ɔ]. Indeed, in some Jamaican speakers a word like *our* can be realized as [or], and possibly as a consequence is sometimes pronounced as [ɔr] in formal contexts such as that of a radio broadcast. Pre-rhotic back diphthongs occur in Jamaican speech therefore in variation as follows: *poor, more* or *court-*

house is produced as [puor ~ pɔr], [muᵒ r ~ mɔːr], [kᵘothaʊs ~ kɔrthaʊs]; note that JE /ɔr/, as in *forty, horse, north*, also varies with the expected [aː] described for the previous variable ([faːti], [haːs], [naːt]). It is possible, therefore, that the pre-rhotic context is one linguistic constraint on the type of variation identified above for the production of diphthongal allophones in speakers.

Table 2.6: Mid tense vowels and variants (all environments) in the total sample

uo	o	ie	e
246 (11%)	2041 (89%)	748 (26%)	2145 (74%)

The data here does support Alleyne's view and Beckford-Wassink's findings about the higher incidence of [ie] in Jamaican speech when all linguistic contexts are analysed together. However, when pre-rhotic occurrences are excluded from the data, there is a noticeable difference in the way the diphthong patterns. As in Beckford-Wassink's data on careful speech, in these JAMPRO interviews we observe a predominance of monophthongal forms generally. However, I find there are some speakers who do allow diphthongs, and typically only in the pre-rhotic environment.

The data in Table 2.7 shows how the pre-rhotic diphthongs occur at JAMPRO.

Table 2.7: Comparison of mid-tense vowels and variants in the total sample

	[ɔ]	[uᵒ]	[o]	[ⁱe]	[e]
pre-rhotic (court) – (beer)	453 (73.2%)	116 (18.7%)	50 (8.1%)	485 (45.5%)	579 (54.5%)
pre-consonantal (coat) – (babe)		130 (8.0%)	1538 (92.0%)	263 (14.0%)	1566 (86.0%)

For the back vowel set, most speakers produce the [ɔr] in *poor* type words, with a little over quarter of the sample using the other variants. The pre-rhotic environment for the back vowel then seems to inhibit diphthongization in ways that it does not for the front vowel. And the /o/: [uo] allophone is also very infrequent pre-consonantally in my sample. Close to half of my informants, however, use the diphthong variant of the front vowel before [r]. Essentially these speakers tend not to produce [uo] in any contexts, selecting either forms like [bot] *boat* or [pɔr] *poor* in formal speech. In the same stylistic situation front diphthongs occur more frequently in all environments, but particularly pre-rhotically.

2.3.6 The word initial velar stops /k/, /g/

In Jamaican speech, before the low central vowel /a/, the /k/ and /g/ have the variants [kʰ] and [kj], as in *cat* [kʰat ~ kjat] or *card* [kʰaːd ~ kjaːd]); or [g] and [gj], as in *gap* [gap ~ gjap] or *guard* [gaːd ~ gjaːd]. The /kj/ and /gj/ are contrastive in Creole before /a/ - [gjaːdn] *garden* and [gaːdn] *Gordon*; [kjaːf] *calf* and [kaːf] *cough*; but *[gjaspl] *gospel*, *[kjaːk] *cork* . It is non-contrastive in JE, as the items *garden* and *Gordon* are distinguished instead by the vowel a/ɔ contrast. The palatal glide in words such as *garden* or *card* was, up to the end of the 18ᵗʰ century, regarded as "smooth and elegant (...) sufficient to mark the speaker as either coarse or elegant, as he adopts and neglects it" (Mugglestone 1995: 233 citing Walker 1781). By the middle of the next century its status had changed (Cassidy & Le Page 1967: lviii) and descriptions such as "affected", "old-fashioned" and "rapidly dying out" were used for this feature, though its association with "proper" female speech seemed to have persisted somewhat longer (Mugglestone ibid.).

Current analyses of Jamaica tend to label [kj] a "Creole" or basilectal variant (Akers 1981: 33; F. Miller 1987: 89; J. C. Wells 1982c: 569; but cf. Patrick 1999: 96 and 2000: 11). However, in her AJE sample, F. Miller found that the [kj] was produced for 44.3% of items and more by upper middle class men than by other groups. She states that, "no linguistic constraints on this variable were observed" (pg. 118). Interestingly, she cites a letter to the local newspaper by a reader who wished to point out to Jamaicans that the "correct" pronunciation of a word like *Canada* is [kjanɪdʌ]. This possibly indicates that some speakers hold a competing idea of the standard pronunciation that differs from modern MSE norms.

In a previous study (A. Irvine 1994: 69), I found that educated, affluent speakers avoided the [kj] before the long vowel, but more consistently produced /kj/ before the short [a] (see Table 2.8).

Table 2.8: The incidence of the palatal glide in eight male speakers

kj + a	kj + aː	kʰ + a	kʰ + aː
61 (94%)	10 (6%)	4 (9%)	41 (91%)

Patrick does acknowledge the importance of vowel length for the incidence of the palatal variants, but argues instead for *-ar* words as a separate class for analysis from *-at* type words. So, for example, the prestige pattern of [kj] use (found in the urban, upwardly-mobile, middle class speaker) will permit [kjat] *cat* but inhibit [kja:r] *car*. I have found in my sample, however, that speakers do produce forms like [kjarɪ] *carry*, [kjaraktʌ] *character*, [kjarɪbiən] *Caribbean*; and there is a prominent insurance company locally that advertises its [gjaranti] *guarantee* of good service. Moreover, the -AR class he identifies (pg. 107) of lexical items like *cards, car, guards* and *garbage* all have long vowels, and it is therefore not clear why they are analysed as an exceptional word class. Dyer & Beckford-Wassink (2001) conclude in their study that: "where the status of the upwardly mobile speaker was once marked by the absence of Creole forms, certain Creole forms such as (KYA) are now welcomed" (31). They find (pg. 23) palatal glide insertion to be constrained by the number of syllables in the word (occurring typically in mono- and disyllables). I have also not found this pattern in my sample, as attested to above.

The pattern of use among my informants was as described in Table 2.9.

Table 2.9: Word initial velar stops and variants in the total sample

kja	kʰa	kja:	kʰa:
119 (56.9%)	90 (43.1%)	19 (19.8%)	77 (80.2%)

In this data, *can* (the modal auxiliary) was excluded in the many instances it was produced as [kɛn] and therefore was not comparable with other items in the data set. This reduced the token count for this feature in the data. I have therefore collapsed the voiced and voiceless velar stop in this analysis under the general heading of /k/. The palatal velar before the short vowel occurs frequently in the informants' speech. Notably, the incidence of the feature before the long vowel is much lower, and comparable to the more stigmatized variants [nat] and voiceless TH stopping. The pattern in the sample, which shows variation before the short vowel, suggests that [kʰ ~ kj] is linked to /ɔ/ use in JE and may be a phonetic feature that draws attention to possession of distinct /a/ and /ɔ/ sounds (see Cassidy & Le Page 1967: xlix). Arguably, use of [kj], which is prohibited before [ɔ], more sharply distinguishes [a] from [ɔ] in a sociolinguistic context where the two vary in many speakers' production.

The data on TH stopping, [e ~ ie] and [kj ~ kʰ], raises an interesting question about sociolinguistic variation in pairs of variables. It is possible that speakers pay "attention" to only one member of the pair of related phonological variables when prestige/stigma are at stake. While the incidence of word initial voiceless TH stopping is very low in the sample with a 14% rate of occurrence, the voiced counterpart was produced 54% of the time for the variable. And the incidence of the front diphthong before /r/ is more than four times that of its counterpart elsewhere. Here again we find one of a pair of variables being singled out and being used to index prestige/stigma, as [kja:] is seldom produced in a sample in which [kʰa ~ kja] freely vary. This issue will be explored fully in the final section of Chapter 3.

2.4 Features not widely discussed in the literature (Group B)

Brodber (1989) identifies at least two types of speakers of Jamaican English – one group "generally displays a command of a variety of formal and informal styles [of JE]", while the other, an "adherence, in speech, to spelling pronunciation, and careful, somewhat measured, articulation" (46). The former tend to be vernacular speakers of English who acquire Creole later, the latter learn English in the school system.[6] Mugglestone (1995: 158) and J. C. Wells (1982a: 229) describe a similar distinction in RP English, with speakers of adoptive RP i.e. "those who did not use this accent as children" tending to avoid features that occur naturally in the speech of "mainstream" speakers. I take the first three variables dealt with below to be instances of the kind of articulations Brodber discusses for adoptive JE. This section on Group B variables is completed by an examination of rhoticity and final cluster simplification in the JAMPRO sample.

2.4.1 The word final unstressed vowel in words that end in -er

In some speakers, pronunciations such as [ʤʌmekʌr] *Jamaica* and [bʌtʌr] *butter* occur. This may be explained in two ways. Firstly, there seems to be a generalized sensitivity to the (perceived as) Creole [a] discussed above, which occurs at the end of words like [mada] *mother*, [tiʧa] *teacher* and [tiela] *tailor*. Some speakers use a spelling pronunciation to avoid the [a] ending, and this has been extended even into words that do potentially end in [a] and have no -er in the orthography (like *Jamaica*).[7] This kind of spelling pronunciation is a consequence of avoiding a stigmatized item, and in that respect is different from the phenomenon of

---

[6] According to Hernández-Campoy & Jiménez-Cano (2003) the implementation of the standard variety usually follows the same route. As such, the greater the frequency of standard forms in informal/familiar styles, the greater the degree of standardisation.

[7] However, the kind of hypercorrection being discussed here is attested to elsewhere in the English language community. Mugglestone (1995: 100) cites texts from the late 19th century which have this sort of complaint: In a young author's first volume I found "Italy" made to

speakers in some (principally L$_2$) communities saying for example [dɛbt] *debt* and [θɪŋg] *thing* (Trudgill & Hannah 1994: 123), which does not typically appear in Jamaican English varieties. Secondly, retroflexion of an *-er* ending is an aspect of rhotic varieties of English – for example General American (Giegerich 1992: 64f) – which JE is said to be (see Table 2.10). The [ʌr] variant may reflect either this general rhoticity or the adoptive JE spelling pronunciation or both. No one in my sample produced forms like [dʒʌmekʌr] *Jamaica*, which suggests that the retroflexion for the JAMPRO informants is spelling pronunciation rather than the targeting of a generalized rhoticity.

Here I am looking at the production of lexical items that do have a final spelled *-er* in the written form (illustrated by the word *butter*). See Table 2.10 for what the informants in my sample produced.

Table 2.10: Final articulation of *-er* words in the total sample of informants

butt[a]	butt[ʌ]	butt[ʌ r]
237 (18%)	958 (72.9%)	118 (9.1%)

Very few occurrences of the [ʌr] variant are produced in these informants. Interestingly, this feature (and the one in the following discussion) is one aspect of a register that has been called "teacher English" by some Jamaicans (see also Christie 2003: 19). The label carries with it a number of associations: overly careful speech due to linguistic insecurity, an unvarying classroom formality, and femaleness.

In the sample, there were six informants with a high frequency of [ʌr] in their speech, but only two speakers who used this variant more frequently than any of the other variants (M15, F52).

2.4.2 The vowel in the final syllable *-tion*

In words like *education* four possible variants occurred in the sample for the final syllable – [ʃan] ~ [ʃʌn] ~ [ʃɔn] ~ [ʃən]. Shields-Brodber (1996: 4) mentions this [ʃɔn] pronunciation in her article on the changing voice of public, formal

---

rhyme with "bitterly". Now "Iterly", in the mouth of a public speaker, would condemn him as a thorough Cockney (Carpenter 1868).

She concludes that in England, and as suggested by the quote, there was a widespread standard ideology that "literate speech" meant a rhotic articulation, notwithstanding the reality of evolving mainstream RP production.

discourse in Jamaica. Her impression is that [ʃɔn] is also an aspect of what she calls "adoptive JE" (Brodber 1989: 46), use of which indexes both the learning of English and length of stay in the school system. I suggest that [ʃɔn] is an example of distancing from the form associated with Creole ([ʃan]). Just as the stigma attached to voiceless TH stopping and non-contrastive /h/ generates production which is regarded as hypercorrect by some users of JE, the association of [a] with its "correct" reflex [ɔ] in stressed syllables has thrown up a variant which exaggerates backness and rounding in syllables that are typically unstressed in MSE. To avoid saying something like *educa*[ʃan], or being perceived as someone who does, some speakers produce *educa*[ʃɔn] even in unstressed syllables, thus over-extending the conversion of /a/ to /ɔ/.

The JAMPRO informants produced the data in Table 2.11.

Table 2.11: Articulation of final *-tion* in the total sample

educa[ʃan]	educa[ʃʌ n]	educa[ʃɔ n]	educa[ʃən]
149 (20.9%)	377 (53%)	120 (16.8%)	65 (9.3%)

The [ʃɔn] variant, like the retroflex variant in Table 2.11, was used by a small subset of speakers (11 informants) with high frequency. However, this group of 11 has only one speaker in common with the group of 6 who produced [ʌr] (F52). The sociolinguistics of these sub-groupings in the JAMPRO sample will be explored in the following chapters. Generally, there seems to be much less focussing around a particular norm for this feature (unlike the data in Table 2.11), with close to half of the attestations of *-tion* varying among the possible phonetic options. What is noticeable, however, is that the [ʃɔn] variant occurs with greater frequency than the MSE (schwa) variant.

2.4.3 The alveopalatal affricate

In words like *creature, culture, soldier* and *procedure*, some informants produce a palatalized alveolar stop variant and not an affricate, e.g. [kritjʌ], [kʌltjʌ], [sol-djʌ] and [prəsidjʌ] *procedure.*[8]

I propose it is partially the form of the written word that influences the production of [tj] and [dj], which appears to be a fairly widely used pronunciation for *culture* type words in my sample. Speakers would seem to be using English

---

[8]This last item is frequently pronounced with syllable initial stress, as in [prɔsɨdjʌ] *procedure.*

Table 2.12: Articulation of *culture* type words in the total sample

dj	ʤ	tj	ʧ
34 (75.5%)	11 (24.5%)	73 (35.4%)	133 (64.6%)

orthography as a guide to "correct" pronunciation. Words such as *teacher* or *bleacher*, that pattern the phonemic shape of *creature* in MSE, but with a written symbol <ch> that suggests affricate pronunciation, never exhibit this variation between affricate and palatalized stop. However, the spelling pronunciation itself may function in another way in these cases. It also distances speakers from a stigmatized JC feature, the use of an affricate in words such as *pleasure* [plɛʤa] (F91, F23), *usually* [juʤəli] (F71) and *division* [dɪvɪʤʌn] (F57). Notably, these JC pronunciations seem to occur typically with the voiced affricate, and this may explain the greater frequency of palatalized voiced alveolar stops used by informants in my sample. The phoneme inventory described at the start of this chapter identifies /ʃ/ in JC but not /ʒ/. Arguably, the stigmatized affrication in JE items that would have the voiced fricative /ʒ/, has perhaps resulted in the higher incidence of [dj]. Moreover, two of my informants (F6, F10), on more than one occasion, produced the form [djunjʌ] *junior*, an extension of /ʤ/ → /dj/ even when the orthography suggests the former. Interestingly, Devonish (pers. comm.) also cites [tju:] *chew* as occurring.

Additionally, it is possible, based on Marshall's study (1983), that Creole is associated with the use of affricates generally. He found spirantization, in forms such as [ʒəmeka] *Jamaica* and [ʒɛnərʌl] *general*, to be increasingly a feature of some formal speech, an avoidance of the affricate even when the orthography requires it. Another two informants at JAMPRO (F58, F59), produced [wɪt] *which* and a third item [ʧa:rd] *charge* was recorded (F52).

In at least these speakers, I suggest, "good English" is not producing the affricate, notwithstanding its use in MSE. (Note again that in *-tion* words, the MSE schwa variant is also not as widely used as [ʃɔn]). For the variable in *creature* type words, the Creole form and the MSE form are similar. These informants, in favouring [tj]/[dj], are responding to local patterns of language use and to local notions of what is Creole and what is English, not to a remote standard of English that is external to their speech community. Discussions about the "metropolitanization" of speech in social contexts like Jamaica (Trudgill 2002: 70, for example[9]) seem to disregard the local ideologies of language that must mediate any changes in language use that speakers are seen to make. Shields (1987) bears repeating,

> though some phonological features are shared by mainstream RP and Ja-
> maican Creole these are often eliminated from the speech of [English speak-
> ing] informants because of their obvious associations with Creole (119–120).

Historically, in MSE, the literature does point to pronunciations such as [kritjʌ], [kʌltjʌ] and [soldjʌ] as variants of 18th century British pronunciation, though its status in terms of prestige was unclear by then (Lehmann 1973: 178). Certainly, in the late 17th century the recommendation was that *pastor* and *pasture*, *pick't her* and *picture* should be pronounced the same (Freeborn 1998: 365). Beal (2002: 146) discusses a number of prescriptions on the matter from a number of contemporary sources and concludes that, for some:

> This pronunciation [as in ne:tju:r *nature*] would have been beyond reproach
> in the late eighteenth century (...) This is almost certainly the style that
> Spence would have heard in the rhetorical style used by the clergymen who
> seem to have provided his model of "correct" speech.

Moreover, the recommendation from Sheridan's dictionary that favoured the affricate was criticized as follows: "...if a foreigner or native be ambitious for passing for an English gentleman, let him avoid with utmost care, Mr. Sheridan's -SH-" (Beal 2002: 147, citing a source from the 1790's).

This historical data may point to the reputed conservative nature of colonial Englishes (Fisher 2001: 84, for example), so that the variation in my sample may represent continuity from the patterns discussed above for 18th century English. But that explanation would possibly have more traction if this kind of variation was observed in other such speech communities; I have not been able to find any reference to it, though my own impression is that it occurs in Trinidad English as well. Interestingly, the association of the [tj]/[dj] feature with clergymen may suggest an early model of educated JE, given the historical connection between education and the church in Jamaica (see Campbell 1996: 262, for example). It

---

[9]Hancock (1994) uses the term to mean "the replacement of creole features by those from the coexistent metropolitan language" (97) – which is initially confusing because it would be difficult to argue that Jamaican Creole and any metropolitan variety of English coexist. However, Hancock's definition of metropolitan English ("any native variety of non-creole English", 97) suggests that his use of the term *metropolitanization* may be interpreted as the replacement of Creole features by those from JE.

is probable that this pattern in JE is a coincidence of all three influences: an aspect of what Coye (1998) calls "orthoepic piracy" – when a spelling form is more frequently used (181) – reinforced by the avoidance of the stigmatized "Creole" affricate, and an earlier prestige norm that also disfavoured the affricate.

Nearly all my informants varied the palatalized alveolar stop with the affricate when voiced. 17 informants used only the [dj] variant and 22 the [tj]. Interestingly, informant F52, whose speech patterns are singled out above in the discussions of [ʃɔn] and [bʌtʌr] as one informant who produced these consistently, used only the affricate and not the spelling pronunciation that would perhaps have been predicted by her language use in those cases.

2.4.4 Post-vocalic rhoticity

The seminal work on rhoticity in the Jamaican continuum is Aker's implicational scale (Table 2.13).

Table 2.13: Rhoticity in the Linguistic Continuum, adapted from Akers (1981: 73)

	Stage						
	0	1	2	3	4	5	6
Intervocalic		x	x	x	x	x	x
Word Final			x	x	x	x	x
Before Coronal liquids/nasals				x	x	x	x
Before other Coronals					x	x	x
Before Consonants						x	x
After Schwa							x

Aker's description idealizes a rhotic acrolect (stage 6), largely an extrapolation of a system maximally divergent from a non-rhotic basilect (stage 0), and is not based on the actual production of acrolectal speakers. There is general agreement that Jamaican Creole varieties are generally non-rhotic pre-consonantally (Beckford-Wassink 1999a: 184; J. C. Wells 1982c: 577). Non-basilectal varieties show more variation, as typified by Well's description:

> ...in *start* and *north* words, sporadic pre-consonantal rhoticity is characteristic of many mesolectal and some acrolectal speakers: thus short, basilectally [ʃaːt], may be pronounced either [ʃɔːrt] or, more commonly, [ʃɔːt].

Post-vocalic rhoticity does function as a sociolinguistic marker in Jamaican speech. Beckford-Wassink (1999a) found that male informants in her acrolect-dominant urban sample were less likely to be rhotic than their female counter-parts. In an earlier study (A. Irvine 1988: 142, see §1.4 in this book), I found factors like parent's background and speaker's level of education to also show correlations with rhoticity. For example, speakers were more likely to be rhotic when they were highly educated; those whose parents were relatively affluent were typically non-rhotic, unless they had spent a long time in the school system. My conclusion then was that education in Jamaica had normalized a rhotic variety of English. Indeed, r-insertion was observed in two informants, who produced forms like [wɔrn] *one* and [ɔrpətjun] *opportune*, which suggested that rhoticity is perceived to be "correct" JE.

In the JAMPRO sample, speakers were almost categorically rhotic word finally where the syllable is stressed (as in *car* or *more*), and following the vowels in words like *bird* and *beard*. The data for sociolinguistic variation here concerns rhoticity before coronal consonants and after the vowels /a/ as in *party,* and /ɔ/ as in *forty.*[10]

Table 2.14: Rhoticity in the total sample of informants

party type words		*forty* type words	
[partɪ]	[paːtɪ]	[fɔrtɪ]	[fɔːtɪ]
114 (44.4%)	143 (55.6%)	210 (66%)	108 (34%)

r-insertion did occur in one informant (F16), who produced the forms [ɔrtɔrɪtɪ] *authority* and [masarʤ] *massage*; and according to F. Miller (pers. comm.) one of her informants produced the form [mɔrðʌr] *mother*. In light of the findings in the earlier study, for some JE speakers at least, such as those with considerable formal education, "correct" English is rhotic. Generally, however, as in Wells' description above, speakers at JAMPRO varied in relation to rhotic and non-rhotic post-vocalic productions after the low central vowel. However, there is a much higher incidence of rhotic productions after [ɔ] in the same sample.

---

[10]Historically, loss of rhoticity in this phonetic environment is first attested in 1640, but is more widely a feature of 18th century British prescriptions (Beal 2002: 164f; J. C. Wells 1982a: 218). Indeed, according to Beal, such rhoticity became as stigmatized as h-dropping in the 19th century. Wells suggests that the pattern of rhoticity in YS varieties reflects the different historical influences on American English, with the rhotic varieties reflecting earlier contact with norms from Britain and the non-rhotic varieties later contact with new prestige pronunciations.

2.4.5 Word-final clusters

In this study I wish to compare the patterns for two word-final clusters, [st] and [nt], distinguishing for the latter between its use when only a phonological cluster (as in *government, rent, important*) and when it also has morphological function (as in *don't, can't, aren't*). I am not including [nt] clusters that have past reference (as in *sent*) in this set, as analysis sometimes proved problematic. For example, in the sentence "*when I sen' for the report...*" it is not always clear whether [d] or [t] is the absent consonant in the cluster, particularly in a speaker's longer narrative text. I cannot necessarily assume past tense marking as it is very possible that on some occasions speakers produced an invariant verb form as is done in Jamaican varieties. I will also analyse separately the extent to which clusters with past tense reference (as in *looked* or *kept*) occur in my sample. In my data I have collapsed regular bi-morphemic past tenses (*passed, believed*) and semi-weak forms (*felt, meant*) together to furnish enough data for analysis. The literature would suggest that in varieties of English, the former will be more consistently marked than the latter (Guy 1980: 5; Neu 1980: 47, for example); but speakers of educated (standard) varieties are said to generally delete grammatical clusters less than they do purely phonological clusters. Additionally, a preceding nasal in a phonological cluster is one environment where it is not clear whether clusters tend to be promoted or inhibited in varieties of English (the table in Patrick 1999: 131 summarizes a number of findings in other studies). In contrast, a preceding sibilant (as in *fast* or *most*) is a more favourable context for simplification. In that respect, it will be interesting to see what occurs in the acrolect and compare it to findings from other varieties.

I am interested in three specific aspects of cluster production in the acrolect: whether it is more frequent than has been found in studies of basilectal/mesolectal speech, as would be expected if we accept the notion of continuum; whether it is socially distributed in the acrolect and associated with factors like education, gender and the like; and whether it is a salient feature in identifying one as a speaker of "good" JE.

The literature on final clusters in varieties of English is detailed and rich, suggesting that there are two important phonological constraints on the rate of presence/absence of CC##:

1. the following segment, so that clusters are less likely to be produced when the following segment is a consonant (Labov 1972: 217);

2. the preceding segment, so that clusters are less likely to be produced after a sibilant (Santa Ana 1991, cited in Patrick 1999: 131).

In addition, the data for (mesolectal) Jamaican also suggests that clusters with morphological content are least likely to be produced when they function as a negative -*n't* (Patrick 1999: 150). The data in Table 2.15 summarizes Patrick's findings for mesolectal[11] Jamaican; his analysis assumes that mesolectal Jamaican is a variety of English with underlying CC## that can have morphological content.

Table 2.15: Percentage of (TD)-absence in mesolect (Patrick 1999: 140, 150, 157)

Preceding segment	Absence rate
Nasal	74%
Sibilant	85%
Grammatical function	
Regular past	56%
Semi-weak	59%
Negative *n't*	87%

Patrick's data on mesolectal Jamaican varieties suggest that absence of clusters is the general tendency, overall only produced on the surface about a quarter of the time. Moreover, the cluster is typically absent in words like *can't* or *don't*, most often heard as [kjã:] or [duon]. Importantly, the rate of past tense marking in the mesolect is similar for regular and irregular forms, which Patrick interprets as substrate Creole influence on the morphology. Akers's (1977: 130, 140) results for tense marking in Jamaica, with a 53% absence on regular verbs in the wordlist test, suggest that clusters with morphological content are more likely to show t/d absence than purely phonological (i.e. mono-morphemic) ones.

Shields (1984) provides data from interviews with Jamaican teachers in formal contexts (the classroom primarily), and therefore her findings are specific to the acrolectal pattern for the general treatment of consonant clusters. She notes that,

> [i]n SJE (...) it is not uncommon to find [cluster] reduction [before a following vowel] at a very high rate even in very formal contexts. In SJE, the

---

[11]Patrick1999 defines the mesolect as "an intermediate [between the acrolect and basilect] variety or range of varieties" (16); the mesolect is therefore a necessary variety or set of varieties in a continuum, but varieties intermediate to an idealized JE and JX do not require a continuum to exist. Indeed, Meade (2001: 25) argues for the mesolect as a separate mixed system, given that speakers may have "a narrow linguistic range [of competence] that does not extend to include the acrolect or basilect".

(...) following vowel only partially rather than totally inhibits simplification (...) resulting in acceptable variation between SJE *last evening & las' evening*, with [the former] being preferred in most formal contexts (3).

Additionally, speakers are conscious of the need to preserve the clusters and therefore produce exaggerated forms like [la:st^h] *last* or [se:nt^h] *saint* or [hand^ə] *hand*. Shields explains both the high rates of cluster simplification (45% of 1389 tokens, p. 128) and the exaggerated forms by relating them to a fundamentally Creole open syllable structure in most of her informants, notwithstanding the relatively superficial acquisition of English forms (14). Indeed, Devonish (1992: 2) has argued that perhaps the term TD *insertion* might more reflect the realities of the Jamaican situation, suggesting that speakers acquire rules that insert the final element in the cluster rather than delete (as happens in English) in the production of an underlying CC##. This would perhaps explain the following hypercorrect forms that I have heard in JE: 1) the government put a [band] *ban* on cigarettes; 2) I have a pain in my [mɪdrɪft] *midriff*; 3) Chomsky discusses the under[laɪnd] *underlyin'* level of representation; 4) [and] *an* analysis of population movement; and 5) the staff are trying to underm[aɪnd] *undermine* me. Such forms do not occur in a variety like AAVE (Labov 1972: 217), nor have I seen them reported elsewhere. Interestingly, these are all hypercorrections that generate well-formed English items, as I have rarely heard hypercorrect non-English forms as seen in the examples from TH stopping or avoiding affricates. One informant, F16, did produce [ondlɪ] *only* once in her text, which may suggest the hypercorrect insertion of a stop. If an insertion rule is operating in some speakers, then it seems to be a phonological rule that is also lexically constrained, typically substituting already heard/existing well-formed English morphemes like *drift* and *band*, and not merely converting C## → CC##. With the exception of F16's [ondlɪ] none of my informants produced any of the forms discussed above.

Notably, hypercorrect insertion of stops word finally was also a feature of some 17th–18th century varieties of British English, particularly in London (Pegge 1814: 57–73).[12] He cites the following examples: *attackted, sermont, drownded, paragraft* and *sinst*. Mugglestone (1995: 238) also cites the use of "oust" *house* as an example of how vulgar speakers were depicted in the contemporary literature of that period.

The data for all speakers shows the following. I have excluded following alveolar stops, as in *pay rent to*, but have not excluded interdental fricatives from the data as the typical pattern in this sample is production of [θ].

---

[12]Le Page (1960: 11–12) gives London and the ports of London as one source of early Jamaican settlement, particularly the deportation of prisoners from Newgate.

Table 2.16: Phonological clusters in the total sample of informants

Before a following vowel C(C)##V					
-nt	-nt^h	-n	-st	-st^h	-s
166 (68.3%)	34 (14%)	43 (17.7%)	99 (41.5%)	14 (6%)	125 (52.5%)
Before a following consonant C(C)##C					
-nt	-nt^h	-n	-st	-st^h	-s
149 (45.5%)	29 (9%)	149 (45.5%)	44 (11%)	12 (3%)	356 (86%)

The data for -nt clusters in Table 2.16 does not include -n't negative clusters. That data is presented separately.

As the literature would predict, the frequency of cluster simplification is much higher before a following consonant (e.g. $\chi^2 = 48.48$, p < .001 for -nt clusters). Speakers are more likely to produce clusters before a vowel. Also, perhaps not unexpectedly given his sample of mesolectal speakers, Patrick's absence rate of 74% for [nt] is higher than the rate of 34% in my sample. However, for [st] clusters, the absence rate in my data is 74% and is much closer to his mesolectal sample and lower than what Shield's described in her teachers. One possible explanation for these teachers' productions is the "teacher English" referred to in an earlier section of this chapter (§2.4), characterised by its overly careful speech and recourse to spelling for "correct" pronunciation. For clusters with morphological function, the data for all speakers is as follows. I will use the label -ed in this study to refer to the cluster final [t]/[d] produced for the past suffix.

Table 2.17: Morphological clusters in the total sample of informants

Before a following vowel C(C)##V			
-n't	-n'	-ed	Ø
31 (51%)	30 (49%)	156 (77%)	47 (23%)
Before a following consonant C(C)##C			
-n't	-n'	-ed	Ø
89 (16%)	480 (84%)	86 (44.5%)	107 (55.5%)

Before a following vowel segment, 40 informants produced -ed categorically and 5 speakers not at all. Before a consonant, the results were strikingly different, with only 8 informants producing -ed all the time in their interviews and 17 never doing so. Most informants varied in their production of clusters. Comparison of rates of deletion of bi-morphemic past tense clusters with other studies suggests that JAMPRO informants are less likely to consistently mark past tense than speakers of Trinidad English (Winford 1997: 269) or any North American varieties (Labov 1972: 222; Neu 1980: 43), but are more likely to do so than the mesolectal speakers in Patrick's sample. And the data would indicate that phonological constraints on cluster production are important even for tense marking in JE, a phenomenon noted for a variety of non-standard varieties of English such as Puerto Rican, Tejano, Appalachian and the like.

For words like *can't, don't* and the like, arguably the general pattern is to simplify the cluster. Indeed, these two specific items, even in the formal speech here, are frequently produced as [kʰã:(n)] and [dõ(n)]. It is possible that these two items have become or are becoming lexicalized without [t]. This would explain the consistent production of non-morphological [nt] before a vowel (82.3%) but the variation that occurs when it functions as a negative.

2.5 Discussion

The lists below show the rates at which all features are absent/present in the speech of informants. The number of informants varies according to the presence of a particular variable in the recorded interview.

The shaded cells in Tables 2.18–2.19 show where a considerable number of speakers produced a particular variant of a variable, and they suggest an idea of good Jamaican English that can be positively defined in terms of having certain features: having (voiceless) interdental fricatives, pronouncing /h/, using [kʰ] before the long vowel, articulating past tense clusters and -nt before a following word that starts with a vowel. Notably, in spite of the reputed status of the back vowel [ɔ] and the hypercorrection that has been identified with it, most speakers show some variation between it and [a].

The distribution of Group B variants is much more diffuse than for certain Group A variants and speakers cannot be said to consistently use any variant here except the two aforementioned consonant clusters. This is well illustrated in the distribution of *-tion* pronunciations in the sample. At best, the data suggests that most speakers will vary [ʌ] with some other possible variant. I suggest that some features seem not to be salient in producing JE – for example [st] clusters

Table 2.18: Group A variables and distribution in the sample of informants

		Variant			
Feature	Informants taped	Never use		Always use	
/h/	82	11	(13.0%)	31	(38.0%)
Initial [ð]	82	2	(2.0%)	0	
Initial [θ]	82	2	(2.0%)	40	(49.0%)
[ɔ] *not*	82	0		1	(1.0%)
[o] *boat*	82	0		32	(39.0%)
[e] *face*	82	1	(1.0%)	27	(33.0%)
[ɔ r] *poor*	81	0		28	(34.5%)
[ber] *beer*	82	4	(5.0%)	3	(4.0%)
[kʰ a]	64	13	(20.0%)	14	(22.0%)
[kʰ a:]	48	7	(14.5%)	33	(69.0%)

and -n't clusters. More clearly, JE speech as reflected in these informants is *not* having certain JC features, such as an invariant low vowel [a]; for other variables, and particularly [kja] and [d ~ ð], speakers of JE seem to be characterised as not having *only* JC pronunciation.

Most of these areas of variation were identified elsewhere in the English language world, and most from the time that English was also being established in Jamaica. So, for example, the 'illiterate speaker' of the 1850's in Britain was said to use hypercorrect 'h' and to drop 'h' (Mugglestone 1995, Ch. 2). And the refined speaker produced [dj] in *soldier* words or [kj]. Further, prescriptions on postvocalic rhoticity or the distinction between *chap* and *chop* words were changing at the time. Such ideologies would have also arrived and evolved in Jamaica, given the phonology of Creole varieties occupying the same social space and the desire for social differentiation. A good illustration of this is the pronunciation of *culture* type words. The pattern of use in my sample includes the palatalized stop variant, notwithstanding the affricate (now) in use in MSE. Though I do not necessarily attribute this to historical continuity, it is clear that the metropolitan norm has changed. The use in my sample is as much an avoidance of "bad" English, i.e. JC affricates, even when the feature is an aspect of MSE, as it is a response to spelling and therefore a signal of being literate and educated. Clearly, there is considerable variation for most features in this sample of speakers. As such, the social distribution of variants must be important for any discussion of

Table 2.19: Group B variables and distribution in the sample of informants

Feature	Informants taped	Variant			
		Never use		Always use	
-er *butter*	82	35	(43.0%)	0	
[ʌ] *butter*	82	0		7	(8.5%)
[a] *butter*	82	27	(33.0%)	0	
[ʃan] *-tion*	81	39	(48.0%)	6	(7.0%)
[ʃʌn] *-tion*	81	6	(7.0%)	7	(9.0%)
[ʃɔn] *-tion*	81	41	(51.0%)	0	
[ʃən] *-tion*	81	43	(53.0%)	0	
[tj] *culture*	65	6	(21.0%)	17	(61.0%)
[dj] *soldier*	28	13	(20.0%)	14	(22.0%)
[r] *party*	79	29	(37.0%)	21	(26.5%)
[r] *forty*	78	8	(10.0%)	29	(37.0%)
-nt## V	71	3	(4.0%)	41	(58.0%)
-nt## C	77	11	(14.0%)	14	(18.0%)
-st## V	71	19	(27.0%)	12	(17.0%)
-st## C	81	47	(58.0%)	2	(2.0%)
n't## V	33	12	(36.0%)	10	(30.0%)
n't## C	78	34	(43.5%)	0	
-ed *before V*	71	5	(7.0%)	40	(56.0%)
-ed *before C*	62	17	(27.0%)	8	(13.0%)

the acrolect, as the association of variants with factors like education, or gender, can suggest one type of normalisation of features that index "good" English among or for these speakers.

Certainly, as Devonish (2003) points out, "with reference to the Jamaican situation, in the face of two abstractions, Standard Jamaican English and "basilectal" Jamaican Creole, the first is accepted (...) by the society at large as real" (164). But this abstraction is fundamentally defined in terms of written SE, as it is elsewhere in the English language community. Data on the spoken norms of this idealization called SJE, as reflected in use that Allsopp (1996: lvi) calls "considered natural in formal contexts" can reveal received pronunciations of SJE, in the sense of (an) institutionally disseminated accent of an influential minority (Yallop 1999: 31). What is it that determines which of two prospective qualified employees will be selected during an interview? What judgements are being reflected when someone is said to be "well spoken" or "having a good command of English"? The abstraction that is SJE is realized for members of the speech community in the language actually used in these formal contexts. Recourse to external norms of speaking for a description do not reflect the reality. In this sample, use of [h] is widespread and the norm in JE. But, equally, use of [d] *there* and [kj] *carry* is also widespread. The [d], no doubt, would be excluded if most speakers were *asked* which of the two, [d] or [ð], is standard. It is not as clear that norms about the latter feature [kja] are as focussed. Moreover, when others in the speech community hear successful and/or influential people using some of these features and not others; when people who use some of these features are employed and successfully so, then the idea of what is spoken SJE must be informed by such practice.

3 Sociolinguistic variation in Jamaican English

3.1 Level of education

As noted in Chapter 1, DeCamp's original characterization of the acrolect was the speech of "the well-educated urban professional" (1961: 82). And in any reading of the literature on the Caribbean, education is the single most important social factor used to locate the speaker of the standard variety of English.[1] This is not peculiar to the Caribbean, however, as educatedness is important for locating the standard speaker elsewhere. Trudgill (1999: 118) can be used as an example:

> ...it is the variety associated with the education system in all the English-speaking countries of the world, and is therefore the variety spoken by those who are often referred to as "educated people".

This, of course, implies that the perception of a speaker as "educated" can influence the way we evaluate their language use as standard, possibly as much as the structures used in speech (Thakerar et al. 1982).

As stated earlier, the *Revised primary curriculum* 1999, published by the Ministry of Education in Jamaica, conceives of a locally legitimised target variety for the school system, SJE.

Historically, English has been the one compulsory exam taken in Jamaica, and the data indicate that, on average, roughly 40% of CXC candidates achieve grades acceptable for tertiary education (E. Miller 1989: 222). A similar percentage of students, according to the Ministry, passed in 2000:[2]

---

[1] Other factors like social class (typically indexed by occupation and income), urban provenance and, to a lesser extent, race/skin colour have also been used (see the discussion in §1.4 of this book). However, with the possible exception of race/skin colour, factors like class, residence and occupation are themselves inextricably linked to the speaker's level of education.

[2] These results are controversial as they reflect the percentage of students allowed to sit the exam, not students eligible to sit. When students eligible to sit are analysed, then the percentage of students achieving the appropriate English Language grade is halved. For example, in 2003, by reason of pre-selection, 16,000 students were not allowed to take the CXC exam in English, an average exclusion rate of about 50 percent (*The Daily Gleaner*, November 21, 2003).

In English Language, the passes moved from the 41.2 per cent in 1999 to 47.9 this year [2000]. Grades 1, 2 and 3 are the acceptable grades for entry into tertiary institutions (*The Daily Gleaner*, September 2, 2000).

The SJE described by the Ministry of Education and Culture (1999: 17) has only a handful of phonological prescriptions for the teacher/student:

- distinguish between false homophones in JC and SJE e.g. *at/hot, an/on, doze/those*

- clarify JC/SJE confusion of words such as *file/foil*

Interestingly, in light of the discussion in the previous chapter, these pinpoint for the teacher and the student – phonemic /h/ usage, control of the [ɔ] vowel and TH stopping. This might suggest some predictable outcomes in any correlation of language use and education in this study. We might, for example, expect a greater degree of uniformity in the use of the variants [h], [ɔ] and [θ/ð], focussed by the prescriptions of the school system. Additionally, the informants with higher education and more prolonged exposure to the school system might produce fewer non-standard variants of these variables.

Within JAMPRO itself, education was the most important of the criteria mentioned for employment and success at the agency. Of the 104 informants in this study, 77 (74%) specifically said that having at least a (University) degree was essential, and they suggested the following reasons why:

- [it gives you] an ability to see the bigger picture and think a little differently (F50)

- if you're well educated and everything your social class tends to be middle class (F56)

- it equips you to have a good command of the English language (F7)

- it gives you an edge (F21)

- it impresses (F46).

One consequence of this agency policy is that JAMPRO staff is highly educated relative to the wider society (STATIN 1991: 15:22).[3]

---

[3]The category "post-secondary" refers to those employees who have completed high school and gone on to do courses, diplomas or certificates at some institution; "tertiary" then refers specifically to a university degree. The Jamaica data does not add up to 100%, as I have not included the uneducated (i.e. unschooled) in the table.

Table 3.1: JAMPRO and Jamaican educational attainment compared

	JAMPRO (All) (%)	Jamaica (%)
Primary	4	50
Secondary	10	29.4
Post-Secondary	42	18.6
Tertiary	21	1.3
Postgraduate	23	0.7

Most of the staff has post-secondary as minimum level of education, with close to half of the total sample being university educated. All but the primary level informants have therefore achieved Grades 1, 2 or 3 or equivalent in English examinations at least at the CXC or GCE "O" level standard. Those with a university degree, will also have completed tertiary level English language courses such as UWI's English for Academic Purposes.

Of those informants whose speech was recorded, the distribution is as in Table 3.2.[4]

Table 3.2: JAMPRO educational attainment and informants compared

	JAMPRO (All) (%)		Jamaica (%)	
Primary	4	(3.9%)	4	(4.9%)
Secondary	10	(9.7%)	9	(11.1%)
Post-Secondary	43	(41.7%)	36	(44.4%)
Tertiary	22	(21.4%)	16	(19.8%)
Postgraduate	24	(23.3%)	16	(19.8%)

It should be mentioned that for many members of staff, the importance placed on "having a degree" was a contentious issue. Two attitudes were observed. The first was a resentment that JAMPRO placed more stock in the "piece of paper" than it did on actual performance. A few informants expressed the perception that the requirements for promotion, in particular, stressed further education over an ability to do the job. This was a decidedly minority view from 5 informants. A more common feeling was that JAMPRO favoured candidates with foreign degrees, earned outside of the Caribbean. Twenty-three (23) informants

---

[4]One informant did not give a response and therefore the total for JAMPRO adds up to 103.

specifically said that having a foreign degree meant a greater chance of being hired and better prospects in the company. Of the 46 informants with tertiary level qualifications, 12 (26%) had degrees from either the USA or the EU and, not surprisingly, neither they nor senior management shared this perception.

Level of education will of course be an intervening variable in a number of the other social categories discussed in this study, such as status in the company and frontline position. In this section, however, I am only interested in any correlations that can be made with education alone, and where it is relevant in subsequent sections it will be discussed there. The educational categories have been collapsed into "primary", "secondary+" and "tertiary+", for in many correlations tokens were not enough to support a more nuanced stratification. The statistical analyses that follow *exclude* primary educated speakers; by inspection their patterns of use are very different and, when included in the chi-squared tests, they tend to distort the results. Moreover, as there were only four such informants in the agency, sufficient data could not be collected for many variables.

In the tables below the data for the 4 primary educated informants will be displayed so that their patterns can be compared to that of the other informants.[5]

3.1.1 Group A variables and education

Table 3.3: h-drop by education level ($p < .001$, $\chi^2 = 59.72$)

	n	h-drop	h
Primary	4	18 (37%)	31 (63%)
Secondary+	45	127 (17%)	636 (83%)
Tertiary+	32	39 (5%)	729 (95%)

There is a clear correlation between frequency of h-drop and level of education, with less of the feature used as the level of education rises. University graduates almost never h-drop, though all informants generally produce relatively

---

[5] All correlations were done using a chi-squared test of association. My interest here was not to weigh the relative influence of several factors on the production of informants or groups of informants. Indeed, the ultimate purpose of the study is to describe the speech of a particular subset of the JAMPRO sample, who constitute a specific, select set of employees (see Chapter 4). For that, and because of the type of data collected (frequencies and not scores), I used a non-parametric statistical procedure. I accept as statistically significant any association that yields a probability value of less than 5% (<.05). However, I also comment on data that produces results close to that value.

low frequencies of the feature. Of the four primary informants, one (M40) never dropped [h] (see Table 4.16 on page 147 on frontline staff). The few attestations of hypercorrect use, – that is, "incorrectly" adding [h] – were most typical in the "secondary ı" cohort (6 of the 9 informants who produced it), along with one "ter-tiary+" informant (M101), and two primary educated speakers. Seemingly, there were no h-less lects in my sample, though one informant (M88) produced [h] only once in his discourse.

Table 3.4: TH stopping by education level

Word Initial	d	ð	t	θ
Primary	111 (92.5%)	9 (7.5%)	13 (59.0%)	9 (41.0%)
Secondary+	1205 (56.0%)	940 (44.0%)	78 (18.4%)	345 (81.6%)
Tertiary+	920 (49.0%)	965 (51.0%)	25 (7.0%)	341 (93.0%)
	(p < .001, χ² = 21.86)		(p < .001, χ² = 23.24)	
Word Middle	d	ð	t	θ
Primary	10 (71.4%)	4 (28.6%)	2 (100.0%)	0
Secondary+	36 (23.0%)	120 (77.0%)	13 (18.6%)	57 (81.4%)
Tertiary+	27 (21.0%)	100 (79.0%)	7 (15.6%)	38 (84.4%)
	(p > .70, χ² = 0.117)		(p > .50, χ² = 0.17)	
Word Final	d	ð	t	θ
Primary	6 (100.0%)	0	0	0
Secondary+	12 (20.0%)	48 (80.0%)	11 (29.0%)	27 (71.0%)
Tertiary+	15 (27.0%)	40 (73.0%)	8 (18.0%)	36 (82.0%)
	(p > .30, χ² = 0.8)		(p > .20, χ² = 1.27)	

Word finally and in middle position there is no statistically significant difference between "secondary+" and "tertiary+" informants. Both sets of speakers have similarly low levels of TH stopping, whether voiced or voiceless, though the data set per speaker is small and generalizations must be cautiously made. Word initially, the more educated the speaker the lower the incidence of TH stopping, particularly when voiceless. Only one informant (M14) produced a high proportion of the voiceless stop variant. He alone accounted for 7 of the 25 tokens of [t], suggesting that for most speakers in this group a more accurate characterization would be absence of voiceless TH stopping. Importantly, tertiary+ informants who almost never use the voiceless stop variant, have close to half of their productions of the voiced variable as stops. While we can say that tertiary+ educated speakers, who almost never vary [t ~ θ], produce much less of the Creole form, we cannot say that their speech is characterized by more consistent use of the PJS form [ð] in this case.

Table 3.5: The low back vowel and variants by education level

	nat	nʌt	nɔt
Primary	23 (46%)	10 (20%)	17 (34%)
Secondary+	263 (25%)	184 (17%)	610 (58%)
Tertiary+	96 (12%)	127 (16%)	573 (72%)

In productions of *not* type words, primary educated informants show a great deal of variation in their use of the low back vowel variants – with [a] used most frequently – though it cannot be said that this use is focussed around the Creole variant as more than half their attestations of the vowel are not the JC variant. At the other educational levels, what distinguishes the groups is a greater frequency of use of the [ɔ] as level of education increases, and less use of the [a] ($p < .001$, $\chi^2 = 53.5$). The more central vowel [ʌ] is produced by all levels of informants at a similarly low rate.

Table 3.6: Mid-vowels by education level

	uo	o	ie	e
Primary	3 (5.6%)	51 (94.4%)	11 (27%)	30 (73%)
Secondary+	89 (9.0%)	918 (91.0%)	174 (16%)	883 (84%)
Tertiary+	37 (6.0%)	545 (94.0%)	76 (11%)	623 (89%)
	($p < .10$, $\chi^2 = 3.08$)		($p < .001$, $\chi^2 = 15.75$)	

The statistical difference between speakers when it comes to the back diphthong is below the critical level. The tertiary educated do not use significantly fewer diphthongs than the secondary educated; and importantly, the primary educated informants also follow the general pattern of these speakers and more consistently use the monophthong. In this formal context all speakers produced few [uo], though as discussed earlier, in Beckford-Wassink's study, the pattern in informal speech is somewhat different. It is use of the front [ie] that distinguishes speakers from the various levels of education, and as with initial voiceless TH stopping, h-drop and the low vowel [a], the higher the level of education the lower the incidence of the Creole variant and the more the [e] is used. However, it appears that not all Creole features are evaluated in the same way. Speakers generally are more likely to say [fies] than they are to say [guot]; and it is the more frequently used Creole form that does distinguish educational groups at JAMPRO. If the [ie] is in wider use (see the previous section) then it may be more likely that judgements of social place will be linked to that variant, given a general avoidance of [uo] in the data. This avoidance demonstrates a consensus across all educational groups here that [o] is the JE form. Contestation about what is JE takes place with [e ~ ie], with education one factor determining frequency of use. It is also just as likely that use of [uo] may index some other social difference, as in Beckford-Wassink's (2001: 155) study which showed a link to gender.

Table 3.7: Pre-rhotic mid-vowels by education level

	poor type words			*beer* type words	
	[ɔ]	[uᵒ]	[o]	[iᵉr]	[er]
Primary	6 (40%)	5 (33%)	4 (27%)	17 (81%)	4 (19%)
Secondary+	246 (77%)	47 (15%)	26 (8%)	241 (51%)	234 (49%)
Tertiary+	192 (70%)	62 (23%)	20 (7%)	222 (40%)	332 (60%)

Higher education was correlated with fewer front diphthongs overall, and in pre-rhotic environments we find a similar pattern ($p < .001$, $\chi^2 = 11.71$). However, the incidence of diphthongization is noticeably higher in *beer* type words, with educated speakers varying almost freely between the two variants. In *poor* type words, educated speakers overwhelmingly select the [ɔr] variant and therefore have fairly low frequencies of dipthongization ($p < .02$, $\chi^2 = 5.92$). However, those with tertiary+ education produce more of the diphthong than the secondary educated. Higher education then does not necessarily disfavour use of the [uᵒ] variant, though we can identify which of the three is the JE variant. The secondary educated, in particular, are more likely than any other group to use the [ɔr] variant, perhaps approximating more to a prestige pattern that, from the data, seems to be use of the /ɔ/ rather than /o/. Arguably, the stigma attached to using [uo], which speakers tend to avoid, as well as the prestige attached to the [ɔ] vowel in JE, have reinforced the selection of the [ɔr] variant.

Table 3.8: Word initial velar stops and variants by education level

	kja	kʰa	kja:	kʰa:
Primary	5 (50%)	5 (50%)	2 (100%)	0
Secondary+	65 (61%)	41 (39%)	13 (28%)	34 (72%)
Tertiary+	46 (52%)	43 (48%)	4 (9%)	41 (91%)
	(p > .30, χ^2 = 1.8)		(p < .05, χ^2 = 5.36)	

The data set for this feature is small, at best 2 to 3 tokens per speaker recorded. The discussion of these results is done with a full awareness of the problems of generalizing from such a small sampling. The creation of word-lists to test informants, however, would not have been useful here to add to the data set. Word-lists do not reflect the way people normally use or hear spoken language, even in formal contexts. Moreover, they test what the informant perceives to be, for example, the standard form when it is isolated and made the focus of attention. This does not necessarily reveal how the form is used when it is just one of a number of variables that the speaker uses/varies when producing discourse.

The relatively high incidence of [kja] in the speakers with higher education is in sharp contrast to the incidence of [kja:], in particular for university graduates. It is the production of the latter feature that distinguishes the two groups statistically. Indeed, it is possible that the secondary educated pattern, with 61% use of [kj] before the short [a], may reflect the type of quantitative hypercorrection typically described for the LMC (Labov 1980: 254). This suggests either that [kja] is not perceived by speakers as Creole, or that it is a feature that is found across the continuum, even in acrolectal speech (see §3.4 on age). If so, in a linguistic culture in which perceptions are binary, then this feature cannot be regarded as Creole, even though it occurs in JC. When the tertiary educated are analysed in terms of presence/absence of features, the following obtains. In all cases the speakers had the opportunity to produce a particular variant.

For the "tertiary+" speakers, [kja:], voiceless TH stopping and h-drop are the three features that most do not produce in formal speech. To a lesser extent, diphthongs (except the pre-rhotic [ie]) are also not an aspect of many informants' texts. But voiced TH stopping, [kja] and [nat] all occur in spoken JE, though the data above suggest that in tertiary educated speakers the latter is infrequent in the individual's speech even as it is a universally present variant.

Notably, the pattern for primary educated speakers is clearly different (with a caveat about high percentages in a small sample). Only h-dropping and [uo]

Table 3.9: Group A variables and distribution in the highly educated ("Tertiary+" speakers)

Feature	Informants taped	Variant Never use	Variant Always use	
/h/	32	0	17	(53%)
Initial [ð]	32	0	0	
Initial [θ]	32	0	19	(59%)
[ɔ] *not*	32	0	0	
[o] *boat*	32	0	15	(47%)
[e] *face*	32	0	15	(47%)
[ɔr] *poor*	31	0	11	(35%)
[ber] *beer*	32	0	1	(3%)
[kʰa]	27	3	7	(26%)
[kʰaː]	20	2	17	(85%)

were absent from the speech of anyone with primary education. Interestingly, informant F96 produced no [uo] in her recording (for 15 instances of the variable), but produced [ie] for 6 of 13 instances of that variable (46%).

3.1.2 Group B variables and education

Table 3.10: *-er* word ending and variants by education level

	butt[a]	butt[ʌ]	butt[ʌr]	
Primary	38 (76.0%)	12 (24.0%)	0	
Secondary+	150 (22.0%)	473 (69.0%)	60	(9.0%)
Tertiary+	48 (8.5%)	463 (81.5%)	57	(10.0%)

The suggestion made earlier in this section, that it is possibly only in the features perceived to be along the Creole/English dimension that level of education is indexed, can be examined in relation to this set of variables. Here, variation is not only between Creole/English options but also includes alternants of JE as well, though in many cases the phonetic options themselves can be explained in terms of avoiding certain Creole forms (notably [a ~ ɔ] and affricates). The data in Table 3.10 show that production of the JE *butt*[ʌr] form is not what distinguishes the tertiary from the secondary educated; rather it is use of less [a] (the stereotypically Creole variant) and more [ʌ] (p < .001, χ² = 42.38). This would seem to confirm the importance of the Creole/English relationship in defining "good" or standard English in Jamaica, as reflected in the speech of the most educated. Retroflexion of the word ending does not distinguish groups with higher education.

Table 3.11 below further illustrates the effect of Creole avoidance strategies on speakers' productions, but also lends support to the earlier comment that MSE norms are not necessarily the only target of speakers either.

Table 3.11: *-tion* word ending and variants by education level

	educa[ʃan]	educa[ʃʌn]	educa[ʃɔn]	educa[ʃən]
Primary	11 (85.0%)	2 (15.0%)	0	0
Secondary+	102 (30.0%)	171 (50.0%)	39 (11.0%)	31 (9.0%)
Tertiary+	31 (9.0%)	201 (59.0%)	76 (22.0%)	34 (10.0%)

The frequency of use of the schwa is similar for the two higher education levels. What accounts for the value of the χ² is the difference in the use of [ʃan] and [ʃɔn] (p < .001, χ² = 52.23). Tertiary educated speakers use less of the Creole variant, and more of the JE alternant [ʃɔn]. Educatedness, arguably, is more clearly indexed by use of the locally evolved variant, not the MSE schwa.

Interestingly, if the 7 informants with foreign degrees are isolated for discussion, their patterns of variation are, by inspection, different from the locally educated (see Table 3.12).

Table 3.12: Articulation of word endings by place of education

	educa[ʃan]	educa[ʃʌn]	educa[ʃɔn]	educa[ʃən]
Foreign	3 (4.0%)	48 (68.0%)	11 (15.0%)	9 (13.0%)
Local	28 (10.25%)	153 (56.5%)	65 (24.0%)	25 (9.25%)

	butt[a]	butt[ʌ]	butt[ʌr]
Foreign	4 (4.0%)	87 (83.0%)	14 (13.0%)
Local	44 (9.5%)	376 (81.0%)	43 (9.0%)

For these variables, the variation evident in the foreign educated informants is phonetically more akin to MSE. In the first table, there is a marginally greater frequency of schwa; the locally educated produce more [ʃɔn] and [ʃan] (p > .10, χ^2 = 5.93). And in the second table, "locals" produce fewer retroflex endings, and more [a], than those with overseas education (p < .10, χ^2 = 4.9). Among informants whose education has been entirely in Jamaica we find use of the Creole variant and use of the local JE variant(s) to be the main areas of difference between them. Higher education in Jamaica then cannot necessarily be correlated with an increased use of the metropolitan norm, but, as the data here would suggest and as would be expected, such norms are more likely in those who have been exposed to them.

Table 3.13: Articulation of *culture* type words by education level

	dj	ʤ	tj	ʧ
Primary	1	0	2 (40.0%)	3 (60.0%)
Secondary+	19 (76.0%)	6 (24.0%)	36 (51.0%)	34 (49.0%)
Tertiary+	14 (70.0%)	6 (30.0%)	33 (26.0%)	93 (74.0%)
(Foreign)	2 (40.0%)	3 (60.0%)	8 (33.0%)	16 (67.0%)
(Local)	12 (80.0%)	3 (20.0%)	25 (24.5%)	77 (75.5%)

The difference between the secondary+ and tertiary+ speakers use of the voiceless palatalized stop variant is statistically significant (p < .001, χ^2 = 12.56). Speakers with secondary+ education typically vary between affricate and palatalized stop variants, with no evidence that one or the other is favoured here. Tertiary+ educated informants clearly produce more of the affricate, and this whether with a foreign education or local education (p > .30, χ^2 = .77)[6]. When the sample is entirely made up of the locally educated, the results show a similar association between use of the palatalized stop and level of education, with less of the feature in informants with higher education (p < .001, χ^2 = 11.73). The data for the voiced variable are inadequate for more than a tentative comment on production. Speakers here generally do not use the affricate, and this at both levels of education. Discussion of this feature will focus on the voiceless variable. There seems to be consensus that JE has [dj] in items like [gradjʊɛt] *graduate* or [ɪndɪvɪdjəl] *individual,* and it is noteworthy that one of the hypercorrect forms in my sample

---

[6]Because the data for the voiced variable is small, I have not run any statistical tests on it. I include it only so some impressionistic comparison can be made.

involves the replacement of [ʤ] with [dj] as in [djunjʌ] *junior.* The other replaces [ʤ] with [d] as in [dʌs] *just.* However, it is with the voiceless variable that social differences here can be correlated.

Typically, hypercorrection suggests that a speaker perceives X in her vernacular to be Y in the prestige variety. All Xs are converted to Ys, even when not required. But if the speaker has X in her vernacular and X in the prestige variety, and X is stigmatized, then Y becomes the option merely because it is not X, and not necessarily because it has prestige. In the process items are converted from X to Y, even though X is the PJS form. Moreover, the data here raise an interesting question. Given that some speakers may perceive affricates to be "Creole", as demonstrated in the discussion in the previous chapter, what happens when conversion of the stigmatized item takes place in a context where there is no focussed prestige reflex? In this study the following variants occurred in words like culture or structure: [ʃ], [ʧ], [t] and [tj]. So all these pronunciations were produced, either by a few or by many of the informants – [strʌkʃʌ], [strʌkʧʌ], [strʌktʌ] and [strʌktjʌ] *structure.* The variation that is evident for this variable suggests that not only is there competition among features for selection by speakers (Mufwene 2001: 143), but the preferred variants are either the one used by the highly educated speaker [ʧ] or the one which indexes education perhaps because of its clear association with literacy [tj].[7]

A final comment that can be made concerns this and some of the other features discussed so far: the interdental fricative, the mid-vowels and the palatalized velar stop. In all these cases, a pair of related variables has been analysed and distinguished, for example, by voicing or phonetic environment. What emerges is that speakers seem to pay more attention to one of the pair, in the sense that its distribution in the sample is sociolinguistically significant, while the other tends to be produced with a very similar pattern by speakers. Informants freely vary [d ~ ð], but voiceless TH stopping distinguishes speakers' levels of education, with those of higher education using more of the fricative. All informants produced the [o] monophthong, but [ie ~ e] can also be correlated with level of education. In much the same way, there seems to be some consensus about use of the voiced palatal stop, but the voiceless stop in variation with the affricate is again distributed in the sample in relation to speakers' levels of education.

For both variables, higher education can be correlated with more rhotic articulation. In addition, the hypercorrect rhoticity identified in the previous chapter,

---

[7]My impression is that a lexical item like *nature* seems to be more consistently produced with the affricate than items like *structure.* The former item is part of the Creole lexicon ([nieʧa] *libido*), and therefore the [tj] variant might be more frequent in words that are thought of as "English".

Table 3.14: Rhoticity by education level

	poor type words		beer type words	
	[partɪ]	[paːtɪ]	[fortɪ]	[fɔːtɪ]
Primary	1 (11.0%)	8 (89.0%)	6 (50.0%)	6 (50.0%)
Secondary+	57 (39.5%)	87 (60.5%)	105 (73.0%)	39 (27.0%)
Tertiary+	54 (53.0%)	47 (47.0%)	94 (61.0%)	61 (39.0%)
	(p < .05, χ^2 = 4.61)		(p < .05, χ^2 = 5.03)	

does suggest that speakers hold the idea that good English is rhotic. However the pattern for the back [ɔ] is somewhat different from the pattern for [a]. Firstly, speakers tend to be more rhotic after the former vowel, in particular the secondary+ educated cohort. Their production is similar to the data for *poor* words and [kja], possibly showing the quantitative hypercorrection of the linguistically insecure who tend to produce "too much of an indexically good thing" (Silverstein 2000: 138). However, when the foreign educated are removed from the tertiary+ count, there is a clear association between high levels of locally attained education and rhoticity after [ɔ] as well (p < .02, χ^2 = 5.67).

Table 3.15: Rhoticity after [ɔ] by place of education

	[fortɪ]	[fɔːtɪ]
Local	62 (87%)	9 (13%)
Foreign	32 (38%)	52 (62%)

This may also be another example of the effect of the JE vowel [ɔ] on acrolectal phonology – for I suggest that a rhotic articulation makes clear that the speaker does have this vowel, in a context where not being rhotic, as in [faːtɪ ~ fɔːtɪ] *forty*, the speaker may not be as clearly distinguished from the Creole speaker. As such it is the local ecology, and not an increased exposure to a (rhotic) North American model of speech (A. Irvine 1994: 67), that explains the pattern of rhoticity in JE. While there is a general increase in rhotic articulation as education increases, speakers (in particular the locally educated) more consistently rhoticize [ɔ].

The data for the production of word final consonant clusters are shown in Table 3.16.

Table 3.16: Phonological clusters by educational attainment

C(C)##V:[a]	-nt	-nt^h	-n	-st	-st^h	-s
Secondary+	74 (70.0%)	7 (6.5%)	25 (23.5%)	52 (44.0%)	4 (3.5%)	62 (52.5%)
Tertiary+	89 (67.0%)	26 (19.5%)	18 (13.5%)	46 (40.0%)	10 (9.0%)	59 (51.0%)
	(p < .01, χ^2 = 10.95)			(p > .20, χ^2 = 2.8)		
C(C)##C:	-nt	-nt^h	-n	-st	-st^h	-s
Primary	5 (62.5%)	0	3 (37.5%)	0	2 (11.0%)	16 (89.0%)
Secondary+	58 (39.0%)	11 (7.0%)	79 (53.0%)	27 (13.0%)	6 (3.0%)	180 (84.0%)
Tertiary+	85 (50.0%)	18 (11.0%)	66 (39.0%)	17 (10.0%)	4 (2.5%)	148 (87.5%)
	(p < .05, χ^2 = 6.6)			(p > .70, χ^2 = .7)		

[a]No data were available for the primary educated.

The data here reveal that [nt] clusters can be correlated with level of education; the same is not the case for [st] clusters, whether before a following vowel or consonant. The tertiary educated produce more [nt] phonological clusters, and more exaggerated articulations of these clusters, than do those with secondary qualifications. We would expect such a result, given the relationship between speaker's level of education and language use revealed in the data above and in other studies. However, for [st] clusters the two groups are very similar, suggesting perhaps that the two clusters are not sociolinguistic equivalents for speakers. An alternative explanation is also suggested by LaCharité (1996) who argues that [st] is not to be analysed as a cluster in Jamaican (non-acrolectal) phonology at all, but as an illicit segment that undergoes repair by having its [−cont.] feature removed.[8]

The data show that use of morphological clusters does not really distinguish groups either, though as education level increases, past tense t/d before a following vowel segment is marginally more consistently used (p > .10, χ^2 = 2.31), see Table 3.17.

Most speakers recorded use -n't before a following consonant infrequently, and like past marking, rates of presence/absence are sensitive to following segment. The surface forms of -n't clusters are similar in my informants, either [n] or a nasalized vowel like [õ]. What distinguishes speakers is, in some lexical

---

[8]LaCharité's arguments for the status of [st] in Jamaican Creole are interesting, but [st] does occur, at least medially, in (newer?) Creole words like [mɛstɪko] *mexico* or [fɛstɪval] *hush puppy* (YS) or [rasta] *Rastafarian* (the latter syllabified ras•ta). Her argument suggests that [st] cannot be syllabified heterosyllabically (5).

Table 3.17: Morphological clusters by educational attainment

C(C)##V:	-n't	-n'	-ed	Ø
Primary	0	1	3	0
Secondary+	16 (52.0%)	15 (48.0%)	65 (71.0%)	26 (29.0%)
Tertiary+	15 (52.0%)	14 (48.0%)	87 (80.5%)	21 (19.5%)
C(C)##C:	-n't	-n'	-ed	Ø
Primary	0	14	1	3
Secondary+	41 (13.0%)	274 (87.0%)	35 (45.5%)	42 (54.5%)
Tertiary+	42 (18.0%)	189 (82.0%)	49 (44.5%)	61 (55.5%)
	(p = .10, χ^2 = 2.7)		(p > .80, χ^2 = .017)	

Table 3.18: Group B variables and distribution in the highly educated

Feature	Informants taped	Variant	
		Never use	Always use
-er *butter*	32	10	0
[ʃɔn] *-tion*	32	10	0
[tj] *culture*	25	10	6 (24.0%)
[r] *party*	30	10	9 (30.0%)
[r] *forty*	30	2	8 (27.0%)
-nt## V	31	1	19 (61.0%)
-nt## C	32	4	5 (16.0%)
-st## V	29	7	2 (17.0%)
-st## C	32	17	1 (7.0%)
n't## V	15	5	5 (33.0%)
n't## C	30	11	0
-ed *before V*	29	1	16 (55.0%)
-ed *before C*	32	6	4 (12.5%)

items, the preceding vowel, i.e. *don't* as either [duõ(n)] or [dõ(n)]; or the onset consonant – *can't* as either [kjã:] or [kʰã:].

Most tertiary educated speakers produce [nt] clusters and past marking, at least before a following vowel. In addition, most speakers do not produce [st] clusters when followed by a consonant segment. For all other Group B variables the situation is diffuse, with much intra-idiolectal variation. A number of patterns though are interesting, such as the rhoticity after [a] and [ɔ], with more speakers being less likely to rhoticize the former; and the general relationship between articulation of any type of cluster and the phonological environment in which it occurs. An overall comment that can be made is that there is much more focussing around certain features stereotyped as Creole; and more focussing around not using particular variants rather than trying to produce others.

3.2 Gender

There are a number of reasons why the dynamics of gender and language use at JAMPRO are important areas of study in this book. Firstly, this agency is overwhelmingly staffed by women. In total, there are 37 men and 116 women employed in the New Kingston office, with males comprising roughly one in four of the staff population. Of the 104 informants interviewed for this study 22 are male and 82 female (85%), and therefore a proportion comparable to the population at the agency was reasonably maintained. This, of course, in no way reflects the male:female ratio in the national or regional (KMA) population statistics, which is 49:51 and 47:53 respectively (STATIN 1991). Nor does it reflect the percentage of the national population of employed persons who are female, which stands at 53% (PIOJ 2000: 86). When analysed with reference to the statistics available from previous studies (D. Gordon 1986; E. Miller 1991), the gender distribution at JAMPRO becomes less remarkable.

Table 3.19: Sex and white collar employment: 1943–1994 (Male:Female of 100)

Type of Occupation	1943	1984	JAMPRO (1994)
Senior Management/Professional	96 : 4	68 : 32	43 : 57
Junior Management/Professional	78 : 22	59 : 41	26 : 74
Clerical/Secretarial	28 : 72	25 : 75	1 : 99

Table 3.19 shows the population by sex and relevant occupation in the island over a 40-year time span and the distribution in JAMPRO at the time of data collection. What is apparent is that more women over time, and fewer men, are being employed in clerical, administrative and managerial positions. Clerical/secretarial work is now almost exclusively female, while middle and senior management positions have become increasingly feminized. Moreover, roughly 74% of graduates from the University of the West Indies (Mona) are female, making a high level of education stereotypical of women in the wider Jamaican society.

The high proportion of female informants is then not inconsistent with the proportion of women employed in similar occupations in the wider society. Moreover, as was discussed earlier, the interview process of weeding out "unsuitable" candidates, seems to result in a greater number of female staff hired into JAMPRO. It may well be that factors like the expectation of better education in women and the already overwhelmingly female workforce predispose those making the selection to opt for the female candidate.[9]

When gender and status in the company is looked at, it becomes clear that this issue is complicated by factors like education, access to mobility and representation in senior management and other supervisory positions.

Table 3.20: Gender and education in JAMPRO (One informant did not give a response)

	Primary	Secondary	Post-Secondary	Tertiary	Postgraduate
Female	2 (2%)	8 (10%)	38 (47%)	17 (21%)	16 (20%)
Male	2 (9%)	2 (9%)	5 (23%)	5 (23%)	8 (36%)

Proportionately, men at JAMPRO generally tend to be more educated (close to 60% with at least tertiary level qualifications compared to 40% of women). Men do not, however, hold a proportionately higher number of positions with authority (see §4.2). It therefore bears repeating that JAMPRO is an essentially female agency, but that this is not atypical in the Jamaican workplace context, particularly in the public sector. JAMPRO is, therefore, an agency that is female-

---

[9]However, Cameron's discussion (2000) of gender and the commodification of language, suggests that in service industries where interaction with a client is crucial, female norms of language use tend more and more to be favoured. She attributes this, in part, to the type of work being done, "emotional labour – the management of feelings" (338); in part, it is a reflection of a popular adoption of some of the discussions of gender and language in academic circles (333).

dominant. This is not merely a matter of distribution of staff in terms of num-bers. In its recruiting and promoting practices, indeed in its culture generally, the agency is not gender neutral.

The effect of gender on language use in a number of societies has been widely discussed in the sociolinguistic literature. Traditionally, sociolinguists have re-marked on women's greater (reported) use of the standard form, explained in terms of their lower status (Labov 1972: 243; Trudgill 1972) and the pragmatics of politeness and face (Deuchar 1988). In these studies, conducted in societies that consider themselves to have clear norms of good English reflected in a widely used standard, prestige variety and standard variety were assumed, with some justification, to be synonymous. Indeed, the style shift that occurred in Labov's studies of New Yorkers (1972 *passim*), for a number of phonological variables, il-lustrated the extent of the generalization of this idea of the standard. This was an idea which, it was shown, was most clearly held by women. Women, it has been argued, are more sensitive to the distribution of power in the society and to the norms that index membership in the groups that have this power.

Subsequent work showed that this sensitivity is not a function of gender *per se*, but of sociological factors like mobility aspirations, access to employment and education or social-psychological issues of identity and group membership. For example, Nichols (1983) concluded that it is patterns of employment that explain a greater use of standard forms by young women in Gullah speaking areas of South Carolina. Young women in the community she studied are more likely to stay in school longer, and use more standard forms, as they are the group finding employment in the wider society that requires ability in Standard English. Male patterns of employment in the same study were typically found to be in more self-employed, blue-collar jobs, such as trucking. Earlier work by L. Milroy (1980: 184) also showed that more standard use, in both men and women in Belfast, could be related, in part, to employment outside of communities in which non-standard forms were normative and the consequent network structures in which men and women operated.

Walters' (1996) discussion of English speaking women newly arrived in Tuni-sia revealed that choice of language use is also closely related to the linguistic markets in which one is operating and the identities that are indexed by the use of particular varieties. These women, finding themselves in a sociolinguistic context that uses French, Standard Arabic and "kitchen" Arabic, are discouraged from using the latter variety because of its association with lack of education and sophistication, even as it is the variety of Arabic to which they have most access and which, arguably, is of most use to them in their daily routine. French and Standard Arabic more reflect the status positions of their husbands, returning university graduates and professionals trained in the US/UK, and membership in the groups to which they aspire.

In Caribbean continuum situations like Jamaica, the acrolect is the label traditionally used in most studies to describe the unmarked prestige variety, the local standard. In brief, command of this variety indicates higher levels of education, socio-economic class, and the like. In the workplace, where an ability to speak English is necessary at nearly all levels, the issue is about the precise linguistic characteristics that constitute for speakers "proper" English. As was suggested in the previous sections, there are no general pronunciation prescriptions for Standard English and reference to metropolitan norms cannot shed much light on local speech patterns.

F. Miller (1987: 112), who has to date done one of the few descriptions of the Jamaican acrolect, concludes that women in this social context are *not* as sensitive to the prestige pattern as men seem to be. She attributes this to an insecurity in men who are more careful to project "being educated", given its lack of association with being male, by more frequent use of MSE forms.

F. Miller uses British and American norms as reference points for both what she calls the standard and the prestige variety in Jamaica (177), and, as noted in Chapter 1, this is problematic in her analysis. Local norms of English have been found to be more apparent in the speech of women in the Caribbean (Le Page & Tabouret-Keller 1985, for St. Lucia; F. Miller 1987, A. Irvine 1994 for Jamaica). Two examples from Jamaica can be used to illustrate this: a) Use of [kjat]-type words has been correlated with socio-economic class. They are found with greater frequency in the formal speech of informants labelled UC/UMC (F. Miller 1987, A. Irvine 1994), and in the speech of women (A. Irvine 1994). b) A rhotic variety of English, which has been correlated with level of education, is more common in acrolect(-dominant) women than men (Beckford-Wassink 1999a: 184; A. Irvine 1994: 72) and there is some evidence to suggest that the local educated norm is rhotic (see the previous chapter). The choices women make in the Jamaican sociolinguistic context will not therefore be said to be approximating the prestige pattern, if prestige is synonymous with metropolitan standard. However, if we reinterpret the acrolect as a legitimate national standard, Jamaican English, with its own norms, then we can re-examine the analysis of the speech of women and its relationship to prestige varieties in the Jamaican society.

3.2.1 Group A variables and gender

15 men and 67 women were recorded during interviews, roughly proportionate to the 1:4 ratio of men to women in the agency.

Table 3.21: h-drop by gender

	n	h-drop	h
Male	15	56 (19%)	239 (81%)
Female	67	128 (10%)	1169 (90%)

Men in the sample were much more likely to produce forms such as [ɛvɪ] *heavy* than their female counterparts (p < .001, χ^2 = 19.64). For this feature, women were more likely to use the JE form, though the generalized pattern of [h] discussed for the total sample in the previous chapter does suggest that hypercorrect use of [h], i.e. insertion of [h], is the more socially diagnostic variable. Moreover, most informants regardless of speaker sex used [h] most of the time. Of the nine informants who did show a hypercorrect pattern of [h] use two were men, a distribution which does not suggest a particular tendency to this in either men or women in the sample here.

There is no statistically significant difference between men and women when it comes to word final TH stopping. Both groups of speakers generally use more of the interdental fricative variants. For word middle [t ~ θ] there is no statistically significant difference between men and women either, with both groups favouring the fricative. Where the groups differ is in their frequencies of, primarily, word initial TH stopping, with women more likely than men to produce the fricative variants. For women, greater use of the fricative is clearly more consistent with the word initial voiceless TH. Even if we place less importance on initial [d ~ ð] for the reasons already discussed (see §2.3.3), women's greater use of [ð] in word middle position does support the generalization made about women's greater use of standard/prestige forms.

Table 3.23 shows that both men and women have similar patterns of [a] production, with both having a low incidence of the Creole variant. Where the two groups differ is that women are more likely to use the [ɔ] variant than men, who use greater frequencies of [ʌ] (p < .001, χ^2 = 15.23). Four informants, 2 males and 2 females, could be described as using hypercorrect [ɔ].

M47 – [rɪlɔks] *relax* and [strɔp] *strap*, F53 –[fɔːma] *farmer* and [sɔlərɪ] *salary*, F11 – [strɔktʌ] *structure*, and M89 [dʒɔs] *just*. Again, it cannot be said that gender correlates with this hypercorrect pattern. Arguably, if we take hypercorrect use as an indication of what speakers perceive to be standard/prestigious, then here again women were more likely than men to use the standard [ɔ] variant. Greater use of the standard form, however, must be clearly distinguished from avoidance

Table 3.22: TH stopping by gender

Word Initial	d	ð	t	θ
Male	510 (66.0%)	259 (34.0%)	41 (30.6%)	93 (69.4%)
Female	1780 (52.0%)	1665 (48.0%)	76 (11.0%)	600 (89.0%)
	(p < .001, χ^2 = 54.33)		(p < .001, χ^2 = 33.96)	
Word Middle	d	ð	t	θ
Male	25 (45.0%)	30 (55.0%)	2 (22.0%)	7 (78.0%)
Female	51 (20.0%)	198 (80.0%)	20 (18.5%)	88 (81.5%)
	(p < .001, χ^2 = 14.96)		(p > .70, χ^2 = 0.073)	
Word Final	d	ð	t	θ
Male	7 (37.0%)	12 (63.0%)	4 (31.0%)	9 (69.0%)
Female	26 (25.0%)	77 (75.0%)	16 (23.0%)	54 (77.0%)
	(p > .30, χ^2 = 0.99)		(p > .80, χ^2 = 0.36)	

Table 3.23: Low back vowel by gender

	nat	nʌt	nɔt
Male	69 (21.4%)	76 (23.5%)	178 (55.1%)
Female	316 (19.5%)	249 (15.4%)	1052 (65.0%)

Table 3.24: Mid-vowels by gender

	uo	o	ie	e
Male	26 (11.0%)	215 (89.0%)	61 (19.5%)	251 (80.5%)
Female	104 (7.0%)	1323 (93.0%)	202 (13.0%)	1315 (87.0%)
	(p < .10, χ^2 = 3.6)		(p < .01, χ^2 = 8.2)	

of the Creole form. For this variable both men and women tend not to use the Creole variant [a].

Women use fewer of the diphthong variants than men, and it is the front vowel, in particular, that distinguishes male from female speech. This finding is in keeping with Beckford-Wassink's data (2001: 153–155) on this feature. Moreover, in her study of two sets of Jamaican speakers, one from St. Thomas (rural-basilect dominant) and the other from Kingston (urban-acrolect dominant), she found that

> [a]cross groups, males produced more downgliding variants than females did in the word list and conversational sessions. It is interesting that males and females pattern together, regardless of group.
>
> (Beckford-Wassink 2001: 154)

Greater use of diphthongs was a male feature, notwithstanding the differences in background between the Kingston informants and those from St. Thomas. In the previous section on education it was shown that it is use of this front vowel [e] that distinguished speakers from differing levels of education as well. Use of the back vowel [o] here is similar between men and women, as it was among primary, secondary+ and tertiary+ speakers.

This pattern is maintained in the pre-rhotic environment, with men producing more diphthongs than women. However, for both groups the incidence of diphthongization is higher than it is elsewhere.

Table 3.25: Pre-rhotic mid-vowels by gender

	poor words			*beer* words	
	[ɔ]	[uᵒ]	[o]	[iᵉr]	[er]
Male	66 (57.0%)	37 (32.0%)	13 (11.0%)	100 (54.0%)	84 (46.0%)
Female	387 (77.0%)	79 (16.0%)	37 (7.0%)	385 (44.0%)	495 (56.0%)

Women are more likely to produce monophthong variants of both variables. The logic of the data on gender so far suggests that female speech is more likely to reflect standard/prestige norms, here less use of the diphthong. Women are much more likely to produce the [ɔ], while the men's speech is more likely to show some variation with [uᵒ] ($p < .001$, $\chi^2 = 20.06$). The use of diphthongs is generally more widespread across speakers of both sexes in *beer* type words. Again, what

Table 3.26: Word initial velar stops by gender

	kja	k^{h}a	kja:	k^{h}a:
Male	35 (59.0%)	24 (41.0%)	4 (23.5%)	13 (76.5%)
Female	84 (56.0%)	66 (44.0%)	15 (19.0%)	64 (81.0%)
	(p > .50, χ^2 = 0.18)		(p > .50, χ^2 = 0.17)	

distinguishes male from female speech here is women's more frequent use of the [e] than men (p < .01, χ^2 = 6.89).

No statistically significant difference was found between men and women and their use of either of these two variables. Both men and women pattern the same, with a much lower incidence of [kj] before the long vowel. It is not possible to say what is the standard or prestige form before the short vowel. Neither can we say that [kja] is the Creole variant, as suggested by avoidance of a feature; though arguably, this label is much more plausible for the [kja:] variant.

Table 3.27: Group A variables and distribution in women

			Variant	
Feature	Informants taped	Never use	Always use	
/h/	67	0	26	(39.0%)
Initial [ð]	67	0	0	
Initial [θ]	67	0	36	(54.0%)
[ɔ] *not*	67	0	0	
[o] *boat*	67	0	23	(34.0%)
[e] *face*	67	0	22	(33.0%)
[ɔ r] *poor*	66	1	24	(36.0%)
[ber] *beer*	67	3	3	(4.0%)
[k^{h}a]	51	12	11	(21.5%)
[k^{h}a:]	39	6	27	(69.0%)

Table 3.27 describes female use of Group A variables. What can be generalized from the above data is that many of the women interviewed consistently used voiceless interdental fricatives and [k^{h}a:]. And as with the data for the tertiary+ educated, there are a number of speakers who always used the PJS variant, but

many more who show much variation. On the whole, unlike in F. Miller's data, I find women to be more likely to use PJS forms than men at JAMPRO. This may be due to the specific context of working in this agency, with its overwhelming female majority. Certainly, the comments detailed earlier (in the introduction to Chapter 2) specifically state that women's language use tends to make them more acceptable candidates for JAMPRO employment.

Additionally, it is important to mention that the interviews for this study were all done by a woman – an interaction context that might favour more non-standard male speech and/or language use that asserts masculinity through non-standard forms (Trudgill 1978). Holmes (1997: 38), citing a number of studies done in the framework of accommodation theory (Giles & Powesland 1975), suggests that men are less likely than women to converge to their addressee's style of speech. Moreover, the pattern for inter-sex and other kinds of talk in Jamaica, even in situations of asymmetrical status, is for speakers to use prestige forms in the opening phases of interaction. However, a shift in code to more non-standard or Creole forms is more likely in male speakers than in women (Shields-Brodber 1998: 200).

3.2.2 Group B variables and gender

In *butter* type words, both sets of speakers tended to produce the variant [ʌ] with no retroflexion. However, the patterns for men and women differed ($p < .01$, $\chi^2 = 11.3$). Men had a less focussed selection of variants and were also more likely to use the [a], typical of Creole varieties, and [ʌr] word finally. The association of this "overly precise" articulation with women, mentioned in the previous chapter, is not apparent in this sample.

Table 3.28: Final articulation of -*er* words by gender

	butt[a]	butt[ʌ]	butt[ʌr]
Male	58 (24.0%)	157 (64.0%)	29 (12.0%)
Female	179 (17.0%)	801 (75.0%)	89 (8.0%)

For the other feature, [ʃɔn] in *education* type words, there was no statistically significant difference in the speech of men and women at JAMPRO ($p > .30$, $\chi^2 = 2.22$). Men and women showed similar distributions.

Table 3.29: Final articulation of -*tion* words by gender

	educa[ʃan]	educa[ʃʌn]	educa[ʃɔn]	educa[ʃən]
Male	29 (21.0%)	76 (54.0%)	19 (13.5%)	16 (11.5%)
Female	120 (21.0%)	301 (53.0%)	101 (17.5%)	49 (8.5%)

Arguably, women showed a slight tendency to favour the more back and round variant [ʃɔn], while men produced more of the schwa.[10]

For the third variable, the results were as shown in Table 3.30.

Table 3.30: Articulation of *culture* type words by gender

	dj	dʒ	tj	ʧ
Male	18 (69.0%)	8 (31.0%)	14 (38.0%)	36 (62.0%)
Female	16 (84.0%)	3 (16.0%)	59 (28.0%)	97 (72.0%)

The correlation between gender and use of the [tj] shows no statistically significant difference between men's and women's speech ($p > .20$, $\chi^2 = 1.57$). A more detailed breakdown of informants' productions presents a different picture of variant use ($p < .001$, $\chi^2 = 15.83$); see Table 3.31.

Table 3.31: Articulation of *culture* type words in informants who vary

	n	tj	ʧ
Male	7	10 (24.0%)	31
Female	22	50 (62.5%)	30

Among speakers who tended to use both variants in their recorded speech, women are more likely than men to use palatalized stops more frequently. Recall that use of palatalized stops was more frequent in the secondary+ educated informant, a class of informants overwhelmingly made up of women. It is perhaps this association with education that may explain the pattern of variant use here. However, among speakers who were categorical in their use of either affricates

---

[10]Le Page & Tabouret-Keller (1985: 145) describe a pattern of use for boys in St. Lucia, with fewer of the local forms studied occurring in their formal speech sample.

or palatalized stops, more women can be classified as [ʧ] speakers – 21 of 30 women (70%) as opposed to 2 of 6 men (33%). I can therefore make no conclusive statement about this feature and its relationship to gender, except that the coincidence of lower levels of education and female speakers in this sample may be apparent in the greater use of palatalized stops in female informants.

For nearly all features analysed so far in this section on gender, where variation is more clearly along a Creole-English dimension (Group A), women have been more likely than men to produce PJS variants of variables, to use the forms also associated with the highly educated. In that respect, this would be in line with traditional sociolinguistic descriptions of women's speech and its relationship to prestige forms, at least in this more formal workplace context. However these three Group B variables also have variants that are not associated with Creole, but represent JE phonetic variation. One could simply argue, of course, that the women's patterns here also reflect what is to be considered "proper" Jamaican English, i.e. non-retroflexion on butter type words, perhaps [ʃɔn], both of which are also associated with higher levels of education. But the data on affricates show a difference between female speech in general and that of the highly educated. Among women who vary in their use of the [tj ~ ʧ], the tendency is to produce the [tj] variant, typically more than men do.

When education level and [tj] use are examined in more detail the data in Table 3.32 emerge.

Table 3.32: Speakers with categorical articulation of *culture* type words by education

	Categorical use of	
	[tj]	[ʧ]
Secondary+	15	13
Tertiary+	6	14

Roughly equivalent numbers of the secondary+ use affricates only and palatalized stops only. Given that I have a sample of 45 secondary+ informants, a similar number vary between [tj ~ ʧ]. Affricate use then is more focussed in, and an aspect of, the tertiary+ educated speaker. Among speakers that do vary [tj ~ ʧ], 17 secondary+ and 12 tertiary+ speakers, there is no statistically significant association between use of variants and differences in level of education ($p > .95$, $\chi^2 = .001$). Secondary+ speakers' patterns are therefore diffuse and show much variation both inter-idiolectally and intra-idiolectally.

The results here suggest [tj] use may be more an aspect of female speech, as 29 or 43% of female informants use [tj] either all or more of the time. It is not that women at JAMPRO proportionately have lower levels of education and this is why they use more of the palatalized stop variant. Rather it is that proportionately more secondary+ informants are women and this explains the frequencies found in this educational cohort. Palatalized stops represent a local variant that coexists with the affricate. Certainly the hypercorrect example, [djunjʌ] *junior,* cited earlier does suggest this. Men, on the other hand, show a different pattern – 9 male informants, or 69% of men, use affricates most of the time.

The results for rhoticity after the vowel are shown in Table 3.33.

Table 3.33: Rhoticity by gender

	party type words		*forty* type words	
	[partɪ]	[pa:tɪ]	[fɔrtɪ]	[fɔ:tɪ]
Male	19 (28.0%)	49 (72.0%)	39 (62.0%)	24 (38.0%)
Female	95 (48.0%)	103 (52.0%)	171 (67.0%)	83 (33.0%)

Beckford-Wassink in her study found women to be more rhotic generally than men in their productions (1999a: 184). In my data, there was no statistical difference in the frequencies of variants used after the back round [ɔ] (p > .30, χ^2 = 0.6). Rhoticity after this vowel seems to be a normalised feature of JE, given a generally rhotic articulation among the highly (locally) educated speakers. However, I find men are significantly less rhotic after [a] than women (p < .01, χ^2 = 8.3).

Women generally, and regardless of level of education, tend to be rhotic – 11 of the women are rhotic in all phonetic contexts tested here and 43 of them are rhotic in one of these contexts, typically after [ɔ]. Men generally are more likely to be non-rhotic, as only 1 of the male informants is fully rhotic in both vowel environments (M100) and 11 of them are non-rhotic in one of the contexts, typically after [a].

The results for gender and phonological cluster production are interesting, in light of the association of higher education with use of nasal + stop but not with [st] clusters. Here, there is little correlation between gender and [nt] (in any environment), but production of final [st] does distinguish male from female speech. Note that the frequencies and proportions of [nt] clusters are very similar for the educated and for both men and women. For [st] clusters, men produce very few, regardless of following segment. Women, however, pattern the tertiary+ ed-

Table 3.34: Phonological clusters by gender

C(C)##V:	-nt	-nt[h]	-n	-st	-st[h]	-s
Male	34 (61.0%)	9 (16.0%)	13 (23.0%)	7 (16.0%)	5 (11.0%)	33 (73.0%)
Female	132 (71.0%)	25 (13.0%)	30 (16.0%)	92 (47.5%)	9 (4.5%)	92 (47.5%)
	(p > .30, χ^2 = 2.06)			(p < .001, χ^2 = 16.31)		
C(C)##C:	-nt	-nt[h]	-n	-st	-st[h]	-s
Male	32 (40.0%)	10 (12.0%)	39 (48.0%)	3 (5.0%)	0	59 (95.0%)
Female	117 (47.0%)	19 (8.0%)	110 (45.0%)	41 (12.0%)	12 (3.0%)	297 (85.0%)
	(p > .20, χ^2 = 2.46)			(p < .10, χ^2 = 4.75) (-st and -st[h] collapsed)		

ucated in their use. It must be remembered that women make up the overwhelming majority of this sample, and therefore the norms identified for the educated are essentially going to be educated female norms, with the possible exception of [tj] use. One could therefore ask whether it is that women approximate more to standard/prestige forms here or whether women's language use is more of an influence on what is considered the standard/prestige form, particularly where there is a less focussed norm. This is a sample in which men are proportionately better educated than women, at least in terms of formal qualifications. It is women in this sample, even those with lower levels of education, whose variant production is more similar to that of the highly educated as a group. And certainly it is women who are stereotyped in this speech community as "educated". Moreover, it is how women present themselves during the interview that is explicitly preferred by management at JAMPRO.

The data show that production of morphological clusters, specifically past tense marking, is more a feature of women's speech. The female pattern also correlates closely with the rate in those with higher levels of education. Similar findings are described in Neu (1980: 52). This finding suggests that women at JAMPRO do tend to produce more standard variants, when they function in the speech community as such, assuming that more educated speech represents the standard. The results for -n't clusters, for both education and gender (and the mesolectal pattern in Patrick 1999), do not suggest that production of [don't] *don't*, say, is necessarily salient for the production of spoken JE in Jamaica.

A significant number of women are rhotic after the back vowel and produce both phonological and past tense clusters. It is women, at the interview stage of applying for JAMPRO employment, that management reported "seemed to do better". And when the patterns of the tertiary+ woman are analysed, the features

Table 3.35: Morphological clusters by gender

C(C)##V:	-n't	-n'	-ed	Ø
Male	6 (54.5%)	5 (45.5%)	25 (66.0%)	13 (34.0%)
Female	25 (50.0%)	25 (50.0%)	131 (79.0%)	34 (21.0%)
	(p > .70, χ^2 = .07)		(p < .10, χ^2 = 3.32)	
C(C)##C:	-n't	-n'	-ed	Ø
Male	9 (12.0%)	65 (88.0%)	11 (29.0%)	27 (71.0%)
Female	80 (16.0%)	415 (84.0%)	75 (48.0%)	80 (52.0%)
	(p > .30, χ^2 = .73)		(p < .05, χ^2 = 4.68)	

Table 3.36: Group B variables and distribution in women.

Feature	Informants taped	Variant	
		Never use	Always use
-er *butter*	67	28	0
[ʃən] *-tion*	66	31	0
[tj] *culture*	52	21	9 (17.0%)
[r] *party*	64	20	17 (26.5%)
[r] *forty*	65	5	26 (40.0%)
-nt## V	58	3	36 (62.0%)
-nt## C	63	11	13 (21.0%)
-st## V	58	14	11 (19.0%)
-st## C	67	35	2 (3.0%)
n't## V	24	7	6 (25.0%)
n't## C	64	25	0
-ed *before V*	60	3	35 (58.0%)
-ed *before C*	51	13	5 (10.0%)

shown in Table 3.37 are consistently used by most. For the purposes of comparison, relevant tertiary+ male patterns are in brackets.

Table 3.37: Selected variables and distribution in tertiary+. For the purposes of comparison, relevant tertiary+ male patterns are in brackets.

Feature	Informants taped	Always use variant	
[h]	25 (7)	56.0%	(43.0%)
Voiceless TH	25 (7)	68.0%	(0.0%)
[o] in *boat*	25 (7)	10.0%	(71.0%)
[e] in *face*	25 (7)	48.0%	(43.0%)
[ɔr] in *poor*	24 (7)	42.0%	(28.5%)
[kʰ a:]	15 (5)	87.0%	(80.0%)
[nt]##V	24 (7)	67.0%	(43.0%)
– ed ##V	22 (7)	64.0%	(28.5%)

Tertiary+ educated men are more likely than their female counterparts to have TH stopping and consonant cluster simplification in their speech here. Additionally, these men are more consistent users of [o] before a following consonant. Most educated speakers tend to produce [kʰa:] as in *card*, [h] in words like *help*, [e] in *face* and [nt] in words like *decent*. For all other variables used in this study, there is less consensus and variation can be correlated with either level of education or gender. Specifically, women tend to be rhotic after vowels, notably [ɔ], and more likely to produce palatalized stops in *culture* type words. It is in the use of these two variables, rhoticity and affricates, that we see the clearest examples of gender differentiation in the sample.

3.3 Parent's background

Informants were asked to state the occupation of the breadwinner in the household in which they were raised. In spite of the problems of using occupation as an index of class and status, it remains a useful tool. It allows, implicitly, some comparison of income and status levels in societies and therefore relative standards of living and access to opportunity (Crompton 1993: 120). A person's occupation also indicates their level of education, to some extent, and therefore their exposure to the norms of the school system. An informant whose parent is/was a teacher is more likely to have been raised in a JE speaking context than an informant whose parent is/was a peasant farmer or casual labourer. Moreover, that informant would have had more access to the facilities and environment that would support success in the school system, such as equipment, physical space and parental assistance.

As an example, Table 3.38 shows patterns of final level of attained education in two neighbouring communities, separated only, to some extent, by the University campus (STATIN 1991: 2–150).

Table 3.38: Level of education and residence in two selected communities

	Population	Primary	Secondary	University
Mona Heights	4644	948 (20.0%)	1927 (41.0%)	1062 (23.0%)
August Town	7359	2955 (40.0%)	2875 (39.0%)	71 (1.0%)

The first, Mona Heights, was built in the 1950s as a government housing scheme for middle income families headed by occupational groups like civil servants or teachers; August Town is a much older low income community. Bryan (2000: 43) cites evidence that suggests it was established well before 1890. Not unexpectedly, residents of Mona Heights have attained higher levels of education, even as the same numbers of schools and the university are (geographically) available to both communities. Undoubtedly this is partially a function of household income, but also less obvious factors like the ability to assist children with their education. Occupation of parent, therefore, can suggest the type of access to education each informant would have had in both their formative years and at higher levels of the school system.

A number of answers on parental occupation were given by informants, too many for any successful correlation, and I therefore initially abstracted 5 occupational categories from the raw data:

(1) **"Cleaner"**: This group included all informants who said their parents had low paying, unskilled work which enabled them to live at subsistence level (small farmer, household helper, gardener, manual labourer). These occupations are also typically low status ones, either because of their link to peasant agriculture or servitude and, of course, poor remuneration (Nettleford 1970: 138–140; Stone 1980: 20).

(2) **"Artisan"**: A group of skilled workers who are self-employed but whose income and status in the society, while higher than "cleaner", is still relatively low. Generally, skills are acquired through apprenticeship rather than in

any formal system of education. Included here are such occupations as carpenter, plumber, mechanic, dressmaker and so on.

(3) "Teacher": Members of this group (also nurse, secretary, junior civil servant), while not necessarily very high income earners, are afforded more status. These occupations are dependent on having access to higher education, as they all require(d) at *least* post-secondary schooling, even at a time when access to schooling was more limited. Historically, for example, the effect of their education among community members was to make people like the teacher typically a leader in communities as well. Importantly, many of the occupations in this group are in the public sector and receive payment from government. This has meant relatively low pay as well as less control over the means to increase their income.

(4) "Doctor": In contrast, this group is made up of self-employed professionals in the private sector who can choose to increase income in response to the possibilities in the market, or better paid employees in the public sector. Informants placed in this group said their parents were lawyers, accountants, business managers, senior civil servants. These occupations therefore combine the relatively high status given to group 3 and relatively high income levels as well.

A fifth category, "**Business owner**" was identified and excluded from the data. Six informants gave this as their parent's job, mentioning specifically occupations such as contractor, shopkeeper, or developer. In the Jamaican context these labels cannot be consistently associated with any measure of personal income. Though some owners of business do earn more than the other groups mentioned above, many do not. Nor do the occupations reflect a shared level of education or status either. (See Appendix C for the full list of occupations mentioned and how they are grouped in this study.) I have therefore not included these 6 informants in the data presented below.

Parent's occupation was eventually analysed as two categories, which attempted to combine likely income and level of education. Category 1, cleaner/artisan, is made up of parent(s) with relatively low paying jobs that have no or few requirements of formal education (46 informants). Category 2, teacher/doctor, is made up of 28 informants with higher income and well educated parents. By comparing the speech of informants from these differing backgrounds, I am assuming a comparison of informants more likely to be from a bilingual JE/JC speaking household with those from households more likely to be monolingual JC speaking. The cleaner/artisan group would therefore typically have much less exposure to JE at home.

Table 3.39: Informant's level of education and parent's occupation

	Cleaner/Artisan		Teacher/Doctor	
Primary	4	(100.0%)	0	
Secondary+	36	(75.0%)	12	(43.0%)
Tertiary+	15	(36.5%)	26	(93.0%)

Table 3.39 shows the extent to which informant's background correlates with their level of education ($p < .001$, $\chi^2 = 13.2$). There is close to a 40% association between the two social variables, so that a tertiary education is typically more likely in informants with educated and better-off parents ($\phi = 0.38$). This would predict a certain pattern of variant use among the teacher/doctor group, one very much akin to the pattern discussed in the section on education, such as lower frequencies of h-drop or TH stopping.

3.3.1 Group A variables and background

A number of the variables do show the kind of pattern that would be predicted by the literature and the data in the previous sections. Speakers with parents from a teacher/doctor background used fewer "Creole" forms in their interviews than those from the cleaner/artisan background. The results of the correlation for h-drop ($p < .001$, $\chi^2 = 24.7$) are reflected in an avoidance of TH stopping ($p < .001$, $\chi^2 = 47.7$), use of the low vowel [ɔ] ($p < .001$, $\chi^2 = 34.29$) and a low incidence of mid-vowel diphthongs ($p < .05$, $\chi^2 = 5.78$).

Table 3.40: Parent's occupation and h-drop.

	n	h-drop	h
cleaner/artisan	46	123 (15.5%)	668 (84.5%)
teacher/doctor	28	43 (7.0%)	575 (93.0%)

The results for gender and level of education as well suggest consensus on which variants are considered "good" English. This discussion will therefore focus on the one result that did not follow this pattern, and requires closer examination and analysis.

Table 3.41: Parent's occupation and velar stops

	kja	k^ha	kja:	k^ha:
cleaner/artisan	67 (58.0%)	48 (42.0%)	14 (28.5%)	35 (71.5%)
teacher/doctor	47 (57.0%)	35 (43.0%)	5 (9.0%)	48 (91.0%)
	(p.>.50, χ^2 = 0.17)		(p.< .02, χ^2 = 6.08)	

I found no correlation between speakers' background and production of [kj] before the short vowel. What distinguishes the two groups is use of [kja:], which is also the result yielded by the correlation with education as well. Informants, when stratified along a number of social dimensions seem to vary [k^ha ~ kja] but tend to produce [k^ha:] most consistently, particularly those groups traditionally said to use standard forms. My analysis so far has shown that along the Creole/English dimension of Group A variables, level of education, gender and background of household are indexed by more or less use of Creole forms. This would suggest that [kja:], which also follows this pattern, can be analysed as an aspect of this Creole/English paradigm. However, use of the voiceless velar variable here is characterized by [kja ~ k^ha] variation, and this may suggest one of the following possibilities:

a) [kja] is a feature that is generalized throughout the Jamaican continuum and is therefore not a basilectal/mesolectal feature;[11]

b) [kja] is reflective of an emerging norm of Jamaican speech, a Creole feature that is entering JE. This latter explanation has been suggested by Beckford-Wassink (2001: 31) and F. Miller (1987), who describes "a pattern which is emerging where educated speakers are expressing themselves by using linguistic forms which are not part of a [standard] British or American model" (177). One would assume, therefore, that older educated speakers may produce lower frequencies of [kja] if it is indeed an emerging JE norm. This is discussed in the following section.

---

[11]Mugglestone (1995) in fact mentions the "delicate palatal glide" in words like [kjaind] *kind* as an aspect of proper speech for women (206). [kja] may well have been an aspect of acrolectal speech in the same time period (the 19th century).

Patrick (1999: 109) demonstrates that

> [i]n all cases, the incidence of the palatal glide is higher in informal speech than in test [reading passage, word list] situations, supporting the claim that (KYA) is not a marker of prestigious speech but a vernacular variable.

This is no doubt the case, but in this study I wish to examine a somewhat different aspect of language use than Patrick's study. Firstly, when the informant is cued to a particular feature under investigation, as in word lists, we do have some access to the ideal that speakers believe ought to be used in correct speech. However, J. Milroy & L. Milroy (1985: 19) suggest that informants may interpret such tasks as tests of their knowledge of the correct pronunciation. I imagine, for example, that all informants here would report that correct JE has word initial interdental fricatives and not alveolar stops. However, in actual recordings of formal speech the voiced and voiceless fricatives are not sociolinguistic equivalents -saying [derfɔr] *therefore* appears to be much more acceptable than saying 'ting' *thing*, at least in Jamaica.[12] I wish to make a distinction between the speaker's reported ideal of SJE, whether explicitly stated or implicit in test results, and the idea of SJE that members of the speech community can abstract from spoken "model" JE – "the speech patterns of the teachers, religious leaders, media personnel and other high status groups in the society" (Brodber 1989: 47).

Secondly, word lists and reading passages do not necessarily reflect the way language is used in even formal interaction. When a stranger comes into an office and asks for help, when a teacher is explaining a subject, or when an address from Parliament is broadcast, these are formal contexts of language use which other members in a community are more likely to hear than, say, the reading of a list of words. The formal mental construct of idealized Jamaican English is perhaps revealed by the latter. But it is from the former situations, and who is speaking, in their social context that members of the community form their ideologies of acceptable language use and which sets of variants may be selected in certain stylistic and social contexts. And it is in one such context, unplanned formal interaction, that the data here are collected. Speakers in this sample, with differing levels of education, gender and background do produce [kja]; but [kjaː] is much less frequent in the sample, which suggests that only the latter feature is not perceived to be permissible in SJE. Arguably, use of [kja] is an acceptable form in spoken SJE, heard in the actual formal language use of educated Jamaicans

---

[12]The impression I have been given from colleagues from other parts of the West Indies (Guyana, Trinidad) is that Jamaicans focus on this voiceless TH stopping as an aspect of bad English more than is done in their communities.

likely to be linguistic models. Certainly, at this point in the analysis of speech produced here, neither variant, [kja ~ kʰa], emerges as more typical in the formal context in which data were collected; nor is either variant more typical in the speech of those groups said to be more likely to produce standard/prestigious forms.

3.3.2 Group B variables and background

Table 3.42: Parent's occupation and *butter* type words

	butt[a]	butt[ʌ]	butt[ʌr]
cleaner/artisan	159 (25.0%)	423 (66.0%)	61 (9.0%)
teacher/doctor	55 (10.0%)	442 (81.0%)	47 (9.0%)

Speakers can be distinguished here again by more, or less, use of the Creole variant *butt[a]* and the JE *butt[ʌ]* (p < .001, χ^2 = 44.68). There is no difference in the groups' productions of the retroflex ending. The results for -*tion* words show a very similar pattern, with the statistical significance largely the result of the difference between those who produce [ʃan] and [ʃʌn] (p < .001, χ^2 = 38.51). For nearly all other Group B variables there was no statistically significant difference in variants used. Speakers in this sample, regardless of background, tend to produce similar frequencies of affricates/palatalized stops and post-vocalic rhoticity.

The presence of word final stops in phonological consonant clusters also patterns similarly in the two groups, though for [st] clusters before a following vowel those with higher status parents tend to produce more of the final stop (p < .10, χ^2 = 5.4). Interestingly, it is this variable that also distinguished male and female productions, with women more likely to articulate the final stop.

Table 3.43: Phonological -st clusters by parent's occupation

C(C)##V:	-st	-stʰ	-s
cleaner/artisan	42 (36.0%)	6 (5.0%)	70 (59.0%)
teacher/doctor	47 (51.0%)	5 (5.5%)	40 (43.5%)

It is entirely possible that background of speaker can be correlated with gender, and that women tend to come from more affluent households than their male counterparts at JAMPRO. This would go some way to explaining some of the patterns of variant use, either among women in the sample or among informants from teacher/doctor backgrounds. Women's general tendency to use more standard forms of Group A variables, say, might be due to them being more likely to come from backgrounds with a greater JE presence.

Table 3.44: Parent's occupation by gender at JAMPRO

	Male	Female
cleaner/artisan	12 (86%)	34 (57%)
teacher/doctor	2 (14%)	26 (43%)

Table 3.44 shows that females are fairly evenly distributed in terms of background. Men, however, tend to come from less well-off households, backgrounds more typically monolingual in JC. Interestingly, when [tj ~ ʧ] (in *creature* type words) is looked at, taking into account the possibility of gender as an intervening variable, the results suggest another possibility. In Table 3.45, only female informants from the two types of households are compared (with relevant male results in italics for comparison).

Table 3.45: Palatalized stops in cleaner/artisan informants by gender (with relevant male results in italics for comparison)

	[tj]		[ʧ]	
Female cleaner/artisan	23 (43.0%)	*11 (24%)*	30 (57.0%)	*35 (76.0%)*
Female teacher/doctor	32 (30.5%)		73 (69.5%)	

There is no statistical difference in production of [tj] between women from different backgrounds (p > .10, χ^2 = 2.58). And women, among those from cleaner/artisan households, vary [tj ~ ʧ] more than men (in italics in Table 3.45). Significantly, [tj] is not the variant of the highly educated in this sample, who typically produce the affricate. This would support the earlier analysis (see Table 3.31) that this variant, [tj] in *culture* words, is more a feature of female speech generally.

Before a following vowel, those with parents classified as teacher/doctor are more likely to produce a morphological word final cluster.

Again the difference between rates of *-ed* before a vowel and before a consonant, as well as the high levels of cluster presence in the cleaner/artisan group

Table 3.46: Morphological clusters by parent's occupation

C(C)##V:	-ed	∅
cleaner/artisan	60 (74%)	21 (26%)
teacher/doctor	86 (86%)	14 (14%)
	(p < .05, χ^2 = 4.1)	

C(C)##C:		
cleaner/artisan	39 (41%)	56 (59%)
teacher/doctor	37 (52%)	34 (48%)
	(p > .10, χ^2 = 1.95)	

(74%), suggest that this is a phonological difference, rather than a difference in the use of English morphology. Generally, both sets of informants tend to produce the tense inflection when it occurs before a following vowel; and both vary considerably when the following segment is a consonant. This suggests that the use of the morphological cluster is very dependent on phonological context, notwithstanding the difference in production that distinguishes teacher/doctor from cleaner/artisan. The pattern for -n't clusters is similar, though not statistically significant, with simplification of the cluster much more likely before a consonant.

Generally then, informants' backgrounds can be correlated with more or less use of Creole features. This is the pattern apparent in Group A correlations. Background showed no effect, however, on production of post-vocalic [r], palatalized stops, retroflex word endings or most consonant clusters.

When a more refined distinction of parent's occupation is compared with the patterns that distinguish the (locally) educated and women the following picture emerges. In Table 3.47 I analyse separately the 'cleaner', 'artisan', 'teacher' and 'doctor' categories (* indicates statistically significant).

To a great extent all speakers, regardless of background, tend to use most word final clusters and post [ɔ] rhoticity here very similarly and approximate to the pattern of the tertiary+ educated. This suggests that education may normalize a particular use of many phonological variables. One exception to this is the production of past clusters and [st] clusters (before a vowel), most consistently produced by speakers from the "teacher" background. The same observation can be made for use of [tj] and may well reflect the pattern identified for the LMC in other speech communities (Labov 1972: 126). Interestingly, the female tendency

Table 3.47: Variables and distribution by parent's occupation

Feature	Women	Men	Tertiary+	Cleaner	Artisan	Teacher	Doctor
Rhotic [a]		*	*	26.5%	54.0%	48.0%	31.0%
Rhotic [ɔ]			*	62.0%	72.0%	61.0%	76.0%
[tj]	*		*	24.0%	38.5%	53.7%	23.8%
[ʃɔ n]			*	7.0%	19.0%	19.0%	20.0%
[kja]				58.0%	58.5%	51.5%	76.0%
[n't]##V				67.0%	50.0%	55.5%	37.5%
[n't]##C				11.5%	18.5%	15.0%	11.5%
[st]##V	*			36.0%	43.0%	65.0%	38.0%
[st]##C				13.0%	14.0%	16.0%	9.0%
-ed + V				62.0%	78.0%	90.0%	67.0%
-ed + C	*			50.0%	39.0%	53.0%	50.0%

to produce palatalized stops, also more apparent in the mid-strata in the sample, may add support to the possibility of an emerging prestige form. This feature, and the analysis of the data from gender, education and background, is discussed in more detail in the final section of this chapter.

All speakers tend to be rhotic after the back vowel, but the pattern for the groups after [a] is more diffuse in terms of background of speaker. Speakers from widely divergent household types ("cleaner" and "doctor") are more typically non-rhotic after [a] while being rhotic after [ɔ].

Those from the most high status backgrounds use more [kja] and [dõ(n)] than others in the sample. In this same group we typically find most use of the PSJ variants. This suggests a number of things. Firstly, these pronunciations are not of the same sociolinguistic type as h-dropping or voiceless TH stopping and therefore do not necessarily have to be avoided when producing JE. Secondly, it may be that these are features used across the continuum by most speakers in Jamaica, and are not indexical of speaking either Creole or English. A third possibility is that these are Creole features, acceptable in JE and used to show an ability to also speak Creole. These issues are fully explored elsewhere in this chapter (§3.6).

3.4 Speaker age

JAMPRO is an executive agency of the Jamaican government and conforms to the government norm that retires employees at 65. The oldest age cohort in my sample is therefore 50–65 years of age. The youngest speaker interviewed was 18 (a single informant), but there were no others under 20. The youngest age cohort in this study is made up of speakers 20–29 years old. There are a number of reasons why the social and educational influences on these two age groups can be described as different.

Those informants 50–65 years old when data was collected, would have grown up and received most of their formal education before political independence (1962). This would have been in a social context of British colonial rule, when access to education was limited for most Jamaicans. According to the data presented by E. Miller (1989: 218), a high school education was the privilege of a few, with just 6% of primary school leavers advancing to high school in 1960. Prior to that, between 1945 and 1950, an average of 2.5% of students advanced out of primary level education. All 4 of the primary educated informants are in the oldest age cohort; but the majority of informants in that grouping have at least a high school education and many a tertiary education (7 of the 16).

Informants in this age cohort would also have been educated at a time when, according to the Kandel Report on the state of British West Indian Education, "a secondary education [was organized] to serve the purposes of an external [British] system of examinations" (Williams 1970: 462), and to impart British culture. Tertiary education would have been had abroad, as is true for 4 of the 7 informants, or had after the local university was established in 1948 with a largely expatriate staff. The speakers in this age group are more likely to have been exposed to British norms and education than any others in the JAMPRO sample.

The 20–29 year old group would have had their formative (educational) years in the 1970s and 1980s. Starting in 1973 high school and university were fully paid for by the government, with the tuition for both tertiary and secondary school provided for students. Examinations were also made Caribbean with the introduction of the CXC. The teacher:pupil ratio in the period following rose from 1:38 in 1978 to 1:55 in the 1980s. The data in Table 3.48 show the results of high school English examinations and one of the consequences of what E. Miller calls this "retrenchment" (1989: 214).

Table 3.48: English language passes in Jamaica 1976–1984

Year	Number entered (CXC/GCE)	% Passing
1976	7,534	62
1980	6,607	41
1984	11,173	44

Additionally, there has been a perception that standards of English education have declined even further since then. Some of these are outlined in the discussions in Patrick (1999: 60) and Christie (2003). The following from a letter to the local newspaper typifies the concerns about the standard of English in public use:

> ...there is abundant evidence of the rise of *Yahoolish*, that language spoken by Jamaicans who believe and insist, yet fail to so demonstrate, that when the time comes they can produce good English. Whatever the destiny of written English (...) oral English has an uncertain future. The day may well come when, at a forum such as the UN, or WTO, the language used by our representatives will be known as Jamaican.
>
> (Chester Burgess, *The Daily Gleaner*, August 16 2001)

Like Beckford-Wassink and F. Miller suggest in their studies, as discussed in the previous section, the above quote also implies, albeit as criticism, the existence of new or emerging norms of good English that depart from MSE usage, particularly in a social context where the functional distribution of JC and JE is less defined than before. Moreover, the greater access to higher education after independence has also meant a greater number of speakers entering an educational system which, unlike in the 1940s and 1950s, consciously exposed them to local norms and models of English.

I wish, therefore, to compare use of the phonological variables in these two age groups at JAMPRO, and identify any features that distinguish the older from the younger. For the analysis below, the 4 primary educated informants will be excluded, so that both groups will be made up entirely of those with at least a secondary education. The older age cohort therefore has 12 and the younger has 29 informants.

3.4.1 Group A variables and age

For a number of the Group A variables there was no statistical difference found between the younger and the older informants. Speakers in my sample raised and educated in colonial Jamaica do not use more or fewer Creole forms than those raised and educated when access to education was improved or, as has been suggested by some, standards lowered. The data also show that older speakers, at least for these variables, did not produce significantly more of the JE variants either, even for those items that are stigmatized like voiceless TH stopping, h-dropping or the low vowel [a] in *not* words. It cannot therefore be argued in relation to these variables here that these phonological norms of (formal) language are necessarily changing.

The exceptions to this pattern are in the use of the diphthongs.

Table 3.49: Pre-consonantal mid-vowels by age

	uo		o		ie		e	
20–29	49	(7.5%)	596	(92.5%)	139	(20.0%)	566	(80.0%)
50–65	23	(8.0%)	266	(92.0%)	25	(8.0%)	271	(92.0%)
	(p > .80, χ^2 = .039)				(p < .001, χ^2 = 19.23)			

Young speakers at JAMPRO are much more likely to produce [ie] pre-conson-antally than older informants, even while use of the back vowel variable remains similar for both groups, showing little dipthongization. When the data for the front diphthong are disaggregated across the age groups at JAMPRO, the patterns in Figure 3.1 emerged for men and women/secondary+ and tertiary+.

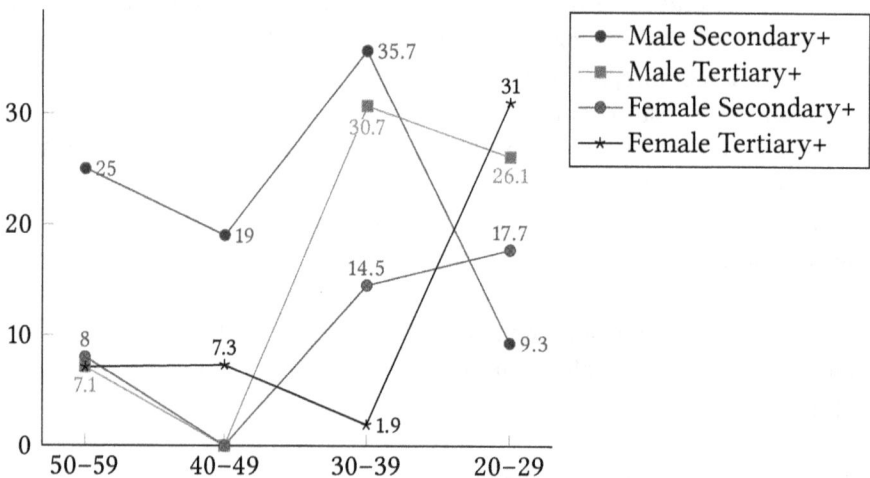

Figure 3.1: Front diphthong use by age, gender and level of education

Younger women generally and younger university graduates use noticeably more [ie] than their counterparts from older age groups. Young less educated men, in contrast, use more [e] than both older men of a similar education level and others in their age cohort in this sample. Indeed, among 20–29 year old in-formants, there is no statistical difference between general male and female use (p > .50, χ^2 = .24). But in the same age cohort, the tertiary educated are much more likely to diphthongize than the secondary educated (p < .001, χ^2 = 11.48), whether male or female. The data therefore suggest that use of the front dipthong may be emerging as a more acceptable feature of JE, as reflected in the pattern for young women and the more highly educated. This pattern is not apparent in the speech of young, less educated men who seem to produce more consistently the [e] that the data in previous sections would suggest is more prestigious. One possible interpretation of the data here is that young men at JAMPRO are more careful in their production of the prestige monophthong precisely because when they use the Creole variant it is more likely to have negative associations than if used by women. Young men in this context here are the group least presumed to be educated and least favoured in terms of how they present as prospective employees of JAMPRO.

Among the older age cohorts note that the data follow a more predictable pattern. For the 30–39 year olds, men use more diphthongs than women and the secondary educated use more diphthongs than university graduates. This would be expected, given the results so far for gender and level of education that correlated fewer Creole forms with women and the highly educated. And for the 50–65 age group, university graduates and secondary educated women showed similar use of the variants, with the latter approximating to the prestige monophthong variant much more than their male counterparts.

Table 3.50: Pre-rhotic mid-vowels by age

	poor words			*beer* words	
	[ɔ]	[uᵒ]	[o]	[iᵉr]	[er]
20–29	179 (80.0%)	31 (14.0%)	13 (6.0%)	173 (49.8%)	175 (50.2%)
50–65	78 (68.0%)	26 (23.0%)	11 (9.0%)	64 (45.0%)	77 (55.0%)
	(p < .05, χ^2 = 6.53)			(p > .30, χ^2 = .73)	

When the pre-rhotic data are also considered, it is clear that the use of the [ie] diphthong is, as Alleyne noted some two decades ago (1980: 41), quite widespread, particularly in younger speakers; and in these same speakers the back diphthong is less produced in all environments. So in this sample of JE speech, front diphthong use tends to be higher in those educated in the 1970s and 1980s than those educated in the 1940s and 1950s, whereas back diphthong use is much less, particularly pre-rhotically where the [ɔ] is favoured.

3.4.2 Group B variables and age

There was no statistical difference between older and younger speakers for either *butter* type words or for the use of palatalized stops in *culture* type words. Where there seems to be some difference in the age cohorts is the -*tion* ending, though the significance is above the critical level (p < .10, χ^2 = 6.5). What difference there is suggests that younger speakers are more likely to have a schwa in *education* type words, while older speakers tend to produce the [ʃɔn] variant. As with the other variables along the Creole/English dimension, age does not correlate here with more, or less, use of the Creole form.

Table 3.51: *education* type words by age

	[ʃan]	[ʃʌn]	[ʃɔn]	[ʃən]
20–29	52 (22.0%)	118 (50.5%)	35 (15.0%)	29 (12.5%)
50–65	25 (21.5%)	59 (51.0%)	26 (22.0%)	6 (5.0%)

Interestingly, while use of schwa did not index higher education, [ʃɔn] did, and has been reported elsewhere as more likely in speakers with longer exposure to schooling (Shields-Brodber 1996: 4). In addition [ʃɔn] is more a feature of the age cohort educated during the colonial period and presumably more exposed to British norms. A more detailed picture of the use of the two variants is presented in Table 3.52.

Table 3.52: *education* type words by age and education

	50–65		20–29	
	Tertiary+	Secondary+	Tertiary+	Secondary+
educa[ʃɔn]	14	11	25	10
educa[ʃən]	4	2	6	23

Older speakers, regardless of level of education, tend to use the variants similarly – here more of the [ʃɔn] variant. It is among young speakers that [ʃɔn] correlates with higher education and therefore a longer stay in the school system. The highly educated young are therefore using the prestige norm of older speakers, and it would therefore be difficult to argue for [ʃɔn] as an emerging variant in JE. Schwa use is highest in the young secondary educated speaker and, given the results for other sociolinguistic correlations, seems to be more periph-eral in the speech community.

Table 3.53: Rhoticity by age

| | *party* type words | | *forty* type words | |
	[partɪ]	[paːtɪ]	[fɔrtɪ]	[fɔːtɪ]
20–29	54 (58.0%)	39 (42.0%)	77 (85.5%)	13 (14.5%)
50–65	13 (41.0%)	19 (59.0%)	38 (63.0%)	22 (37.0%)
	(p < .10, χ^2 = 2.91)		(p < .01, χ^2 = 9.92)	

Younger speakers are more rhotic than older speakers, and in particular after the [ɔ] vowel.

Figure 3.2 compares all age cohorts with education in the production of *forty* type words.

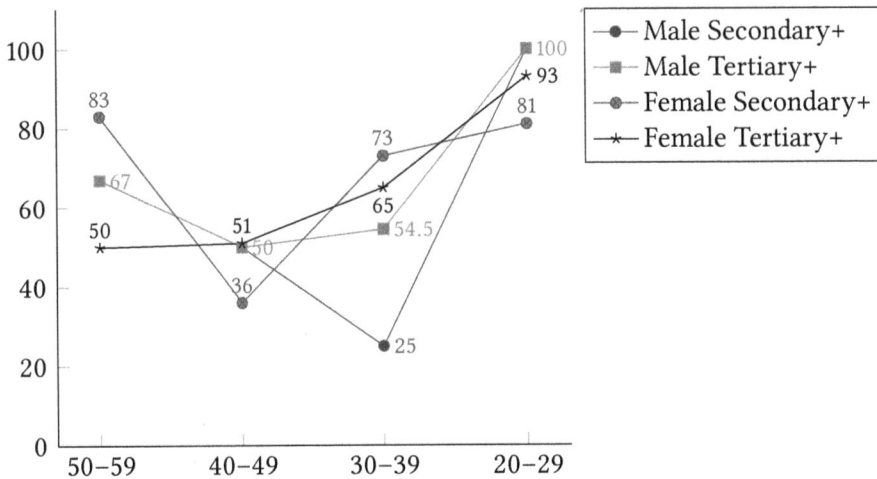

Figure 3.2: Rhoticity after [ɔ] by age, gender and level of education.

With the exception of the 4 primary educated informants, all speakers in this sample seem to be over time normalising rhoticity after the back vowel [ɔ], a pattern which seemed to have been led by less educated females and more ed-ucated male speakers. If we argue that the production of 50–65 year old female graduates, who cannot be characterized as either strictly rhotic or non-rhotic, reflected the instability of the sociolinguistic variable in terms of prestige, then there has been a conscious adoption of a rhotic prestige norm.

When the patterns for the highest educated groups are analysed in terms of gender, we see a divergence between men and women as it relates to rhoticity generally. Young educated men are less rhotic after [a], while following the rhotic pattern of others in the sample after the [ɔ] vowel.

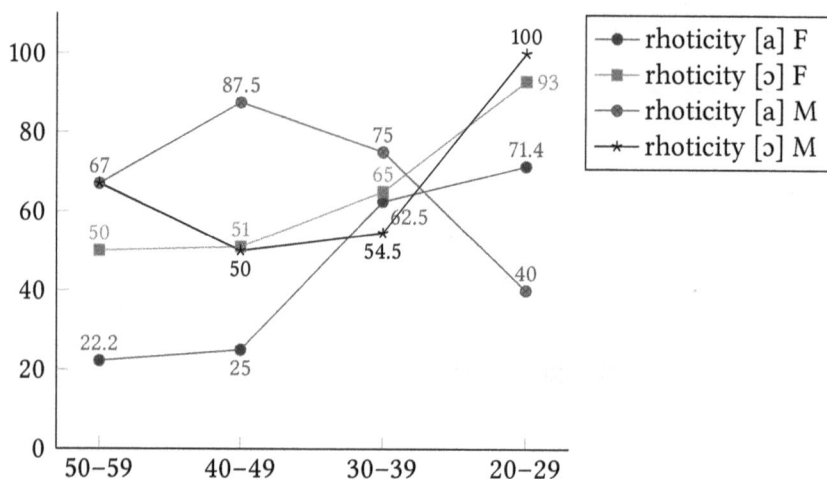

Figure 3.3: Post-vocalic rhoticity after [a] and [ɔ] by age and gender.

There is evidence, in the hypercorrect use of rhoticity, the distancing from non-rhotic Creole forms and the female pattern of rhoticity, to suggest that rhoticity is a normalised feature of SJE. The data for young men, who are less rhotic after [a], suggest two things however. These young men are, as is found in other speech communities, producing more non-standard forms of the variable. Moreover, as with the results for earlier correlations, rhoticity after [a] is much more likely to be the site of sociolinguistic differentiation than after [ɔ]. Arguably, the sociolinguistic significance of having [ɔ] in the idiolect, production of which may be more obvious in a rhotic phonetic environment, is one constraint on variation. Alternatively, the [ɔ] variant is much more likely to have developed focussed norms of use, in this case a rhotic norm. Masculinity may well be projected by "sounding tough" through the use of non-standard forms, to the extent that those forms are not also projecting something which carries greater stigma in the speech community, such as a lack of education or not being able to "speak properly" in a context of white-collar employment.

The results for consonant cluster use suggest that younger and older speakers behave similarly. Generally, both age cohorts have higher rates of cluster production before vowels; and higher rates of -nt clusters than -st clusters. The rates of production of clusters with morphological function are also very similar for both age cohorts in this sample. In all cases, there was no statistically significant difference between the age groups.

3.5 Hypercorrection in the JAMPRO sample

Hypercorrection in speech has been defined in two ways, both relating to an overproduction of particular forms in certain groups of speakers or in individuals. Labov (1972) described a pattern of variant use in the lower middle class New Yorker, such that "...the lower-middle-class speakers go beyond the highest-status groups in their tendency to use the forms considered correct and appropriate for formal styles" (126). In effect, their overproduction was in relation to the linguistic behaviour in other (higher status) classes of speakers and reflected a more consistent production of the prestige or standard variants of a variable such as [θ] or post-vocalic rhoticity. This type of quantitative hypercorrection suggests more than merely which variants speakers in the community consider prestigious; it also reveals that these speakers hold an idea that certain (desirable) social characteristics are indexed by use of such forms, though their patterns of use betray some insecurity about how they do reflect place in the social structure (Silverstein 2000: 138). Quantitative hypercorrection is also "a synchronic indicator of linguistic change in progress" (Labov 1968: 245), in particular the conscious adoption and spread of a perceived prestige form as the standard, noted in the pattern of rhoticity in the JAMPRO sample.

The other type of hypercorrection involves analogical error (Preston 1989: 117). Speakers aim to produce what they have identified as the prestige reflex of a form they have in their vernacular and in the process "replace" too many in the conversion. Trudgill (1986: 66) gives the example of [bʌtʃr] *butcher*, where speakers of Northern dialects of English have over-applied a rule that converts Northern [ʊ] (as in [lʊv] *love*) to [ʌ] for prestigious RP; and Bobda (2001: 277) cites the example of the form [plaktɪs] *practice* in an educated Kenyan speaker who is conscious of the stigma attached to [l ~ r] variation. It is this latter type of qualitative hypercorrection (Janda & Auger 1992) and aspects of its occurrence in speakers of JE at JAMPRO that I wish to discuss in this section.

I should first point out that the features listed below are not the only instances of qualitative hypercorrection in Jamaica. For example, some Jamaican speakers produce such items as:

1. [standʒarin] *tangerine* or [sprɪkl] *prickle*. JC does not allow [st] clusters syllable initially, so that the JC cognates of English 'stone' or 'stop' become

[tuon] or [tap]. In 'tangerine' therefore, by analogy, speakers insert the "missing" onset [s].

2. [aːrva] *harbour,* where [v] is used for cognate English items with either [b] or [v].

3. [amaʊn] *among* or [laʊnz] *lungs,* as [ʌŋ] typically occurs in JC in English cognates like *down* or *town,* the "correct" ending [aʊn] is substituted.

4. [flɪtaz] *fritters,* [talabrɛd] *thoroughbred,* showing the [l ~ r] variation found in, for example, West African varieties of English (Holm 1988: 135). Alleyne (1980: 62) points out that this type of variation is somewhat archaic in Jamaica.

These forms did not occur in my sample and are typically identified with more basilectal varieties of Jamaican speech (Cassidy 1961: 40–47). Possible instances of hypercorrection in my sample occurred with the following variables:

1. Word initial glottal fricative /h/. In my sample of speakers, eleven informants produced the hypercorrect pattern, as in [hoke] *'OK'* (F70) or [hebl] *able* F74), but typically with single attestations.

2. The low back stressed vowel /ɔ/. Forms in my sample like [rɪlɔks] *relax* (M47), [sɔlərɪ] *salary* (F53) and [bɔːtrum] *bathroom* (F96) produced by seven of my informants would suggest the kind of sensitivity to the feature discussed above and a belief that [ɔ] is the "correct" reflex of [a].

3. The interdental fricatives /θ/ and /ð/. In this data word initial voiced TH stopping seemed to be a general feature of JE, but the same informants tended to avoid the voiceless alveolar variant. I have heard hypercorrect use of the voiceless fricative in items in some Jamaican speech. It was produced once in the JAMPRO sample (F76 [θʌg] *tug*). Hypercorrect use of [ð] did not occur in my sample.

4. The alveopalatal affricate. Two of my informants (F6, F10), on more than one occasion, produced the form [djunjʌ] *junior,* a hypercorrect use of the palatalized stop; additionally, 6 other informants typically produced [dʌs] for the word *just,* a possible avoidance of the affricate. It is, however, specifically the hypercorrect use of the palatalized stop that I wish to focus on in this section.

5. Post-vocalic rhoticity. Hypercorrect rhoticity did occur in one informant (F16), who produced the forms [ɔrθɔrɪtɪ] *authority* and [masardʒ] *massage*. In light of this, and the findings in this and earlier studies, for some JE speakers "correct" English is rhotic at least when word internally before a consonant. No pronunciations such as [dʒəmekʌr] *Jamaica*, or [kjubʌr] *Cuba* occurred in my sample.

6. The mid-front vowel [e]. According to Christie (2003: 19),

> [a]nother example of hypercorrection is the pronunciation by some teachers and radio personalities in particular, of words such as *fear* and *here* with the same vowel sound as in *fair* and *hair*, in an unconscious effort to avoid Creole pronunciations such as occurs in *fies* 'face'.

In my own sample, this pronunciation also occurred, and was found in the speech of all but 4 of my sample of 82 speakers. In addition, one informant (F57) produced the item [lez] *liaise*. This relatively new item in the JE lexicon is bisyllabic. This informant might have first converted this to a monosyllabic [liez] and then "replaced" the diphthong with its monopthong reflex [e].

Table 3.54 presents the number and types of informants who did produce the above hypercorrect forms.

Table 3.54: Qualitative hypercorrection in the JAMPRO sample

[h]	[ɔ]	[θ]	[dj]	[r]	[e]	
11	7	1	2	1	78	Number of informants (of 82)
2	0	0	1	1	32	Number with tertiary education (of 32)
3	2	0	2	1	28	Number with tertiary educated parents (of 28)
9	6	1	2	1	64	Number of women (of 67)
2	1	0	0	0	14	Number of men (of 15)

A number of comments can be made about the data presented above. The general pattern in this sample is for each informant to have one or two hypercorrect forms and to produce one or two instances of it in their texts. The data on [e] is clearly different in type from the others, as it seems to be a normalized feature of these JE speakers, used in variation with [ie] by nearly all informants (Allsopp 1996: xlvi suggests this is common in most varieties of Caribbean English). And unlike hypercorrect [h] or [ɔ], for example, [e] in *beer* type words is typical of the speech of the highly educated and of those from likely JE speaking house-holds. In any case, to describe [fe:r] *fear* as hypercorrect is to assume an external (metropolitan) model of English for the Jamaican speech community and to stip-ulate that a vowel distinction between words such as *fear* and *fair* is necessarily standard.

By inspection, hypercorrect forms occur more frequently in female speakers, though there is no statistical difference in the gender distribution of [h] inser-tion. I am unable to make any meaningful comment on this given the dispropor-tionate number of women interviewed. However, Patrick identifies *speaky-spoky*, hypercorrect use of [h] and [ɔ], as perceived to be more associated with female speakers (1997: 45). If women are more aware of the prestige pattern in speech communities, and are more likely to promote what becomes the prestige form, then it is perhaps not unexpected to find more hypercorrection in their speech.

The incidence of [h] insertion and hypercorrect [ɔ] is much higher than for the other features discussed. In light of Patrick's analysis, it appears that the distribution of these two hypercorrect items in the Jamaican population is also much more general than the other five. The historical record (see §3.2) would suggest that they have been aspects of the Jamaican speech community from the earliest days. Indeed, it is possible that their production is only a function of JC-to-JE conversion diachronically, and they have become aspects of one variety of JE selected by speakers from the speech community. It is hypercorrect use of these two items that have emerged as *the* register that indexes the locally pretentious speaker.

Three of the informants produced more than one type of hypercorrect form. Informant F6 used hypercorrect [h], [ɔ] and [dj] (as in the examples [hon] *own*, [kɔ:r] *car* and [djunjʌ] *junior*). She is young (under 30), secondary educated, and comes from a household headed by parents with relatively little education who in Jamaica are called "higglers", roadside or market traders. The other feature of note in her speech is a form like [judʒəlɪ] *usually*, with the affricate more typical of Creole varieties and stigmatized in JE. Informant F74 produced both of the hypercorrect forms described in *speaky-spoky*, as in the examples [hebl] *able* and [mɔ:kIt] *market*. She is over 50 years old, with a primary education and very likely to be a vernacular Creole speaker, given her general sociolinguistic profile. For example, she typically used Creole forms like [dis] *just* and an almost invariant low vowel /a/ in *not* type words in her text. The other informant, F16, produced hypercorrect rhoticity. She also tends to produce [ʃɔn] in *education* type words. Additionally, she does not TH stop, nor does she have "problems" with [h] or [ɔ]. She holds a Masters degree and comes from a household with educated parents (her father is a bursar, her mother an accounts clerk).

The distribution of hypercorrect forms in the sample suggests therefore that:

- Feature 7 (described as "hypercorrect" [e]) should not be included in this discussion which takes an endonormative approach to what is to be termed standard or good English in Jamaica.

- Hypercorrect [h] and [ɔ] are each most common in the sample and, arguably, across the continuum. Indeed, when used together, they are common enough to be considered a stereotype of the comically "elevated" speaker in Jamaica.

- Hypercorrect [h], [ɔ], and possibly [θ], are less likely to be found here among highly educated JE speakers. These are infrequently occurring items, at least in this sample, and therefore such associations must be impressionistic and very tentative. However, most of the informants who did produce these forms were not tertiary educated or from households with educated parents.

- The hypercorrect forms that I find in female speech include more features and may suggest a greater sensitivity to a wider set of prestige variants than held by men. The exaggerated forms in this sample are also more an aspect of female speech. This, of course, would not be unexpected. Greater approximation to and awareness of prestige/standard forms is a well-documented aspect of women in many speech communities.

- The hypercorrect pattern on [dj] may be more a function of correcting a stigmatized form than the targeting of any prestige form for conversion.

This makes this last feature somewhat different from the other instances of hypercorrection in which there is a focussed prestige target. In this sample, as discussed in §2.3 of this study, a number of speakers seem to avoid producing affricates. Possible substitutes are stops [wɪt] *which*, fricatives [ʒɛnərəl] *general* and the palatalized stop mentioned in this section. Certainly the affricate is the preferred variant of the highly educated in the particular lexical items in question; but in this social context, affricates also occur in Creole and can be stigmatized in JE, as in [trɛʤa] *treasure*. I argue that this explains the extent of the variation found in my sample for this feature.

3.6 Constructing the acrolect, Standard Jamaican English

The hypercorrection I describe can be taken as one indication of what is perceived to be standard. In addition, so can the prescriptions of the school curriculum and the variants selected by the most educated and those from backgrounds that predict more access to education. The cumulative data suggest therefore the following is salient for speaking SJE according to this analysis of certain phonological variables:

Consonants

a) the word initial glottal fricative /h/ in words where /h/ has a phonemic contrast with its absence.

b) the voiceless interdental fricative in phonemic contrast with /t/.

c) the word initial velar stop [kʰ] before the *long* low central vowel [aː].

d) post [ɔ] rhoticity, specifically before [+ coronal] consonants in words like *forty*.

e) the word final phonological stop cluster [nt] before a following vowel.

f) the word final morphophonemic cluster when a past tense marker.

Vowels

g) the low back stressed vowel /ɔ/, in words like *not* and *possible*.

h) the mid tense vowel [o] as it occurs pre-consonantally, in items like *goat*.

i) the vowel [ɔ] in *poor* type words.

For all other phonological features there was some interidiolectal variation, certainly correlated with gender and age, or the suggestion of developing norms of use in a context of such variation.

When all the sociological data are considered for these 82 speakers, it is clear that social differentiation is typically located in features along the Creole/English dimension. Group A variables were included in this study precisely because they have been identified in the literature as having clear English and Creole variants of variables. In general the sociolinguistic correlations done for those features reveal that factors such as higher education, a more affluent background and being female are associated with a greater use of JE variants. Moreover, the results for some Group B correlations, specifically the low incidence of [a] in *butter* and *education* type words, are also an aspect of avoiding the Creole variant and favouring the JE [ʌ]. Indeed, the rhoticity in much of the sample may, in part, be due to the coexistence with a non-rhotic JC.

However, the pattern of variation for many of the variables studied here is more interesting, and less predictable, than merely the avoidance of Creole forms. Crucially, for many of the pairs of variables described here, the variant distribution in Table 3.55 can be abstracted from the patterns that tend to occur in actual spoken JE.

Table 3.55: Asymmetrical pattern of variation on certain phonological variables

	Typically used variant(s)	
	Variable 1	Variable 2
Interdental fricative	[d ~ ð]	[θ]
Mid-vowels	[ie ~ e]	[o]
	[ier ~ er]	[ɔr]
Palatalized velar stops	[kja ~ kʰa]	[kʰaː]
Rhoticity	[ar ~ aː]	[ɔr]

Speakers in this sample of formal JE, as used by generally well-educated informants, seem to assign asymmetrical sociolinguistic importance to variants of related variables. One set of variants in their speech, those in the first column, is free to vary in the production of JE. The other set of variants is not, and speakers all seem to demonstrate some consensus in use of one – as shown in the second column. In that respect, the architecture of sociolinguistic variation in this sample of Jamaicans, distinguishes what I will call load-bearing or constructional structures, i.e. those necessary for producing JE, from others that speakers show no imperative to either produce or avoid. I use the term load-bearing here because in constructing an edifice, certain elements are necessary for and essential to supporting the structure; others serve to give the structure its character. I propose that the function of these load-bearing variants is to identify the variety as JE, and that without their presence in sufficient frequency, the speaker will not be interpreted by others as producing "good" English.

An illustration of this asymmetrical pattern of production can be seen in Table 3.56. With the exception of the pre-consonantal mid vowels /e/ and /o/ which vary with diphthongs, for all social groups identified in this study there is a clear contrast between the rate of production of load-bearing variants (highlighted)

Table 3.56: Asymmetrical pattern of frequencies for certain phonological variables

Feature	Education		Gender		Background		Age	
	Secondary	Tertiary	Male	Female	+Affluent	−Affluent	20–29	50–65
[θ] 'thing'	82.0%	93%	69.5%	89%	94.0%	79.0%	86.0%	82%
[ð] 'then'	44.0%	51%	34.0%	48%	40.0%	52.0%	40.0%	47%
[o] 'boat'	91.0%	94%	89.0%	93%	92.0%	89.0%	92.5%	92%
[e] 'face'	84.0%	89%	80.5%	87%	89.0%	85.0%	80.0%	92%
[ɔr] 'poor'	77.0%	70%	57.0%	77%	81.5%	72.0%	80.0%	68%
[er] 'beer'	49.0%	60%	46.0%	56%	63.0%	47.0%	50.0%	55%
[kʰaː] 'calf'	72.0%	91%	76.5%	81%	91.0%	71.5%	73.0%	73%
[kʰa] 'cap'	39.0%	48%	41.0%	44%	43.0%	42.0%	46.0%	44%
[ɔr] 'forty'	73.0%	61%	62.0%	67%	65.0%	69.0%	80.0%	68%
[ar] 'party'	39.5%	53%	28.0%	48%	43.0%	44.0%	50.0%	55%

and non load-bearing ones. A further illustration of this difference is to be found in the productions of 'can't' or 'don't' in this sample. Speakers produced forms such as [kjãː], [kʰãː], [kʰaːnt] or [duõ], [dõ], [dont]. The first in each set is the one that seldom occurred in the data. For the other two in each set, it is the presence of the variant [kʰ] before the long vowel or [o] that identifies the form as JE, notwithstanding the presence of the JC nasal vowel or the cluster simplification evident in the data presented in this chapter. Moreover, I suggest that a speaker who carefully uses forms like [kʰat] *cat* and [ðat] *that* all the time, but produces [kjaːt] *cart* or [tɪn] *thin* too often will not necessarily be seen as using JE.

In the data collected here, the Creole variants of the voiceless interdental fricative, the mid back vowel before [r] and the velar stop before a long [aː] for example are virtually non-existent in the educated speaker's formal language use. Indeed, [uo] is seldom used by anyone in the sample, regardless of level of education. In contrast, those same speakers use both the Creole and JE variants of the voiced interdental, the mid front vowel and /ka/. As such, some features in the Jamaican language continuum starkly distinguish JC use and JE use – keeping the varieties discrete in a linguistic context where there is no sharp discontinuity between a functionally distinct JC and JE.

The logic of this proposition would predict a few things. Firstly, qualitative hypercorrection would be more likely to occur with load-bearing variables than with variables that are not load-bearing. And indeed, the previous section pointed to the production of hypercorrect [θ] but not [ð] for example. Secondly, because variant use is more focussed and more normalised for these load-bearing variables, social differentiation is going to be more starkly signalled by use of these variables, indexing, for example, by their absence the characteristics stereo-typical of the monolingual JC speaker – little education, membership in the lower class and the like. The mid-vowel /o/ is the exception in this sample, as all groups in this study consistently avoid use of the diphthong. As such, and thirdly, group affiliation among JE speakers is therefore typically not going to be signalled by use of these load-bearing variables because they function to show primarily the variety one is speaking. Acts of identity with a group, like gender or age, will more typically occur with the variables in column one – as was seen with male rhoticity after [a] and younger speaker's greater use of [ie].

Devonish & Harry (2004: 271) theorize that the relationship between JC and JE phonology, for most Jamaicans, represents differential convergence, i.e. a type of linguistic convergence that facilitates speakers shifting between the two vari-eties while at the same time maintaining the distinctness necessary for the com-plementary socio-functional distribution of the two varieties. The results here suggest that the mechanism for this involves the selection of one variable of a pair of related variables to attach stigma/prestige, while ignoring the other. The polar lects are kept distinct for speakers through the salient variables, such as [θ], [ɔ], [h], [kʰaː], use of which signals JE and formality for example. This may well be a pattern of variation that distinguishes models of diglossia involving dis-crete varieties from models of diglossia involving varieties on a continuum like that in Jamaica. The distinction discussed by Gair (cited in Paolillo 1997: 272–273), between literary Sinhala and formal spoken Sinhala for example, points to differences between a written and a spoken functionally (H) variety. Educated Jamaicans who write IAE, as with educated Belizeans (Escure 1997: 67–68), pro-duce a formal spoken variety of English, SJE, that displays distinct socio-phonetic characteristics from varieties of English in metropolitan speech communities.

If one examines data from, for example, New York (Labov 1966: 253;1972: 100–104) or Louisiana (Dubois & Horvath 1998: 254) for the interdental fricative, this asymmetrical attention to variants does not seem to occur. Certainly, the dis-cussion in Green (2002: 119) does show that in African American English (AAE) word initial TH stopping occurs principally with the voiced interdental [ð]. AAE speakers do not really produce forms like 'ting' *thing* or 'tree' *three*, unless they are speakers of Gullah, but 'dese' *these* and 'dem' *them* are fairly commonplace. However, the data from all these communities suggest that, typically, style shift or the use of more formal speech is signalled by an across the board reduction in TH stopping, not by reducing TH stopping on one variable and ignoring its coun-terpart. Certainly, in careful speech both voiced and voiceless TH stop variants seem to be minimized, as these studies do not suggest differences in patterning for the two related variables (Ervin-Tripp 2001: 51; Labov 2001: 94). Indeed the two are often analysed as one variable in the published data. And Watt (2000: 86–90) shows that in Tyneside English, variants of the mid-vowels /e/ and /o/ are used with very similar frequencies to each other. Arguably, the speech communities of New York, Louisiana and Newcastle operate within a different ideological framework, one in which there is one language – English – and "best speaker-hood" (Silverstein 1996: 286) is reflected in use of the Standard of that language. Moreover, members of those communities believe there is one language, albeit with dialectal variation that can mark particular sets of speakers.

In Jamaica, there are two related language varieties for speakers, Patwa and English, and best speakerhood is reflected in the bidialectal speaker. Monolingual JC speakers are viewed negatively, as are monolingual English speakers. Both are judged to be deficient in this context, the former "backward" and the latter "not a real Jamaican". These related but functionally distinct varieties are managed through structuring variation in such a way that some variables serve to identify the variety the speaker is using, given the linguistic overlap particularly at the phonolexical level.

Generally, in my sample, the idea of what is JC seems to be focussed around certain features – voiceless TH stopping, [kja:], h-drop, the back diphthong. In large part it is not using these features that defines the acrolect, so that those with higher education, from more affluent backgrounds, and women's language are characterized by very low frequencies or absence of these variants. Additionally, JE is also having a greater frequency of other variants – most importantly [ɔ], being rhotic and with t/d presence before following vowels.

A number of variants are in fact used all the time here by speakers, notwith-standing differences in social group – the voiceless interdental fricative, [kʰa:], [nt] and past tense clusters before a following vowel. In addition, the highly ed-ucated and/or those from backgrounds with educated parents tend to produce /h/ and mid-vowel monophthongs. Interestingly, the data from younger speak-ers suggest that fewer categorically use [h] or [e], but more of them are rhotic, particularly after the back vowel.

Except for one informant in this sample, all speakers vary [ɔ] to some extent with [a]; but with the exception of the 4 with primary education, all informants produce low frequencies of the [a]. I suggest that rhoticity after the back vowel and the palatalization of the velar stop also serve to display possession of this vowel, in a context where not being "able" to distinguish [a] from [ɔ] is "one of the shibboleths of the speech community" (Devonish & Harry 2004: 272). Rhotic articulation may distinguish the [ɔ] vowel in an item like [fa:ti] ~ [f ɔ:ti] *forty* more clearly; and palatalization of the velar only before [a], again reinforces a distinction between [kat] ~ [kɔt] which may be either *cat* or *cot* in some speakers.

Moreover, JE variants like [ʃɔn] in *education* type words are also a function of avoiding [a].

The chapter to come explores the sociology of JAMPRO as an organization and its allocation of staff to certain positions. In doing so I wish to explore how these phonological features are distributed in the speech of JAMPRO staff and, in particular, the speech of staff who are successful in the agency and get promoted into positions that reflect the public face of an agency of the Jamaican state.

4 Sociolinguistic Variation in JAMPRO

4.1 JAMPRO: One site of promoting a SJE ideology

In this chapter I present information on the 82 speakers, not as a sample of educated Jamaicans, but as members of a social collective,[1] and specifically as members of an agency of the Jamaican state, JAMPRO. Following on the discussion
in Chapter 1, in particular on the ideology of language in Jamaica and the normative pressure exerted by institutions in their expectation and practice, I selected
one government agency and the speech of its employees for analysis. The type of
agency, the requirements for employment, and the patterns that lead to success
for staff, can certainly shed light on the phonology of "good" Jamaican English.
As was mentioned at the start of Chapter 2, all advertisements for employment
at agencies like JAMPRO insist on "a good command of the English language" or
"excellent oral and written skills". But the study of staff selection and promotion
can also reveal the type of employee that such an agency perceives and selects
as best able to realize its own image and the image(s) that it constructs for and
about Jamaica. I have selected an agency whose function it is to market Jamaica
to both local and overseas clients, with some of its staff specifically selected as
representatives of the agency through the positions they hold at JAMPRO.

Scollon's comments (1997) are, therefore, a good starting point for this discussion:

> If we think of public discourse in this sense as being outputs of bureaucratic
> structures, then a crucial point of interest is the boundary across which
> the discourse is generated (...) in a business it might be an advertising de-
> partment or a public relations department, in the government it might be a
> public affairs office. In any case, one might always expect to find some for-
> mally constituted institutional structure along with designated members of
> the institution who serve to both generate and legitimate the crossing of
> the organizational boundary into public discourse (45).

---

[1]Sealey & Carter (2001) use the term to describe a grouping whose membership is indicated by
an awareness of, and a kind of commitment to, the conventions that constitute the group in
the first place (4).

Agencies of the state like JAMPRO are, in part, engaged in creating an idea of Jamaica and the Jamaican for a client and therefore a consumer of that construct. What the agency says or implies about a Jamaican must be reflected in the type of employee that it selects to symbolize its public face and to interact with its clients. In its role as one of the agencies that legitimate Jamaica to others overseas, JAMPRO puts into the arena of public discourse certain ideas, one of which concerns language. Its own language use, as reflected by the language behaviour of its staff, therefore becomes important. This language behaviour provides us with actual examples of how the agency's language ideologies become realized in its allocation and selection of staff for certain positions.

A number of Jamaican government agencies provide information about the language situation in Jamaica, JAMPRO being one of them. I wish to discuss the description of the local sociolinguistic situation provided by these agencies of the Jamaican state, and therefore the nature of the *official* public discourse about language in Jamaica. Firstly, this discourse serves as an indicator of the linguistic expectations for staff held by these arms of the state. But such a discussion also brings into focus the ideas held about language in Jamaica and the ways in which they (may) have changed over time. In the previous chapters, some of the comments on the language situation found in the main local newspaper were mentioned. They represent one aspect of public discourse, which Christie (1998a) discusses in her study of this aspect of the language debate in Jamaica. I wish to explore the institutionalised aspect of public discourse, and the image of the Jamaica(n) that can be abstracted from published official documents. The agencies to be discussed here are a) the Jamaica Tourist Board (JTB), b) the Jamaica Information Service (JIS) and c) JAMPRO.

4.1.1 Jamaican institutional discourses on language

The marketing of Jamaica for tourism is believed to have started in 1851 (Taylor 1971: 62), when a pamphlet, ascribed to someone named Anderson, was published urging Americans to come to the island for health reasons, particularly in winter. Tourism then, as now, was geared to the needs of a largely U.S. clientele, as a great deal of initial travel to Jamaica was prompted by the United Fruit Company's ties to Port Antonio through the banana industry. Titchfield Hill was one of the first hotels, a "lost garden of Eden – the incomparable combination of American comfort, English cleanliness and Italian climate" (1903 pamphlet, unnamed author, cited in Taylor 1971: 99).

The Jamaica Tourist Association was formed in 1910, and, as Taylor remarks, scant mention was made of Jamaicans themselves, as they were viewed as more of a liability than an asset in the marketing of the island. Even then there was concern expressed about letting visitors see all aspects of the society. The only mention of Jamaicans cited by Taylor is in a 1914 pamphlet: "the hospitality of the people is proverbial ... demonstrated by the smiling faces and happy laughter of the natives" (4). These are, of course, the production of an association formed during the time of a colonial government. A comparison with post-independence publications, when the agency morphed into the JTB, projects a similar image. Jamaicans are described as: "gentle people named Ivy or Maud or Malcolm who will cook, tend, mend ... who will "Mister Peter, please" you all day long" (JTB 1968, cited in Taylor 1993: 174). Taylor analyses this as marketing for a U.S. sensibility, a clientele more accustomed to and comfortable with the idea of "Negro servants", and persuading them that Jamaica was safe in spite of its majority black population. Language is not mentioned at all, perhaps because interaction was not expected, though the implication here is that English is at least understood.

More recent advertisements do discuss language. A typical example, directed specifically at North Americans again, is contained in a JTB pamphlet (1992) and entitled *Say It Again, Mon,* "mon" being an attempt to represent the Jamaican vowel that is more backed when compared to its General American counterpart. I have numbered particular items for comment.

> Listen to two Jamaicans talk and you'll hear a (1) musical mix of English, patois (a combination of English, African and Welsh (sic)) and island words and rhythms. You might think it's (2) impossible to make sense of it all without being a native. Not so! While it might be tough to wholeheartedly jump into a rocket fast discussion, (3) it's easy to learn a few phrases that might come in handy at the local rum shack or in the marketplace. Here is a mini-glossary to get you started.

> **Cool runnings** (4) No bother, no fuss, it's okay. Also used when parting to mean "goodbye".

> **Gimme a chups** Kiss me.

> **Irie (EYE-re)** (5) Everything is cool.

> **Irie dawta** A (6a) sexy, good-looking girl. "Wat a irie dawta!".

> **Jah God** as in "Praise Jah." From the (7) biblical name for Jehovah; this phrase is most often used by Rastafarians.

> **Kiss me neck** Not to be taken literally, this is an expression of surprise, incredulity or defiance. (8) "Kiss me neck, I can't believe you got married last night and didn't tell anyone you were going to do it".

Soon cum Meaning someone or something will arrive anywhere (9) between the next five minutes and the next five hours.

Tek yuh time Take your time; a favourite (10) in the craft market where you're being invited to browse. Nobody's going to rush you here!

Ting This is a tricky one. First and foremost its simply (11) slang for "thing." However, if someone says, (6b) "Mek we do a ting" to a woman, it's considered a proposition. If it is said to a man, (12) the phrase means "Lets make an arrangement, do business, or have a drink." To make matters more (13) confusing, Ting also happens to be a popular grapefruit soda.

Walk good A farewell meaning, "Take care, stay safe, hope all goes well with you".[2]

Comments made about the language situation to be found readily acknowledge Creole (Patois), suggesting it is a mix of English and other ingredients, and do so in ways that apparently justify adjectives like "musical", "colourful" and "rhythmic". In addition, this mix of language varieties is confused and confusing (2, 3 and 13). Similar terms are used to discuss regional patterns of English, in comparison with the standard varieties of English. These imply "lack of clarity" and "the charm of the humor in confusion" (Silverstein 1996: 292–293). Note, however, that in spite of the idiosyncrasies and slang items, the presentation suggests that it is clear that Jamaicans speak English; though the article offers the tourist the local phrases, the representation of actual Jamaican speech is English (12 & 8). The tourist to Jamaica, for the most part from the U.S., needs only to learn a few simple phrases in order to communicate with the Jamaican he/she is likely to meet. In addition, these phrases are most useful in the rum bar or marketplace (3), which clearly locates the contexts in which Creole is likely to be heard and to be appropriate.

What is also of interest are the phrases themselves that were selected for the article. Four of them project an image of a relaxed, happy-go-lucky people (compare the 1914 pamphlet) with little concern for schedules or time, as in 4, 5 and 9, or serious business, as in 10 and 12. The visitor is also subtly informed that the women are young and attractive (6a and b) and people, however strange looking, are non-threatening and Christian (7 and 10). The latter piece of propaganda, the term used here in its denotative sense, is particularly important, as "visitor harassment" is said to be a problem in the resort areas on the island. More specifically, the arguably negative notion of "defiance" in the Jamaican is reduced to

---

[2]Reprinted from *Bridal Guides Magazine*.

personal concerns that have nothing to do with the tourist or the hardships of living in a relatively poor country. In summary, Jamaica is said to have two language varieties, but the Jamaican is represented as English speaking (with some regional elements). The people are carefree and laid-back. The Jamaican woman is presented only in a sexualized way, and the wider socio-cultural context is Judaeo-Christian and therefore not unfamiliar.

This pamphlet, produced by the JTB, is a reproduction of a collection of articles on Jamaica that appeared in a US magazine. In that respect, it is an *American* image of Jamaica and Jamaicans that the JTB is using to sell the destination to Americans. Other JTB documents, particularly more recent publications, speak of the Jamaican language situation using the same terms: "We speak English, with a few embellishments" (JTB 2001). In that respect, according to the JTB, it is suggested that Jamaicans speak a variety of English not very different from other Englishes except for a few localisms.

A second example is taken from the Jamaica Information Service (JIS), the official information agency of the government. Interestingly, no explicit reference is made to English. The reader is invited to infer from the language in the electronic document that English is the official language of the State. Instead, the following is said:

> The language "patois" is an important part of who we are, giving the people a peculiar accent so much so that even in countries outside the region, we are easily identified. The Jamaican sound is so loved that even persons who do not sound like us are often quite comfortable being called Jamaican. While there may be variations in the patois accent across the island, there are words and phrases that have gone beyond the boundaries of our little island (Jamaica Information Service, accessed 2002 at www.jis.gov.jm).

This naming of Patois as "language" is clearly unrelated to the actual description provided. For Patois is here considered to be only English with an accent and some lexical/idiomatic regionalisms. Moreover, this "sound" of a Jamaican is charming enough to be imitated by others. Since, for the JIS, the difference between Patois and other Englishes is largely a matter of phonology, this may account for no direct reference to English as the language of Jamaica, just as there would be no need to make such a clarification in Australia or the UK.

The sources of these examples represent what Scollon calls the products of formally constituted institutional structures and therefore the language ideologies of the groups that occupy such positions. These are organizations that are staffed by "middle class" Jamaicans, in terms of education levels, income/occupation, residence and the like. They naturally have particular ideologies which, according to Austin (1983), are based on

> the view (...) that the middle class gained and deserved their access to higher education and the professions because their socialization and Christian ways have made them superior to the uneducated, indeed uncivilized, working class (236).

She cites as an example the "middle class" attitude to traditionally working class practices like Pentecostalism and Rastafarianism. The former is seen as "degrading" (233) while the latter was coopted by the middle class and is now approved for use to sell Jamaica. As if in confirmation of this, one member of JAMPRO senior management said in his interview that

> ...if the person don't (sic) portray the middle class features ... am...could be kept back. For example I know of people who are members of the conservative pentecostal and evangelical type religions who have been kept back (M20).

JAMPRO was legally incorporated in April 1990 under an arrangement that merged three previously existing government bodies.[3] These three bodies were created in the first half of the 1980's "precisely in recognition of the fact that investors need to be on a fast track to speed up the investment process" (JAMPRO 1997a), but had a forerunner in the pre-Independence Jamaica Industrial Development Corporation of the late 1950's. The three functioned in overlapping, but different, areas of trade/investment promotion. The first, JNIP, was charged with identifying potential investors and selling Jamaica to them as a safe and profitable location for their business, i.e. its purpose was as a national marketing agency. The second, JNEC, targeted both local exporters and foreign investors, and was created to smooth the way through the maze of the Jamaican trade and tariff bureaucracy. In that respect, it was there to represent the Jamaican government to business and it promised "enough clout in the public sector...that the investor is facilitated as quickly and easily as possible" (op.cit.). The third company, the JIDC, was mandated to oversee the industrial development policy of the government, and therefore functioned as go-between for buyers of land,

---

[3]The three are JIDC (Jamaica Industrial Development Corporation), JNIP (Jamaica National Investment Promotions) and JNEC (Jamaica National Export Company).

equipment and infrastructure and the holders of capital. In 1990 government decided that one umbrella corporation would increase efficiency and inter-agency communication and created JAMPRO.

It is important therefore to emphasise that JAMPRO is an arm of the Jamaican state, crucial in representing Jamaica to other individuals and governments as "the investment capital of the Caribbean" (JAMPRO 1996). It is involved in the serious enterprise of economic growth and development – without which very little else of government policy can be realized.

JAMPRO, to further its purpose, produces a number of publications designed to provide its clientele with information about a) the wider Jamaican social context and b) JAMPRO itself, including the type of employee it selects and that the investor is likely to encounter when dealing with the company. JAMPRO is one such "formally constituted institutional structure" that is a state agency, within which functions its own public relations department. By examining the information put out by this department, we can get a sense of the image of Jamaica and of Jamaicans that JAMPRO constructs for its clientele. In constructing this image for its clientele, JAMPRO also generates and legitimizes a particular idea of the Jamaican society and language situation. It is this ideology that I would like to explore in detail, and how it becomes realized in the allocation of particular staff members in the agency to certain functions.

Firstly, the ideologies of language and society that JAMPRO documents reveal are a projection of the ideas of self held by one class of Jamaicans, vis-à-vis others who occupy the same sociolinguistic space. These ideas are promoted against the background of and in relation to their own ideas of who the client is. To illustrate, there are a number of social and linguistic practices that could be described in JAMPRO publications, but only some are selected. The selection reveals not only what this class perceives itself and the 'marketable' Jamaica to be, but also what they believe will inspire confidence in the client. To do this, certain assumptions must be made about themselves and the client, what they have in common – and can therefore go unexplained – and what is distinctive. To illustrate, no JAMPRO document tells the investor that Jamaicans live in houses, as this would be unnecessary as the class that composes the information would view this as normal for both itself and the client. However, language in Jamaica has to be accounted for, and in ways that we can use to locate what this class perceives as normative.

Secondly, employees of the company, and in particular those who have to interact with clients, will have to reinforce this image or the client will lose confidence in the information provided. JAMPRO cannot project an identity of the country and itself that is dissonant with its own behaviour, reflected in the behaviour of its staff. Clients to the company who are encouraged to place their confidence, and ultimately their money, in this described Jamaica, do so, in part, because of the expectations created by the agency. Its staff, therefore, must be in a position to confirm this image of Jamaica. As I was told by two members of senior management:

> It's not overtly stated as being important, but I think it is a factor. I think that when you consider the sort of image that [the agency] wishes to project, certainly the thinking is, I feel, [that] people from certain backgrounds can give or protect that image, rightly or wrongly (M101).

> A job like this requires a certain type of personality as well as the qualifications you try to find a combination so its not all qualifications ... important consideration of someone here having to go abroad to represent the organization to me that is important and you'll look for the possibility of this with somebody (F55).

The published JAMPRO information and the personnel that the agency employs steer the investor in a particular social direction when advising on where and how to interact with other Jamaicans generally. An analysis of this advice, including some historical discussion of the type of output, can reveal what aspects of Jamaica are considered by agency staff to best conform to the norm that is created in their own publications.

4.1.2 The JIDC/JAMPRO: Their construct of the Jamaican language situation

The JIDC was established in 1952. I was able to find three specific references to the local language situation and the Jamaican people, which I will quote in full (my emphases).

> Jamaica's Alert, Energetic People – The Jamaican is intelligent, self-respecting, and has a keen technical as well as artistic sense. **Jamaicans speak English with a soft, gentle inflection partially reflecting the British accent.** The US, Canadian or British manufacturer will not face the **problem of a foreign-language-speaking work force which he would encounter in many other Caribbean**, Latin American areas. The **advantage of a common language** also facilitates the training of Jamaicans for responsible posts in manufacturing (JIDC 1957: 11–12).

The selling points of Jamaica are that it belongs to the English language community, in common with the US, Canada and Britain, unlike many other Caribbean territories. Moreover, all Jamaicans speak an English that is phonologically somewhat like British English, though "British" is not further defined. It is not unreasonable to interpret this as RP, the variety most likely to come to mind for a Canadian or American reader.

A later publication says much the same thing:

> Jamaica is a land of soft-spoken people (...) Jamaicans speak English. The US, Canadian or British manufacturer arriving in Jamaica does not face a language difficulty in training and supervision. The advantage of a common language is that it speeds up training and production (JIDC 1961: 2–8).

The fact that Jamaicans also speak something else, Creole/Patois, is not addressed. There are a number of possible explanations for this. Firstly, additional information in these pamphlets gives an indication of where and with whom the investor was expected to interact and the strata in the society that the JIDC wished to own. For example, under the heading Cultural Activities, the investor is told of "lectures on music and art sponsored by the British Council and the Institute of Jamaica" (13), despite the local popularity of mento bands and the numbers of venues at which sound systems played (Barrow & Dalton 1997: 7–13). Additionally, the Social Clubs recommended by the documents were exclusive and/or member's only establishments such as Jamaica Club, Liguanea Club and the Garrison Officer's club. Secondly, the idea of Patois as a language was not, at the time, an accepted aspect of public discourse. Indeed, Le Page (1988) asserts that it was the discussion in academia, by David DeCamp, Beryl Bailey and himself, that gave some, however limited, legitimacy to the idea of something called "Jamaican Creole" as a language in its own right. Interestingly, both quotations are careful to suggest the gentleness of the people, perhaps to reassure the investor's anxieties about the social context, in a similar way to Taylor's reading of the JTB information.

Current JAMPRO documents/pamphlets are noticeably different in some ways, at times presenting the language situation in more measured terms:

> The official language of Jamaica is English. However, the majority of the population speak Jamaican creole called patois, which is a mixture of English and derivatives of various West African languages. The Jamaican Creole has been studied by many scholars. There is a Dictionary of Jamaican English published by Cambridge University Press.

There is another variety spoken in Jamaica, legitimised by being in a dictionary. However, the magazine then immediately goes on to reassure the reader, in two other places that: "Kingston [the capital] is the largest English speaking city a) south of Miami and b) in the Caribbean." (JAMPRO 1997b: 2–3). This insistence that Jamaica is English speaking dominates the information available to those interested in more serious ventures – investment, manufacturing or business.

> The official language is English. What we call patois, an English-derived dialect, is widely spoken, though seldom in official or business circles. Patois tends to prove challenging to foreigners, though a number of publications ranging from visitor guides to scholarly dissertations are available on the hotly debated language. Local radio and television dramatic productions also have high patois content, as do some radio call-in programmes from time to time, especially when tempers rise! (JAMPRO 1997a).

> English-speaking, well-educated and competitively priced labour force (JAMPRO 1993).

> Jamaica's English speaking population of approximately 2.5 million represents a diverse mix of ethnic origins (JAMPRO 1994: 15).

> English-speaking, non-unionised and experienced professionals (which include accredited technicians) as [film] crew (JAMPRO 1993: 5).

Here the investor is informed that Creole is widely used but only in specific cultural and discourse contexts. Creole is also not the language of serious business, suggesting the kind of distinction the BBC made between programmes hosted by regionally accented and RP accented broadcasters. Moreover, the fact that the language is "hotly debated" suggests the kind of local controversy about Creole that is not described for English. The investor is further reassured that the pool of labour from which comes his/her workforce speaks English and gets a British-style education:

> English is universally spoken. Education is based on the British system... English is the official language of Jamaica, and this makes communication with off-shore investors and understanding new processes easier... The language of the workplace being English, instruction at all levels is given in English, even where the workers speak patois and not Standard English (JAMPRO 1992).

Two important things are being said here. Firstly, English is *universally* spoken and, it is suggested later in the passage, understood. Even if the investor hears *workers* speaking patois they should not take this to mean that these workers cannot speak or understand English. Secondly, a distinction is being made between English, Patois and Standard English. What the investor will find, and what is being implied, is that the worker's speech, Patois, is not much more than a regional non-standard variety of English, for what workers do not speak is Standard English, the language of official and business circles.

In summary, the JAMPRO documents give the following sociolinguistic information:

- All Jamaicans speak English ("universally").

- Some Jamaicans also speak Patois ("widely spoken").

- Patois is non-standard English, largely distinguished by some items, possibly of West African origin.

- Patois is used by workers, but they also speak and understand English.

- Patois is used in specific (dramatic) contexts and when tempers flare.

- Patois is controversial.

- Official and business circles use (Standard) English.

- Standard English is only a "problem" for workers.

Generally, we can deduce from these documents that Creole enters the public discourse, as generated and structured by these government agencies, as the other: the non-normal, non-universal aspect of the Jamaican socio-cultural landscape. We can further deduce that Patois, being peripheral to the official and business milieu in which JAMPRO operates, is not going to be heard by the investor in his interactions with the agency.

I found only one specific text reference to the staff at JAMPRO. The magazine in which it is contained promises "highly trained professionals [who] provide friendly, experienced assistance" (JAMPRO 1996: 10). If we relate this information to the above discussion, then we would expect JAMPRO staff members, who do operate in official and business circles, at least to speak (Standard) English and to be very well educated. The speech that these employees actually produce must be useful in identifying what JAMPRO management considers to be protective of its image, and conforming to the norms they have described above for Jamaica. This is an agency in which the investor will encounter highly trained and (Standard) English speaking professionals.

4.2 Frontline staff – The public face of JAMPRO

There are certain employees at JAMPRO designated "frontline staff". This label is applied to those employees who actually interact with the public, both local and foreign, in the course of their duties. In certain departments at JAMPRO, certain members of staff are required either to deal directly with the agency's clients or to represent the agency in overseas departments or trade missions. It is this subset of my informants – those in the frontline – who are the focus of this section.

There are a number of reasons why the speech patterns of frontline staff are crucial to the issues raised in this book, particularly in relation to the legitimizing of norms of JE usage. Firstly, as has already been discussed in previous chapters, selection of staff at JAMPRO is heavily dependent on performance during the job interview. And this is especially so for professional and (senior) management positions. Frontline staff positions reflect an even more subjective set of selection criteria on the part of the agency, as these are employees who are the public face of JAMPRO. As explicitly stated by senior management, those in frontline positions are selected because they are perceived to be the type of person who can represent both the agency and the agency's idea of a well educated, competent and professional Jamaican.

Secondly, in selecting some employees for frontline positions and rejecting others, JAMPRO management is communicating the type of Jamaican they think best fits the desired image, one which may well be informed by the speaker's use of English. JAMPRO, as shown at the beginning of this chapter, operates in precisely the socio-cultural milieu that it advises is reserved for (Standard) English. Frontline positions indicate a positive judgement made by some Jamaicans, i.e. the senior management who assign staff to jobs, on the way other Jamaicans present to them in interviews. This forms, in large part, the basis on which certain members of staff are selected to interact directly with clients (both local and foreign) and to represent "Jamaica" and the upper end of the construct of the local language situation described in JAMPRO publications. Their promotion into the frontline provides us with some means of indexing the reactions of others to the English they produce, for they have been selected from a pool of speakers who themselves had been chosen from a pool of educated Jamaicans with

English language qualifications. In that respect, the analysis of the speech of frontline staff allows me to add an evaluative dimension, albeit an implicit one, to this study. Within the organization, at least, the kind of behaviour that comes to be perceived as suitable and successful for many, in terms of advancement and employment prospects, can be taken to be reflected in frontline staff.

Thirdly, informants themselves held perceptions about the kind of person who is in the frontline. I would like to examine these perceptions and compare them to relevant data on the sociology of the agency. For if staff perceptions about frontline staff are reflected in the findings, then it gives added credence to those perceptions less amenable to examination – most importantly the ones about language and speaking "good" English.

In the course of interviews, a number of the informants made comments on their perceptions of the type of employee who gets selected for frontline positions. An asterisk indicates that the speaker is in senior management.

> yes I think so, am there's a particular look which you must have, which I think, you know, I think fair...fairer skin people tend to, especially in terms of overseas officers...it's as if they want to portray a certain look of a Jamaican (F13).

> there are some reasons for it in that you are talking about a promotional organization and sometimes you will buy into that...somebody with a particular social background, somebody who has been exposed early has the ability to present themselves and to cut a dash...but I think it happens a little bit too much in that some are excluded where they shouldn't get (inaudible) as sophisticated they'll step over her (F64).

> I remember once a skin thing came up and it was more in relation to the film division, there was a time when the perception was that only fair skin people can deal with movie stars coming from abroad and the colouration there tended to seem to reflect that (F87).

> ...but for example if they want persons to go on say overseas assignment...if you're going to Korea or one of those you know eastern countries right they prefer male to go they specifically ask for male (F71).

> Yeah I think sometimes...deciding they probably notice the way you act and the way you speak if you can really represent well at a standard (F73).

I think it does I think it does because one has to have a certain amount of command a certain amount of respect from the people that you have to interact with and it [a certain background] does help it opens a lot of doors put it that way...and that's [education] important because it it equips you to have a good command of the English language...the subject matter and it sort of helps you to be able to help the client better (F7).

race especially pigmentation is important, the brownings, I feel so but you know that fits within the, you know, more with the profile you see some of these things can be justified on the basis that we are a promotional organization so the investors are likely to be impress (sic) by a certain type...it's just that we want to present the right image and the image would include a certain kind of, of diction and good looks too...if that person is not obviously from the middle class and if the person's manner and, and dress don't portray the middle class features [they] could be kept back...(M20*, Public Relations).

[language] is very important it's very important in that in JAMPRO you have to interface a lot with your external clients your ability to deliver is very important (F32*).

It's not overtly stated as being important, but I think it is a factor. I think that when you consider the sort of image that [the agency] wishes to project, certainly the thinking is, I feel, [that] people from certain backgrounds can give or protect that image, rightly or wrongly (M101*)

at the stage of the interview I ask is this person somebody I could send away next week to go and talk to an investor or to go and sell Jamaica. (F55*).

This is a place where you interact a lot with the public, with international agencies...if you have a, well, you're well educated and everything your social class tends to be middle class (F56*)

Generally, these comments speak to a perception among staff, that those in the agency who interact with the public, especially foreign clients, are selected on the basis of a) certain social backgrounds, i.e. from the middle class, b) light skin colour c) "good looks" and d) language. The one mention of gender is specifically related to assignment to some Asian countries where men are specifically requested by the host country. That suggests an issue outside of JAMPRO's control, one which they attempt to accommodate.

The first set of data presented discusses those social factors which proved to have a statistically significant association with having frontline status. The data is presented in percentages, but the statistical significance was calculated on the raw data.

Table 4.1: Level of education and selection to frontline duties at JAMPRO

Position	Education (%)					
	Primary	Secondary	Secondary+	Tertiary	Tertiary+	no data
+Frontline	1.5	3	36.5	27	32	
−Frontline	8	21.5	46	11	11	2.5
no data			3	1		

By inspection, it is clear that selection for a frontline position becomes more likely if one is better educated (p < .001, χ^2 = 10.91 when analysed as secondary+ and tertiary+). Here, to accept the null hypothesis (H_0), we would expect to find more primary and secondary school leavers in the cadre of frontline staff members. What we do have is a greater proportion of university graduates in these positions (almost 60%). The one primary educated informant is M40, the driver/chauffeur for the agency. Staff perceptions that education is important for frontline positions are confirmed by this data. JAMPRO does cream off its better-educated employee for interaction with the public.

Table 4.2: Parent's occupation and selection to frontline duties at JAMPRO

Position	Parent's Occupation (%)		
	Cleaner/Artisan	Teacher/Doctor	no data
+Frontline	46	44	10
−Frontline	65	24	11
no data	3	1	

Tests of association suggest that there is some relationship between family background and selection for a frontline position (p < .05, χ^2 = 4.09), when categories are collapsed to cleaner/artisan and teacher/doctor. Specifically, those who come from the lowest income/occupation bracket are under-represented in the ranks of frontline staff; 76% of the teacher/doctor group are in frontline positions. This may be what senior management refers to when it speaks of a preference for people of "certain backgrounds", and the implication is that the requisite presentation for a JAMPRO representative is least likely to be found in the employee who came from a low income/education household (indeed, only 8% of frontline staff). Crucially, informants from the more affluent backgrounds are better educated, most likely to have tertiary level qualifications (§3.3). It is therefore difficult to delink level of education from background and household. "Background" is of course a loose term that attempts to capture both linguistic and cultural practice (see informant F64's comment on "sophistication"). However, frontline staff at JAMPRO typically come from households of relative advantage, probably because they are, in this sample, also highly educated.

Table 4.3: Type of transport to work and selection to frontline duties at JAMPRO

	Transport (%)		
	Bus	Lift	Own Car
+Frontline	21	17	62
−Frontline	46	30	24
no data		2	2

How one gets around in Jamaica is a fairly reliable measure of personal income and, to some extent, type of social contacts maintained. The public transport system, certainly at the time of data collection, was chaotic, crowded and unreliable. Jamaicans, therefore, used the public bus system only if there was no other option, such as a lift to work. The categories above can be used to reflect both access to income as well as interaction with other people of a certain income. Informants who took the bus to work were not only low income earners, but they operated in networks with similarly low income earners. Those informants who got a lift to work might not themselves have a car, but they knew people who did. This suggests a somewhat different socio-economic situation, one with at least some personal contacts to people of a higher income. Most frontline staff, however, were able to buy and maintain their own car, and most of these would not have had access to JAMPRO's company car salary package. This data supports the stated perceptions about the preference for "middle class" frontline staff – they are better educated, from more affluent backgrounds and tend to have better incomes than non-frontline staff ($p < .001$, $\chi^2 = 13.2$).

Table 4.4: Age of informant and selection to frontline duties at JAMPRO

Position	Age (%)			
	20–29	30–39	40–49	50–65
+Frontline	22	38	21	19
–Frontline	57	16	8	19
no data		3		1

Grint (1991: 259, citing research by Jenkins 1985) points out that those involved in exclusionary recruitment, which is what frontline hiring and promotion is about, tend to have a hierarchy of criteria for acceptance – "the primary criteria involve appearance, manner (...) and maturity. Secondary criteria relate to 'gut feeling' employment history (...) age, speech style".

But while middle-aged employees are most typical of those in the frontline ($p < .001$, $\chi^2 = 14.01$), this does not necessarily mean that JAMPRO selects employees with most company experience.

Table 4.5: Years with the agency and selection to frontline duties at JAMPRO

	Years in JAMPRO (%)		
	10+	–10	New
+Frontline	33	38	29
–Frontline	19	32	49
no data	2	2	

There is no statistically significant correlation between years in the agency and frontline status ($p > .10$, $\chi^2 = 4.49$), though there is a tendency to use more experienced workers. Importantly, new recruits were hired into frontline positions, suggesting that having JAMPRO experience is neither necessary nor sufficient for frontline employment. Eighteen (18) members of staff were hired into posts that entail interacting with the public, notwithstanding their lack of agency experience. Something in their interviews and qualifications prompted recruiters/management to do this. Clearly, socialization to JAMPRO linguistic or corporate norms is not a factor. What may be at issue is socialization to educated linguistic norms, as evidenced by longer stay in the formal education system. On closer examination, these 18 had the following profile:

Education post secondary 9 (50%), tertiary 3 (17%), graduate 6 (33%);

Parent's background cleaner/artisan 6 (33%), teacher/doctor 12 (67%);

Transport to work bus 6 (33%), lift 2 (11%), own car 10 (56%);

Age 8 under 30 (44%) and 10 over 30 (56%);

As such, at least half of the new staff who entered the frontline ranks were university graduates, from relative affluence, had their own car and were over 30. Most of them were hired into professional or managerial positions.

Initially informants were asked to name the racial group to which they belong, an effort to collect self-ascriptive data. For a number of reasons this proved to be problematic. Some informants were reluctant to discuss the issue at all – typical responses were *I don't know* or *you put what you think*. This is not unusual, as other studies of race in Jamaica have also recorded a similar discomfort with the subject. As Alexander found in his survey:

> This ambivalence is expressed in the touchiness with which the subject is discussed. Informants all framed the matter the same way: race is a subject people do not discuss freely and openly; it remains understood (1977: 427).

Additionally, those that did answer did so in terms that would have been difficult for further sociolinguistic analysis. The first 10 informants gave 5 different answers, such as *Maroon, dark, mixed, Jamaican* and *Negro*. Apart from an inability to correlate such a diversity of answers, it is not at all apparent that even when informants used the same term to describe themselves that they necessarily refer to the same thing. It is entirely possible that two informants who describe themselves as "black" may have differing ideas of what [use of] that label means. I found (1988), for example, that one informant who described himself as "white" also included Chinese, Syrians and Lebanese people in the group as the label referred as much to socio-economic status as it did to race.

In order to have some control over the number and semantic range of labels, I assigned informants to racial groups. I am aware, however, that by doing so I am imposing my own perceptions of race on the sample, and that this can yield misleading results. Labov's work (1972: 298) in New York City and his analysis of Italian-American vowel production can be used to illustrate the point. Along similar lines, Horvath & Sankoff (1987) found that refinements in method revealed a somewhat different picture of ethnic variation in Australian English than previously described.

Informants in the JAMPRO sample were grouped according to my perceptions of skin colour as there is some historical and contemporary justification for believing that race in Jamaica is essentially defined phenotypically: by colour, hair type and the like (see Lewis 1968: 20; Nettleford 1972: 24;, 374; Witter & Beckford 1980 for typical discussions). The labels black and brown are used primarily to refer to dark brown and light brown skin colour respectively.

Table 4.6: Skin colour and selection to frontline duties at JAMPRO (%)

	Black	Brown	no data
+Frontline	44.5	41.25	14.25
–Frontline	65	16	19
no data	1	3	

The data in Table 4.6 shows that a smaller percentage of the informants who I view as "brown", i.e. have lighter skin, are in non-frontline positions (p < .02, χ^2 = 6.52). Put in another way, there are 32 brown informants for whom I have data on their position, 26 of them are in the frontline, and therefore more than four times the number behind the scenes at JAMPRO. In contrast, there are 52 black informants, with 28 in the frontline and 24 behind the scenes. Brown people therefore are over-represented in the frontline of the agency.

It is important to point out that staff with lighter skin colour are not better educated; their selection cannot necessarily be explained as a preference for the highly educated in frontline positions (p > .50, χ^2 = .31). However, it is entirely possible that such a perception exists as part of the cultural traffic (Alvesson 1993: 80) that flows in from the attitudes held in the wider society. In an earlier matched-guise study of 100 educated, affluent Jamaicans (A. Irvine 1994: 61), I found that the guise of JE judged to be that of a black person was also ranked lower on the intelligence/competence dimension. And while not statistically significant, there seems to be some association between skin colour and background/household (p > .10, χ^2 = 1.68). Brown members of staff are, for example, much less likely to come from households with parents who are "cleaners".

Arguably, brown members of staff are also less likely to come from monolingual JC households and consequently it is possible that an assumption is made that their use of JE is not as dependent on formal education; moreover, they are more typically from the backgrounds that JAMPRO seems to favour for frontline staff.

Table 4.7: Gender and selection to frontline duties at JAMPRO

	Gender (%)	
	Female	Male
+Frontline	78	22
−Frontline	78	22
no data	4	

The only specific reference to gender and position in the company suggests that, for certain Asian markets, men are more likely to be selected as overseas officers and at the request of the host country's agencies. The data show men and women having virtually the same chances of being selected for the frontline, since gender does not correlate with position in the agency ($p > .95$, $\chi^2 = .004$).

The social factors that show some degree of association with membership in the ranks of frontline staff are social class – as indexed by parent's occupation and transport – age, level of education attained and skin colour. The perceptions of staff and the statements of senior management about the type of employee who tends to be in the frontline did mention background, class, colour and education. I argue then that since there seems to be some validity to and empirical support for these perceptions, those that speak specifically to linguistic criteria are also to be taken as important. Frontline staff are those employees whose English is believed to be suitable for a representative of JAMPRO, displaying the attributes of diction, talk and English "at a standard".

4.2.1 Group A variables in frontline staff

Along the Creole/English dimension we would expect frontline staff to use fewer Creole forms than those not so selected. The results for a number of Group A variables are in line with this expectation. Frontline members of staff are much less likely to drop [h] ($p < .001$, $\chi^2 = 38.54$); they also produce fewer low central vowels in *not* words and more of the JE [ɔ] ($p < .05$, $\chi^2 = 50.4$). For other Group A variables the results are somewhat less predictable, as some Creole features are used more by frontline staff or in a similar way by both classes of employee.

Voiceless TH stopping, which I argue is the more indexical variable in this pair, is produced less by frontline staff, in line with h-dropping and the low vowel ($p < .05$, $\chi^2 = 4.43$). The hypercorrect use of these three features in JE speakers would suggest a sensitivity to their use and their importance to any idea of good English. But voiced TH stopping is more apparent in the same select speakers

Table 4.8: Word initial TH stopping in frontline staff

Word Initial	d	ð	t	θ
Frontline	1472 (52%)	1373 (48%)	63 (12%)	478 (88%)
Non-frontline	818 (37%)	1369 (63%)	54 (17%)	269 (83%)

($p < .001$, $\chi^2 = 102.44$), which suggests that less attention is paid to its production in a context of spoken JE (although I would predict that in a word list test the results would be very different). Arguably, the more speakers are cued to the variants that matter – here the [θ] – there is less of a requirement to pay attention to the ones that do not. Certainly, voiced TH stopping does not seem to preclude promotion to the frontline.

A similar pattern is evident in words beginning with a velar stop.

Table 4.9: Word initial velar stops in frontline staff

	kja	kʰa	kja:	kʰa:
Frontline	77 (56%)	61 (44%)	9 (13%)	60 (87%)
Non-frontline	42 (59%)	29 (41%)	10 (37%)	17 (63%)
	($p > .50$, $\chi^2 = .19$)		($p < .01$, $\chi^2 = 6.97$)	

Frontline staff produce much fewer instances of [kja:] than do those in the background; but use of [kja] does not distinguish the two groups, and it is freely varied, as has been the case in nearly all correlations with this feature in this study. Three possible conclusions can be drawn from this. The first is that some Creole features are perfectly acceptable in spoken JE and have been normalized as such (as are [kja] or [d ~ ð]). The second is that [kja] and [d] are not necessarily perceived to be Creole features. The third is that [kja] and [d] are peripheral to the issue of speaking JE. As such, their use by a speaker who consistently produces say [θ] is of little import to members of the speech community when making judgements about "good" JE. When speaking with another Jamaican, as was the case in their interviews both for selection to frontline duties and for this study, informants' use suggest [kja] is an aspect of Jamaican speech attested to in spoken formal JE.

Table 4.10 shows that the back diphthong is seldom used by any speakers either pre-consonantally or before [r]. This would confirm the theory, presented

Table 4.10: Mid vowels in frontline staff

	uo	o		ie	e
Frontline	87 (8%)	960 (92%)		141 (12%)	994 (88%)
Non-frontline	42 (7%)	537 (93%)		114 (18%)	522 (82%)
	(p > .30, χ^2 = .56)			(p < .01, χ^2 = 10.04)	

		poor words			*beer* words	
	[ɔ]	[uᵒ]	[o]		[iᵉr]	[er]
Frontline	303 (73.0%)	77 (18.0%)	37 (9.0%)	316 (42.5%)	426 (57.5%)
Non-frontline	127 (72.5%)	35 (20.0%)	13 (7.5%)	149 (52.0%)	138 (48.0%)
	(p > .80, χ^2 = .42)			(p < .01, χ^2 = 7.29)	

at the end of the previous chapter, that back diphthong use is the more *linguistically indexical* variable of the pair – a necessary element for being perceived as speaking good JE. The front diphthong, however, is less likely in the speech of frontline staff, as would be expected from previous results that also support the view that [ie] use is more *socially indexical* in JE than [uo]. Front diphthong use is more apparent in the young, a group under-represented in the ranks of frontline staff.

4.2.2 Group B variables in frontline staff

The statistical results for *butter* type words point to the difference here being who uses an [a] as opposed to an [ʌ] ending, along the Creole/English dimension characteristic of Group A variables (p < .001, χ^2 = 85.9). As we would expect, frontline staff use less of the Creole variant. A similar analysis can be made for that aspect of Table 4.11, but the [ʃɔn ~ʃən] variation is much more interesting.

Table 4.11: Articulation of final – *tion* in frontline staff (p < .001, χ^2 = 61.8)

	educa[ʃan]		educa[ʃʌn]		educa[ʃɔn]		educa[ʃən]	
Frontline	69	(14%)	286	(57%)	103	(21%)	41	(8%)
Non-frontline	80	(38%)	91	(43%)	17	(8%)	24	(11%)

Frontline staff are more likely to use the [ʃɔn] that is associated with higher education and not the schwa typical of MSE. Clearly here speakers are being selected for interaction with the public not only on their avoidance of stigmatized items, but also on their production of this JE feature, given the peripheral status of schwa in this speech community. This feature was also correlated with level of education, and was more typical of women. Within this sample, [ʃɔn] is a variant in the speech of most, if not all, groups that can be used to locate standard/ prestige forms.

Table 4.12: Articulation of *culture* type words in frontline staff (p > .10, $\chi^2 = 2.04$)

	dj	ʤ	tj	ʧ
Frontline	25 (76%)	8 (24%)	49 (32%)	102 (68%)
Non-frontline	9 (75%)	3 (25%)	24 (44%)	31 (56%)

Use of either the voiceless palatalized stop or the affricate in *culture* type words does not significantly distinguish frontline from non-frontline staff. Variation in this feature was correlated with gender and level of education – the highly educated favouring the affricate and women more likely to use the palatalized stop variant. As frontline positions seem not to be allocated on the basis of gender, the weak tendency for frontline staff to use the affricate more frequently can be explained by their higher levels of education.

Table 4.13: Rhoticity in frontline staff

	party type words		*forty* type words	
	[partɪ]	[pa:tɪ]	[fɔrtɪ]	[fɔ:tɪ]
Frontline	69 (41.5%)	97 (58.5%)	134 (60%)	89 (40%)
Non-frontline	39 (46.0%)	46 (54.0%)	67 (79%)	18 (21%)
	(p > .50, $\chi^2 = .42$)		(p < .01, $\chi^2 = 9.53$)	

While there is no statistically significant difference in post [a] rhoticity in the two groups of employees, rhoticization of *forty* type words, though clearly the norm in this total sample, is less a feature of frontline staff's speech. Recall that rhoticity after [ɔ] was less a feature of older speakers in this sample (see Table 3.53 for example). Moreover, this feature was seen to be normalised in JE among younger speakers and women. Again, persons in frontline positions tend not to be younger members of staff. The data in total suggests an idea of a rhotic

JE, given both the quantitative and qualitative hypercorrection identified. But it also suggests that frequency of rhotic productions differentiate varying groups in the sample, with younger and educated female speakers generally the most rhotic of the groups in both phonetic environments and younger educated males being less rhotic after [a].

Frontline staff are more consistent in their use of all phonological clusters here than non-frontline staff. In particular, while [nt] clusters before a vowel tended to be generally used in the JAMPRO sample, frontline staff also produce more [st] clusters and clusters before a following consonant (p = .05, χ^2 = 3.8). Use of clusters with morphological content does not distinguish frontline and non-frontline staff.

4.3 Discussion

The patterns for frontline staff, the selected voice(s) of JAMPRO, suggest that certain aspects of language use are normalised as good English.

Significant numbers of speakers never h-drop, use voiceless TH stopping or palatal velar stops before long vowels. And, to a lesser extent, this also applies to diphthongs, though it appears that [ie] is more and more an aspect of younger speakers who do pass the "interview" test. In its expectation and practice, this agency is communicating to its employees that these features of Jamaican speech [h], [θ] and [kʰaː] are necessary linguistic aspects of those that do well; at the same time features like [d ~ ð] or [kja] do not preclude advancement or employment. Indeed they are also features of the successful employee. In this way, by appointing some employees and excluding others, JAMPRO is engaged in constructing and legitimizing an ideology of what are the spoken norms of Standard Jamaican English.

Most speakers who are frontline staff produce affricates in *culture* type words, bimorphemic clusters and [nt], at least before a following vowel segment. But the data here also suggests that saying [dõ wʌrɪ] *don't worry* or [laːs jeːr] *last year* is not unacceptable in a speaker who has been selected by the agency to represent it to the public. Of course, a discussion in terms of presence/absence of features does not reflect the complexity of the situation. While it does show which features are generally widely used or avoided, it cannot suggest the importance of, say, using [ɔ] rather than [a] in JE, whether in stressed or unstressed syllables, or the asymmetrical salience of one variable in a pair of related linguistic variables in the sample.

Table 4.14: Group A variables and distribution in frontline staff

Feature	Informants taped	Variant			
		Never use		Always use	
/h/	51	0		24	(47%)
Initial[ð]	51	1	(2%)	0	
Initial [θ]	51	1	(2%)	28	(55%)
[ɔ] *not*	51	0		1	(2%)
[o] *boat*	51	0		19	(37%)
[e] *face*	51	1	(2%)	20	(39%)
[ɔr] *poor*	50	2	(4%)	17	(34%)
[ber] *beer*	51	1	(2%)	2	(4%)
[kʰaː]	33	2	(6%)	26	(79%)

Table 4.15: Group B variables and distribution in frontline staff

Feature	Informants taped	Variant			
		Never use		Always use	
-er*butter*	51	20	(39%)	0	
[ʃɔn]-*tion*	51	19	(37%)	0	
[tj]*culture*	41	17	(41%)	12	(29.0%)
[r]*party*	49	19	(39%)	9	(18.0%)
[r]*forty*	48	5	(10%)	12	(25.0%)
-nt## C	50	6	(12%)	8	(16.0%)
-st## V	45	8	(18%)	7	(15.5%)
-st## C	50	25	(50%)	2	(4.0%)
n't## C	48	17	(35%)	0	
-ed*beforeC*	43	10	(23%)	6	(14.0%)

Frontline staff are selected because they are perceived to be staff who can "represent well at a standard", and their behaviour provides a concrete model of spoken JE, which at least this institution considers representative of what it referred to as Standard English. Unlike the education system, JAMPRO is not engaged in providing a model for imitation. Rather, the language use of frontline staff here, in this formal interview context, is a sampling of speech from Jamaicans who are considered by other Jamaicans to be speakers of good English.

The individual profiles below are examples of some frontline speakers who used the fewest Creole forms in their interviews.

It would be difficult to argue that any one of the 3 unmarked speakers (M34, F16, F11) is more acrolectal than the other, or that one could be placed on a "higher" level on the continuum than some other one of these informants. M34, for example, is unique in my sample. He was categorical in his use of [ɔ] in *not* words, he seldom produced diphthongs, in fact 2 instances in 31 tokens, articulated [st] clusters (before vowels) and so on. Is he to be placed on a "higher" level on the continuum than F16 for example, given M34's use of [kja] or [tj]/[dj] or [dõ]? If one takes MSE as point of reference for Jamaican linguistic norms, then the answer must be no. In F16's interview she is categorical in her use of morphological clusters and in line with other MSE speakers in her use of phonological clusters. But she also h-drops more and uses diphthongs more often in most environments. Her use of variants, if one takes an endonormative approach, may well be evaluated by others as less acrolectal than his because of the particular features that are found in her speech. But she is a highly educated female and from a household with educated parents; he is a less educated man. Their language use is likely to be filtered through the social perceptions that others in the society hold of members of those groups. Kulick (1998) suggests that

> ...language ideologies seem never to be solely about language – they are always about entangled clusters of phenomena, and they encompass and are bound up with aspects of culture like gender, and expression, and being "civilized" (100).

H-drop in the driver M40's speech, for example, is not therefore sociolinguistically the same as it is in, say, speaker F16. And it would be an interesting extension of this study to see if the occasional h-drop in someone like F16 is even "heard" by the listener. M40 is a speaker who typically uses Creole phonology. The exceptions are the back diphthong [uo] and h-drop. These features were both infrequent in my total sample, and I have classified them both as two of the load-bearing variables in Jamaica. M40 also uses [tj] in *culture* words and past tense

Table 4.16: Group A Variables and distribution in 4 frontline speakers.

Feature	%			
	M34	F16	F11	M40
h-drop	0	3	0	0
Voiced TH stop	30	16	19	100
Voiceless TH stop	0	0	11	100
[a] *not*words	0	9	7	67
[uo] *boat*words	6	8	6	0
[ie] *face*words	0	0	0	100
[ᵘor] *poor*words	0	44.5	0	100
[bier] *beer*words	33	25	28	0
[kja] *cat*words	75	0	67	no data
[kja:] *cart*words	0	0	0	100

Table 4.17: Group B Variables and distribution in 4 frontline speakers.

Feature	%			
	M34	F16	F11	M40
[a]*butter*words	0	0	0	86
[ʃan]-*tion*words	7	0	0	100
[ʃɔn]-*tion*words	21	40	82	0
[ʃən]-*tion*words	7	20	0	0
[tj]*culture*words	100	no data	100	100
[r]*party*words	20	0	100	0
[r]*forty*words	33	no data	100	no data
-nt## before V	33	67	100	no data
-nt## before C	33	33	0	50
-st## before V	100	67	100	no data
-st## before C	33	40	0	no data
-n't## before V	no data	100	no data	no data
-n't## before C	14	33	0	0
-ed before V	100	100	100	100
-ed before C	50	100	33	no data

inflections. In that respect, there are aspects of his speech that index "better English" and this may suggest why he has been selected for a frontline position.[4]

The data from frontline staff, the selected public face of JAMPRO, is taken from speakers who are there because they have been judged suitable to represent the construct of the language situation described by the agency. Patois and Standard English are the varieties described in these publications, the latter, I would suggest, reflected in the formal usage of the majority of professionals appointed to the frontline ranks. And the features present or more frequent in this majority represent what is good spoken SJE, the acrolect in this speech community. In its expectation for staff and its practice of promotion, JAMPRO is legitimizing norms of speech, necessarily mediated by the ideas of those who control it about who the speaker is and what place they are expected/believed to occupy in the society. That the norm is essentially reflected in educated female speech at JAMPRO is also a function of the social context and the place women occupy in that agency.

---

[4]In the ideology of the Jamaican middle-class (Austin 1983: 236) a position like driver/chauffeur cannot be held by someone at the professional level in the agency or a woman and therefore must be occupied by an employee like M40.

5 Conclusion

This study set out to answer a set of questions about English in Jamaica, and to discuss what is called the acrolect or acrolectal in Jamaica. One central point that has been made in this study is that the construct called the Jamaican linguistic continuum, of which the acrolect is an integral part, has to be defined and analysed in relation to local norms of language use and not an external MSE. Approaches that use MSE as benchmark for what is standard in the Jamaican speech community, I argue, can be problematic both in analysis of data and in some of the conclusions that follow from that analysis. For example:

- Forms are typologized as basilectal in Jamaica even though they are attested to in the speech of all Jamaicans generally, irrespective of social context of use;

- Forms are labelled (upper) mesolectal even when found in the formal speech of educated Jamaicans or appear to be accepted as standard locally;

- Conclusions are arrived at that suggest that no one in the speech community speaks Standard English, even as members of the speech community hold to an idea that there is such a thing and that there are such speakers;

- The presence of non-MSE forms in the speech of educated Jamaicans is described as an emerging or new trend even though such variation was identified some two centuries ago;

- Discussions about decreolization and language change are carried out on the assumption of a vaguely defined "local standard" as one target, even though in practice that local standard is typically treated as either RP or General American.

This exploration of the acrolect takes an endonormative approach and seeks to explore the phonology of JE, as used by 82 educated speakers using language in a formal context of interaction. From the data collected, I define what is spoken SJE or the Jamaican acrolect. Further, the speech of select groups of informants was singled out for analysis, most notably frontline JAMPRO staff, in order to present an actual example of good spoken JE as judged by other Jamaicans. In so doing I wished to address the following questions:

- What patterns of use are to be found in this sample of educated Jamaican speakers when in formal interaction?

- How do the various groups identified differ in their use of these phonological variables?

- What is the relationship between acrolectal phonology and other varieties in the speech community?

- Does JAMPRO select speakers of a particular sociolinguistic type for high status positions?

- Is JAMPRO, in its practice and expectation, legitimizing certain speech patterns?

- What, based on all the above, constitutes an endonormatively determined set of phonological features for SJE?

5.1 The architecture of phonological variation in the Jamaican acrolect

Two types of phonological variables were created for the purposes of analysis. One type was a group of variables previously described in the literature as having Creole and English variants (Groups A); the other was a less studied group with variant options that are not solely describable as Creole vs English and which suggest another aspect of JE variation (Group B). The general patterns of use of these variables is shown in Tables 5.1 and 5.2, with reference to particular sociolinguistic correlations.

As shown in Table 5.1, there are some Group A variables that are statistically significant with most of the social categories used to stratify this population. Most of them, for examples [h] in *hot*, [ð ~ d] in *them*, [θ ~ t] in *thing*, [ɔ ~ a] in *pot*, [ɔr ~ uor] in *poor* and [e ~ ie] in *face*, are aspects of education, parent's background and high job status in the same speakers means a high degree of similarity in the way these groups pattern in their use of Group A variants. The Creole variants of the first four are also the features that women tended to produce less of. We can identify the standard and prestige variants of these as [h],

Table 5.1: Overview of Group A data indicating statistically significant associations

Group A	Education	Background	Gender	Age	Frontline	Significant
[h ~ ∅]	*	*	*		*	4
[ð ~ d]	*	*	*		*	4
[θ ~ t]	*	*	*		*	4
[ɔ ~ a]	*	*	*		*	4
[o ~ uo]						
[e ~ ie]	*	*	*	*	*	5
[ɔr ~ uor]	*	*	*	*		4
[er ~ ier]	*	*	*		*	4
[kʰa ~ kja]						
[kʰa: ~ kja:]	*	*			*	3
Significant	8	8	7	2	7	

Table 5.2: Overview of the Group B data including statistically significant associations

Group B	Education	Background	Gender	Age	Frontline	Significant
-tion	*				*	2
culture wds.	*					1
party wds.	*		*			2
forty wds.	*			*	*	3
-ed before V		*				1
-ed before C			*			1
-nt before V	*					1
-nt before C	*			*	*	3
-st before V			*		*	2
-st before C					*	1
Significant	6	1	3	2	5	

[θ], [ð], [ɔ], [ɔr] and [e], the first four also identified as part of the prescriptive SJE of the school curriculum. Further, the patterns of use in the sample indicate that [kʰaː] *calf* and [o] *boat* are also the standard and prestige forms in JE.

Indeed, in the sample of speakers who received at least a secondary level education, there was very consistent use of the JE variants of these variables and very little use of either [kjaː] or [uo].

Further support for this is to be had in the hypercorrect productions of some informants for some of these variables. This hypercorrection does suggest that these variants, for example /h/:[h], /ɔ/:[ɔ] and /θ/:[θ], can be said to characterize and define acrolectal speech.

Among Group B variables, those that also presented variation among JE options, the sociolinguistic variation that occurs is more diffuse than with Group A variables. Notably, only level of education and frontline status distinguish speakers' use of more than a few features. The association of education, parent's background and status in the agency was manifest in Group A variation, where JC and JE variants were typically the speakers' options for use. But with these Group B variables, the patterns of the highly educated were not necessarily a predictor of the patterns of speakers from more affluent backgrounds or high status positions at JAMPRO.

The variants [ʃɔn] – *tion*, and [tj]/[dj] *culture / soldier* reinforce the point that MSE forms cannot be used to identify acrolectal forms. In both instances speakers here do not necessarily use the MSE variant (schwa and the affricate) but are varying with options that reflect the coexistence with Creole and what speakers believe to be Creole forms. These are features that are produced in response to an idea of what is stereotyped Creole (affricates), distancing speakers even when the Creole form is like the non-local standard that the literature has assumed the acrolect to be. As such, the acrolect is not "more or less well-defined and discrete" (Winford 1997: 241), at least phonologically. Forms that are perceived to be Creole, such as [ʃan] – *tion* or [ʤ] *treasure*, affect the productions of some speakers and as a consequence the kind of variation found in the acrolect.

However, the distribution of the phonological variants in the data presented here is more complex than merely a low frequency of Creole forms or high frequency of prestige forms in the speech of formal JE speaking informants. And it is this distribution that turns out to be *the* important feature of acrolectal phonological variation.

There is one category of phonological variables that appears to be salient for producing SJE. Speakers, when producing these variables, show a remarkable conformity in variant use.

These are:

a) the word initial glottal fricative [h] in words like *hand*;

b) the voiceless interdental fricative in words like *thin*;

c) the word initial velar stop [kʰ] before the long low central vowel [aː] in words like *calf*;

d) [ɔ] in words such as *cotton*;

e) post [ɔ] rhoticity, specifically before [+ coronal] consonants in words like *forty*;

f) [ɔr] in words such as *poor*;

g) [o] in words such as *boat*;

h) the word final phonological stop cluster [nt] before a following vowel, as in *hint at.*;

i) the word final morphophonemic cluster when a past tense marker, as in *looked*.

This type of variable I label a *load-bearing* phonological variable in the acrolect, for they seem to function primarily to define the variety the speaker is using. Without these variants being produced in significant quantities, the speaker will not be interpreted in the Jamaican speech community as someone speaking English. Moreover, it appears that it is use of these load-bearing variants, and not English variants *per se*, that defines someone as speaking SJE.

As an example, high status speakers typically produce voiceless interdental fricatives, so much so that qualitatively hypercorrect use of the variant occurred. A different analysis, however, would have to be made of these same speakers' use of [ð ~ d]. The voiced TH stop variant occurs in their speech in high frequencies, and occurs more in the speech of frontline staff than those not selected to interact with the public. The kind of asymmetrical patterning I find for this pair of variables does not seem to occur in spoken MSE.

This same kind of asymmetrical sociolinguistic pattern is found elsewhere in the data, and is evident in the mid-vowels, the velar stops and post vocalic rhoticity. [e ~ ie] is sensitive to social factors here and more frequently varied, but [o ~ uo] is not; [kja] is attested in all speakers, but [kjaː] is seldom produced by anybody; and while speakers vary rhotic productions after [a], they generally are rhotic after [ɔ].

It is important to point out, also, that this is the pattern of production in *careful* speech. This asymmetrical attention to variants produced of related variables is then fundamentally different to the patterns I can identify in the literature on metropolitan English varieties, and is not a function of style shift in speakers. Informants here, when producing speech in circumstances that would suggest care and attention to forms used, focus on *one* variable of the pair and show some consensus on which variant to select. At the same time, use of the other variable in the pair is typically less focussed and is characterized by much greater levels of variation.

This suggests that use of the variants [ð] in *them*, [e] in *face*, [kʰ] in *cat* or the affricate [ʧ] in *culture*, does not necessarily define SJE. This makes these phonological features a different type from their load-bearing counterparts, because their production does not seem to be either necessary for or an indicator of speaking SJE.

The data also shows that speakers, in performing acts of identity or signalling group affiliation, are more likely to manipulate use of these non load-bearing JE variants for such purposes. I argue that this is because their presence or absence is *not* already assigned particular social meaning in the speech community, i.e. an inability to speak English, and therefore the speaker can manipulate these phonological variables in contexts of interaction that require SJE.

Younger informants used the diphthong [ie] in *face* more frequently; in the same speakers there was very little use of the back diphthong [uo] in *boat*. When compared with the oldest speakers, it *appeared* that front diphthong use was increasing. However, Alleyne's observations about the more widespread use of [ie] in Jamaica were made over two decades ago, and therefore I remain cautious about saying that its more frequent occurrence in younger speakers reflects a changing norm. It is possible therefore, that front diphthong use here distinguished younger speakers from older ones, and therefore is an aspect of signalling group affiliation.

Variation in rhoticity, specifically after [a] in words such as *party*, also correlated with age as well as gender. Young men were more typically non-rhotic after [a], distinguishing them from older speakers and women's patterns generally. Males in this sample also more typically produced an affricate in *culture* type words, as distinct from the female pattern which showed higher frequencies of [tj] use.

I argue that because the variables discussed above are not crucial to defining the variety being used, whether JC or JE, the type of variation that occurs is going to be less focussed and therefore more a function of signalling group affiliations like gender, or age. Variation on load-bearing variables will be constrained by their function of either indexing "speaking Creole" or "speaking English" or the identities of "Creole speaker" or "English speaker". But this is not the only type of social differentiation that is marked sociolinguistically.

The question then becomes, how does one project membership in other types of social groups, particularly to an unfamiliar hearer? One cannot manipulate variants to which social meaning is already widely assigned unless one is interacting with intimates. When interacting with intimates, who are familiar with one's background and who generally have information about one's social position, use of JC features is typical, indeed it is expected. However, with strangers, variation in one's use of [h] or [uo] in JE is likely to indicate something undesirable, such as "backwardness" or being "low class" or "uneducated", particularly in a (work) context that favours the English speaking, middle class persona. As such, the pattern of variation on load-bearing and non load-bearing variables is different, more uniform on the former than on the latter.

I wish to therefore to reformulate my initial classification of variables as Group A or B, and instead distinguish load-bearing variables from the other phonological variables used in this study. The absence or low frequencies of the appropriate variant of a load-bearing variable will be negatively evaluated in social contexts where use of SJE is expected.

I further propose that this asymmetrical attention to variants is possibly a function of the coexistence of two varieties for speakers, English and Creole, in an ideological context where use of both is the ideal and not just use of "the standard". Models of language situations like Jamaica point to the structural relationship among varieties, i.e. the linguistic continuum, or the functional relationship among varieties, i.e. diglossia. The variation that occurs here in this JAMPRO data, suggests that these speakers do not merely shift from the L variety JC to the H variety SJE when switching from informal to formal situations. Rather, these are speakers who seem to signal a shift in both variety and function by manipulating *some* variables, those load-bearing variables which are indexical of variety and which therefore signal use of the H code. At the same time, the ability to use JC, the L code, is signalled by the presence of other non load-bearing variables because the ability to use both is ideal in the Jamaican social context.

I can abstract four types of variables from my data, reflecting the general patterns of their distribution in the speech of this JAMPRO sample.

Load-bearing and non load-bearing variables can be further distinguished in terms of whether or not they function as indexing membership in or affiliation with particular social groups.

| Load-Bearing | Variables | | Non Load-Bearing |
	Socially Indexical		
Type 1	Type 2	Type 3	Type 4
/o/:[o]C	/o/:[ɔr]	/e/:[e ~ ie]	
	/h/:[h]		
-ed	-nt:[nt]V	-st:[s ~ st]	-n't:[n ~ nt]
	/ɔ/:[ɔ]		
	/θ/:[θ]	/ð/:[ð ~d]	
	/k/:[kʰ]a:		/k/:[kʰ ~ kj]a
	[ɔ]+rhotic	[a]+/−rhotic	

Not used in Jamaican Creole←——————————————→Used in Jamaican Creole

Figure 5.1: Load-bearing and non load-bearing variables in JE

- Type 1 load-bearing variables typically are produced by speakers with very similar patterns of use. All speakers tended to produce -ed and [o] in *goat* and, in fact these features were seldom statistically significant when subject to the test of association.

- Type 4 non load-bearing variables are also produced with very similar patterns of use. All speakers tended to vary the Type 4 variants [kj ~ kʰ] in *cat* or [nt ~ n ~ õ] in *don't* regardless of how the sample was stratified and analysed.

- Types 1 and 4 are not usually sensitive to sample stratification. What differentiates Type 1 from Type 4 is that the generally used variant of a Type 1 load-bearing variable is *not* used in JC, while the variant used in a Type 4 non load-bearing variable does occur in JC as well.

- In contrast, Types 2 and 3 variables *are* typically sensitive to sample stratification. However, they (are used to) index different things in the speech community.

- Type 2 variables, which are load-bearing, typically can be correlated with social factors like level of education and social status and therefore also index an ability to speak SJE.

- Type 3 variables tend to correlate with factors like gender or age without *necessarily* also signalling an (in)ability to use SJE.

Dyer & Beckford-Wassink's (2001) matched-guise test results, in which a speaker who clearly used Creole forms was judged to be a likely speaker of JE, can be explained in terms of her use of load-bearing and non load-bearing variables[1]. The speaker judged as "uses English", even though she "produced 16 of 19 forms with basilectal variant" (26) in the test, did produce – ed *turned* and [kʰ] (lexical item unclear).

As there is nothing to suggest that the phonology of a system would have patterns of variation peculiar to it alone, which are not also evident in other areas of structure, it is very likely that use of morphosyntactic forms in JE is structured in a similar way to the phonological variation abstracted from the data presented here.

5.2 An endonormative definition of SJE phonological features

The data from this JAMPRO sample reveals that education, social background and gender are the three social factors that have a significant association with speakers productions, a not unexpected finding. Crucially, being female, university educated and from a relatively affluent background to a great extent reflects the type of employee JAMPRO hires; senior management explicitly says so. The JAMPRO data as a whole shows that typically the features that tend to occur in female speech also tend to distinguish the select employees at JAMPRO, i.e. the frontline cohort. Female speech also patterns the variant use that characterizes those with more access to (longer) schooling. This suggests either that the phonology of formal acrolectal varieties is essentially going to be a female/educated norm, or that women at JAMPRO approximate more to the norms considered to be acrolectal in the speech community. It is perhaps one reason why Senior Management at JAMPRO articulates a preference for female employees when selecting from interviewed candidates.

Generally, there are very few, if any, phonological features that are not shared with other varieties along the Jamaican linguistic continuum. What distinguishes acrolectal speech is the frequency of use of these features and what characterizes it is a low production of *stigmatized* Creole items. This suggests that the acrolect, and here I mean the spoken SJE, will be described as either having [h], [θ] and the like or as not having the Creole reflex of these features. It cannot be described as being typified by an absence of [kja] or [ð] *them* or even mid-vowel diphthongs,

---

[1]This data is discussed in Chapter 1, Table 1.1.

although it is very probable that if asked, speakers will describe an idealized SJE that is devoid of these features.

The acrolect, as actual spoken SJE, cannot therefore be located by identifying MSE forms; nor can the features along the linguistic continuum be characterized with reference to MSE without leading to paradoxical conclusions or misinterpretations of data. Indeed, an idealized acrolect as "local standard" can also be problematic. This can be illustrated by looking again at the example of Meade's work (2001), cited at the beginning of this study. In his study MSE phonology was used to determine what he labels acrolectal phonology. But his data on use of dental fricatives and their variants makes no distinction between voiced and voiceless forms. It is entirely possible, therefore, that his sample of Jamaican children with educated caregivers are being exposed to [ð ~ d]. The data I have would suggest that it is the pattern on the voiceless fricative, or other such load-bearing variables, that would need to be examined to determine a time frame for acquisition of JE phonology.

The speaker's notion that two varieties exist in Jamaica, JC and JE, is therefore important. The form English takes in the Jamaican social context, particularly its pronunciation, is shaped in part by the idea speakers have of what Creole is. In an informal survey of 42 students at the University of the West Indies, when asked how they know someone is speaking good English, most responded by saying "because they are not" - dropping aitches, saying 'mi', 'did' a and so on, listing a number of stereotypical Creole practices. For them, English is, in part, negatively defined in relation to what Creole is believed to be and is assessed in terms of the speaker's avoidance of those characteristic items. Wolfram & Schilling-Estes (1998: 12) comment on similar definitions of the standard in the US. But there are other items that are present in the acrolect that have been typically associated with Creole that speakers use as frequently as, if not more than, the variants which also appear in MSE.

Patrick (1999: 9) observes, of his urban, mesolectal sample, that the speakers he interviewed all seem to have

> a rich and nuanced ability to vary their speech (...) but a very limited set of metalinguistic labels for it, essentially binary oppositions of which the bluntest instrument is the English/patois distinction.

He does not take the strong position of DeCamp, who described this belief as a persistent myth (1971: 350), but argues that this distinction, though psychologically powerful, should not form the basis of linguistic description. But the importance of the speaker's distinction should not be underestimated either. It is central to the way variation patterns asymmetrically on a number of phonological variables. Moreover, issues like language acquisition and language change in the Jamaican context are going to be affected by what speakers think is Creole and English, to the extent that they are trying to target the latter. For them, targeting English is not reproducing foreign norms.[2] Many speakers here for example, notably women and the secondary educated, are avoiding affricates, perceived to be Creole, and producing [tj] in *culture* type words.

JAMPRO was specifically selected because of its role as a one of the Jamaican state's promotion agencies, conducting its business in a context that it explicitly states is reserved for Standard English. JAMPRO is one of many agencies that select receptionists, broadcasters, managers and the like and reject or pass others over. In its practice of selecting some staff for frontline positions, Jamaicans who represent the agency in this milieu, JAMPRO is implicitly favouring some patterns of speech over others and determining which features are acceptable or unacceptable as spoken SJE.

The data here demonstrate that a number of social and linguistic factors inform their selection. Frontline staff are typically highly educated, they come from households more likely to be JC/JE speaking and they are perceived by others in their work environment to be selected because they can represent JAMPRO well, socially and in the way they speak English. Arguably, frontline staff reflect the agency's idea of "best speakerhood" (Silverstein 1996: 286) – at least of the upper end of the bidialectal/diglossic construct JAMPRO says exists in Jamaica. Their speech shows the pattern of variation uncovered in this study – little if any voiceless TH stopping, but freely varied [d ~ ð]; a virtual absence of [kja:], but frequent use of [kja]; little use of diphthongal variants for the back mid-vowel and variation between [e ~ ie], especially pre-rhotically. In addition, frontline staff are more likely to produce [ɔ] – whether in stressed syllables or in words ending – tion – and seldom h-drop.

I suggest that this frontline data presents an actual example of what "good English" is in Jamaica. Speakers who seek certain kinds of jobs will perhaps target features like [ʃɔn], or even [kja]; certainly they will identify [h] and [ɔ] as aspects of speech that the more successful use, not because they belong to British or American varieties of English but because in Jamaica these are features of speakers presented as having the right diction. Speakers who seek certain kinds of jobs will carefully avoid voiceless TH stopping, [uo], [kja:] because these are "Creole", not because British or American speakers do not use them. And they

---

[2] An early discussion of this preference for and use of local norms is found in Eersel's study (1971: 320) of educated Surinamese use of Dutch.

will perhaps freely vary word final [st ~ s] in a word like *cast*, [d ~ ð] or [e ~ ie] because they do not necessarily index "bad English".

It is important therefore to separate discussion of the (historical) linguistic processes that may have accounted for most of the forms I have described above, from a speaker-driven endonormative discussion of the Jamaican acrolect. Undoubtedly, hypercorrection, distancing from Creole or Creole influence, may explain the presence of most of the features in the production of informants. But the idea speaker hold of SJE, the acrolect, as it occurs now will come from their perceptions of who is successful and how they speak and who is presented as having a good command of the English language in the Jamaican social context. It cannot be assumed, however implicitly, to be a foreign model of English because English is not a foreign language in Jamaica. Mühleisen's (2002) criticism that "CELCs [Caribbean English-lexicon creoles] are (...) never defined in isolation but always 'in comparison with' the high prestige language English" (74) is made more pointed if that English is itself situated outside of the speaker's community.

It is not clear how we can proceed to discuss issues of decreolization, or of language change generally, with assumptions about the acrolect, or for that matter the basilect, that are not based on the norms of speakers in their speech communities. Jamaican English is, after all, a national variety (or set of varieties) in its own right. The speakers in this speech community operate in a social context where their two languages, Jamaican English and Jamaican Creole, have coexisted for centuries. The two are perceived as distinct, but connected elements of being Jamaican. The data presented here demonstrates both – the speaker's differentiation and integration of JE and JC in the Jamaican diasystem.

Appendix A: Prepared script for all interviews of JAMPRO informants

104 informants were interviewed using this script. 82 of these interviews were recorded and transcribed phonetically for later sociolinguistic analysis.

1. Was the informant told of the purpose of the interview? 13 (yes)

A.1 Personal data collected

1. Sex: 82 (female), 22 (male)

2. Age: 35 (20–29), 33 (30–39), 16 (40–49), 20 (50–65)

3. Residence: 65 (Portmore), 4 (Franklin Town), 21 (Liguanea), 9 (Red Hills), 4 (Stony Hills), 1 (no data)

4. Race: 53 (black), 35 (brown), 1 (Chinese), 1 (Indian), 14 (no data noted)

5. Years at JAMPRO: 30 (10+), 38 (5+), 28 (−5), 8 (new)

6. Level of Education: 4 (primary), 10 (secondary), 43 (post-secondary), 22 (tertiary), 24 (graduate)

7. Salary Scale: 7 (ancillary), 31 (secretarial), 42 (professional), 10 (director), 14 (senior management)

8. Spouse's Occupation: 1 ("cleaner"), 7 ("artisan"), 23 ("teacher"), 11 ("doctor"), 2 (business), 60 (none)

9. Parent's Occupation: 17 ("cleaner"), 39 ("artisan"), 30 ("teacher"), 8 ("doctor"), 6 (business) 4 (no data)

10. Floor: 32 (1), 17 (2), 14 (3), 28 (4), 10 (5), 3 (overseas posting)

11. Job Description: 24 (frontline - local clients), 39 (frontline - local & foreign clients), 41 (no clients)

12. Employment History: 26 (never promoted), 37 (one promotion), 30 (multiple), 11 (no data)

13. Transport to Work: 30 (bus), 50 (own car), 24 (lift)

14. Organizational Section: 24 (JNIP), 15 (JNEC), 3 (JIDC), 1 (JNIC), 61 (none)

A.2 Data on patterns of workplace interaction

1. Which members of staff do you lunch with?

2. Which members of staff live in your residential community?

3. Are any members of staff related to you?

4. Which members of staff do you consider friends?

5. Which members of staff do you see outside of work?

6. Are you active on the Staff Association (JSA, hereafter)?

7. Do you hold any (elected) position on the JSA?

A.3 Data on working at JAMPRO

1. What type of person does well and moves ahead in JAMPRO?

2. Why do you think staffers feel as they do about the JSA?

3. Who is responsible for your promotion?

4. Do you see yourself here in 5 or 10 years? 36 (yes), 50 (no), 18 (don't know)

5. How important do you think these are in determining who does well here:

6. gender (36.5%) b) colour (16%) c) class (40%) d) education (87.5%) e) other (15%) (These percentages are calculated out of a possible 104 mentions of a particular social factor.)

7. Which levels in JAMPRO do you think have authority and constitute top management?

Appendix B: Profiles of JAMPRO informants

Table B.1: Profiles of male JAMPRO informants

	Males			
Informant #	Education	Parent's	Age	Status
5	tertiary	tradesman	38	5 (frontline)
8	tertiary	teacher	38	4 (frontline)
9	tertiary	builder	no data	6 (frontline)
14	tertiary	carpenter	51	7 (frontline)
15	graduate	farmer	42	7
18	primary	farmer	52	1
20	graduate	tailor	35	6 (frontline)
27	secondary	farmer	33	1 (frontline)
29	graduate	teacher	55	5 (frontline)
34	secondary+	civil servant	29	5 (frontline)
40	primary	mason	51	1 (frontline)
47	secondary	supervisor	58	1 (frontline)
49	graduate	farmer	27	5
54	graduate	messenger	32	5
86	graduate	salesman	44	6
88	secondary+	shoemaker	42	5 (frontline)
89	tertiary	shopkeeper	45	6 (frontline)
92	tertiary	farmer	27	4
94	secondary+	helper (maid)	26	4
100	secondary+	dressmaker	28	5 (frontline)
101	graduate	teacher	60+	7 (frontline)
102	graduate	no data	49	7 (frontline)

Table B.2: Profiles of female JAMPRO informants

		Females		
Informant #	Education	Parent's	Age	Status
2	secondary+	no data	29	3 (frontline)
3	tertiary	teacher	25	4 (frontline)
4	secondary	higgler	58	1
6	secondary+	nurse	25+	3 (frontline)
7	graduate	no data	40+	5 (frontline)
10	tertiary	contractor	35+	5 (frontline)
11	tertiary	farmer	31	4 (frontline)
12	tertiary	engineer	45	6 (frontline)
13	tertiary	business man	40+	6 (frontline)
16	graduate	bursar	33	5 (frontline)
17	tertiary	overseer	40	2 (frontline)
19	secondary	self-employed	35+	3 (frontline)
21	secondary+	dressmaker	30	3
22	tertiary	civil servant	30	4 (frontline)
23	secondary+	farmer	30	4 (frontline)
24	tertiary	teacher	23	4 (frontline)
25	secondary+	cleaner	27	3 (frontline)
26	tertiary	teacher	30	4 (frontline)
28	tertiary	pub. health insp.	38	6 (frontline)
30	secondary+	mason	24	4 (frontline)
31	secondary+	factory worker	25	3
32	secondary+	civil servant	50+	7 (frontline)
33	graduate	teacher	50+	6 (frontline)
35	tertiary	business man	37	6 (frontline)
36	graduate	financial contr.	40+	6 (frontline)
37	secondary+	carpenter	33	3 (frontline)
38	secondary+	clerk	30+	4 (frontline)
39	secondary+	supervisor	27	3 (frontline)
41	secondary+	farmer	28	3
42	tertiary	civil servant	39	6 (frontline)
43	secondary+	business man	27	3
44	secondary+	clerk	25	3
45	secondary	bus conductor	22	3

Informant #	Education	Parent's	Age	Status
46	tertiary	teacher	32	5
48	secondary+	tobacconist	63	3
50	secondary+	nurse	40	4 (frontline)
51	graduate	civil servant	52	6 (frontline)
52	secondary+	dressmaker	27	3
53	secondary	farmer	36+	1
55	graduate	cashier	42	7 (frontline)
56	graduate	insurance agent	31	6 (frontline)
57	secondary+	prison warder	52	5 (frontline)
58	tertiary	pub. health insp.	40	5
59	secondary+	butcher	60	5 (frontline)
60	secondary+	construction	26	2
61	secondary+	farmer	21	no data
62	tertiary	plumber	37	5 (frontline)
63	secondary	electrician	23	3
64	tertiary	pastor	33	6 (frontline)
65	tertiary	dressmaker	43	3 (frontline)
66	secondary+	secretary	37	5
67	secondary+	cook	30	3 (frontline)
68	tertiary	meteorologist	28	5 (frontline)
69	tertiary	teacher	23	4 (frontline)
70	secondary+	policeman	22	3 (frontline)
71	secondary+	business man	26	3
72	secondary	draftsman	23	5
73	secondary+	carpenter	29	3
74	primary	labourer	50	1
75	graduate	engineer	33	6 (frontline)
76	secondary+	plumber	28	2 (frontline)
77	no data	tailor	57	5
78	secondary+	tiler	26	2 (frontline)
79	tertiary	teacher	25	4
80	secondary+	supervisor	32	4
81	secondary+	dressmaker	64	5
82	secondary+	policeman	24	3
83	graduate	manager	26	6
84	secondary+	no data	23	3
85	secondary	business man	27	3

B Profiles of JAMPRO informants

Informant #	Education	Parent's	Age	Status
87	graduate	farmer	41	7 (frontline)
90	secondary+	matron	26	4 (frontline)
91	secondary+	farmer	27	2
93	secondary+	cleaner	28	3 (frontline)
95	secondary+	self-employed	54	2
96	primary	cleaner	51	1
97	secondary+	teacher	23	2
98	secondary+	clerk	52	4 (frontline)
99	secondary+	doctor	31	4
103	tertiary	policeman	43	3 (frontline)
104	secondary+	cleaner	31	3 (frontline)
105	graduate	doctor	30	4 (frontline)

Appendix C: Parent's Occupation

The following is a detailed list of parent's occupations given by informants in this study. The data has been grouped according to the five headings used in the body of the study.

Table C.1: List of parent's occupations

"Cleaner"	"Artisan"	"Teacher"	"Doctor"	"Business"
small farmer	carpenter	teacher	engineer	contractor
labourer	plumber	policeman	physician	shopkeeper
cleaner	butcher	draftsman	manager	pastor
messenger	tailor	superintendent	accountant	overseer
driver	mason	nurse	financial controller	
cook	electrician	meteorologist		
	tobacconist	clerk		
	dressmaker	supervisor		
	shoemaker	public health inspector		
	tiler	warder		

References

Akers, Glen. 1977. *Phonological variation in the Jamaican continuum*. Harvard University dissertation.

Akers, Glen. 1981. *Phonological variation in the Jamaican continuum*. Ann Arbor: Karoma Publishers.

Alexander, J. 1977. The culture of race in middle-class Kingston, Jamaica. *American Ethnologist* 4(3). 413–435.

Alleyne, Mervyn C. 1980. *Comparative Afro-American*. Ann Arbor: Karoma Publishers.

Allsopp, Richard. 1996. *Dictionary of Caribbean English usage*. Oxford: Oxford University Press.

Alvesson, Mats. 1993. *Cultural perspectives on organizations*. Cambridge: Cambridge University Press.

Austin, Diane. 1983. Culture and ideology in the English speaking Caribbean: A view from Jamaica. *American Ethnologist* 10(2). 223–240.

Bailey, Beryl. 1966. *Jamaican Creole syntax*. Cambridge: Cambridge University Press.

Bailey, Beryl. 1971. Jamaican Creole: Can dialect boundaries be defined? In Dell Hymes (ed.), *Pidginization and creolization of languages*, 341–348. Cambridge: Cambridge University Press.

Barrow, Steve & Peter Dalton. 1997. *Reggae, the Rough Guide*. London: Rough Guides Ltd.

Baugh, Albert & Thomas Cable. 1993. *A history of the English language*. London: Routledge.

Beal, Joan. 2002. *English pronunciation in the eighteenth century*. Oxford: Oxford University Press.

Beckford-Wassink, Alicia. 1999a. *A sociophonetic analysis of Jamaican vowels*. University of Michigan dissertation.

Beckford-Wassink, Alicia. 1999b. Historic low prestige and seeds of change: Attitudes toward Jamaican Creole. *Language in Society* 28. 57–92.

Beckford-Wassink, Alicia. 2001. Theme and variation in Jamaican vowels. *Language Variation and Change* 13. 135–159.

References

Beckles, Hilary. 2000. A "riotous and unruly lot": Irish indentured servants and freemen in the English West Indies, 1644–1713. In Verene Shepherd & Hilary Beckles (eds.), *Caribbean slavery in the Atlantic world*, 226–238. Kingston: Ian Randle.

Bell, Allan. 1984. Language style as audience design. *Language in Society* 2. 145–204.

Bell, Allan. 2001. Back in style: Reworking audience design. In Penny Eckert & John Rickford (eds.), *Style and sociolinguistic variation*, 139–169. Cambridge: Cambridge University Press.

Bickerton, Derek. 1973. On the nature of a Creole continuum. *Language* 49(3). 640–669.

Bickerton, Derek. 1975. *Dynamics of a Creole system*. Cambridge: Cambridge University Press.

Bobda, Augustin Simo. 2001. East and Southern African English accents. *World Englishes* 20(3). 269–284.

Bourdieu, Pierre. 1984. *Distinction*. London: Routledge.

Bourdieu, Pierre. 1991. *Language and symbolic power*. Cambridge: Polity Press.

Brereton, Bridget. 1995. Text, testimony and gender: An examination of some texts by women on the English-speaking Caribbean, from the 1770's to the 1920's. In Bridget Brereton Verene Shepherd & Barbara Bailey (eds.), *Engendering history*, 63–93. Kingston: Ian Randle Publishers.

Brodber, Kathryn. 1989. Standard English in Jamaica: A case of competing norms. *English World-Wide* 10(1). 41–53.

Bryan, Patrick. 1996. The black middle class in 19th century Jamaica. In Hilary Beckles & Verene Shepherd (eds.), *Caribbean freedom*, 284–296. Princeton: Markus Wiener Publishers.

Bryan, Patrick. 2000. *The Jamaican people, 1880–1902: Race, class and social control*. Kingston: The University of the West Indies Press.

Busby, Margaret. 1992. *Daughters of Africa*. New York: Ballantine Books.

Cameron, Deborah. 2000. Styling the worker: Gender and the commodification of language in the globalized service economy. *Journal of Sociolinguistics* 4(3). 323–347.

Campbell, Carl. 1996. Social and economic obstacles to the development of popular education in post-emancipation Jamaica, 1834–1865. In Hilary Beckles & Verene Shepherd (eds.), *Caribbean freedom*, 262–268. Princeton: Markus Wiener Publishers.

Carmichael, A.C. 1833. *Domestic manners and social condition of the White, Coloured, and Negro population of the West Indies*. London: Whittaker, Treacher. Also published in New York by Negro Universities Press, 1969.

Carpenter, Joseph E. 1868. *A handbook of poetry*. London: Sampson Low, Son, & Marston.

Cassidy, Frederic. 1961. *Jamaica talk*. London: Macmillan.

Cassidy, Frederic & Robert Le Page. 1967. *Dictionary of Jamaican English*. Cambridge: Cambridge University Press.

Chaudenson, Robert. 2001. *Creolization of language and culture*. London: Routledge.

Cheshire, Jenny. 1999. Spoken Standard English. In Tony Bex & Richard Watts (eds.), *Standard English: The widening debate*, 129–147. London: Routledge.

Christie, Pauline. 1989. Questions of standards and intraregional differences in Caribbean examinations. In Ofelia Garcia & Ricardo Otheguy (eds.), *English across cultures: Cultures across English*. 243–262. Amsterdam: Benjamins.

Christie, Pauline. 1998a. History and language. *UWILING, Working Papers in Linguistics* 3. 74–90.

Christie, Pauline. 1998b. Trends in Jamaican English: Increasing deviance or emerging standards? *UWILING, Working Papers in Linguistics* 3. 19–34.

Christie, Pauline. 2003. *Language in Jamaica*. Kingston: Arawak Publications.

Coye, Dale. 1998. Orthoepic piracy: Spelling pronunciations and Standard English. *American Speech* 73(2). 178–196.

Craig, Dennis. 1982. Toward a description of Caribbean English. In Braj Kachru (ed.), *The other tongue: English across cultures*, 198–209. Urbana: University of Illinois Press.

Crompton, Rosemary. 1993. *Class and stratification: An introduction to current debates*. Cambridge: Polity Press.

DeCamp, David. 1961. Social and geographic factors in Jamaican dialects. In Robert Le Page (ed.), *Creole language studies 2*. 61–84. London: Macmillan.

DeCamp, David. 1971. Toward a generative analysis of a post-Creole speech community. In Dell Hymes (ed.), *Pidginization and creolization of languages*, 340–376. Cambridge: Cambridge University Press.

Deuchar, Margaret. 1988. A pragmatic account of women in their speech communities. In Jennifer Coates & Deborah Cameron (eds.), *Women in their speech communities*, 27–32. London: Longman.

Devonish, Hubert. 1978. *The selection and codification of a widely understood and publicly usable language variety in Guyana, to be used as a vehicle for national development*. University of York dissertation.

Devonish, Hubert. 1992. On the existence of autonomous language varieties in 'Creole continuum situations'. In Pauline Christie, Barbara Lalla, Velma Pollard & Lawrence Carrington (eds.), *Studies in Caribbean language* II. 178–196. St. Augustine: Society for Caribbean Linguistics.

References

Devonish, Hubert. 2002. *Talking rhythm, stressing tone*. Kingston: Arawak Publications.

Devonish, Hubert. 2003. Language advocacy and 'conquest' diglossia in the 'anglophone' Caribbean. In Christian Mair (ed.), *The politics of English as a world language*, 157–177. Amsterdam: Rodopi B. V.

Devonish, Hubert & Otelemate Harry. 2004. Jamaican Creole and Jamaican English phonology. In Edgar Schneider (ed.), *Varieties of English, volume 1, the Americas and the Caribbean*, 450–480. Berlin: Mouton de Gruyter.

Devonish, Hubert & Walter Seiler. 1991. A reanalysis of the phonological system of Jamaican Creole. *Society for Caribbean Linguistics Occasional Paper* 24.

Dubois, Sylvie & Barbara Horvath. 1998. Let's tink about dat: Interdental fricatives in Cajun English. *Language Variation and Change* 10(3). 245–261.

Dyer, Judy & Alicia Beckford-Wassink. 2001. *Taakin braad and talking broad: Changing indexicality of phonological variants in two language contact situations.* Paper presented at the University of the West Indies (Mona), Kingston, May 7, 2002.

Eersel, Christian. 1971. Prestige in choice of language and linguistic form. In Dell Hymes (ed.), *Pidginization and creolization of languages*, 317–322. Cambridge: Cambridge University Press.

Ervin-Tripp, Susan. 2001. Variety, style shifting, and ideology. In Penny Eckert & John Rickford (eds.), *Style and sociolinguistic variation*, 44–56. Cambridge: Cambridge University Press.

Escure, Genevieve. 1997. *Creole and dialect continua* (Creole Language Library 18). Amsterdam: John Benjamins Publishing Company.

Escure, Genevieve. 2000. Neva: From Caribbean Creoles to meso-acrolects. In, vol. 2000, 141–145. Papers presented at the biennial meeting for the Society for Caribbean Linguistics 2000, Kingston, University of the West Indies (Mona), August 16–19.

Fisher, John H. 2001. British and American, continuity and divergence. In John Algeo (ed.), *The Cambridge history of the English language, vol. VI, English in North America*, 59–85. Cambridge: Cambridge University Press.

Freeborn, Dennis. 1998. *From Old English to Standard English*. London: Macmillan.

Gbedemah, G. 1995. *Fun with phonics: Skill-building*. 7th edition. Kingston: Carlong Publishers.

Giegerich, Heinz. 1992. *English phonology*. Cambridge: Cambridge University Press.

Giles, Howard & Peter Powesland. 1975. *Speech style and social evaluation*. New York: Harcourt Brace.

Gimson, A. C. 1980. *An introduction to the pronunciation of English.* London: Edward Arnold.

Gordon, Derek. 1986. *Class, status and social mobility in Jamaica.* Kingston: ISER.

Görlach, Manfred. 1987. Colonial lag? The alleged conservative character of American English and other 'colonial' varieties. *English World-Wide* 8(1). 41–60.

Graff, David, William Labov & Wendell Harris. 1986. Testing listener's reactions to phonological markers of ethnic identity: A new method for sociolinguistic research. In David Sankoff (ed.), *Diversity and diachrony*, 45–58. Amsterdam: John Benjamins Publishing Company.

Green, Lisa. 2002. *African American English.* Cambridge: Cambridge University Press.

Grint, Keith. 1991. *The sociology of work.* Cambridge: Polity Press.

Gupta, Anthea. 2001. Realism and imagination in the teaching of English. *World Englishes* 20(3). 365–381.

Guy, Gregory. 1980. Variation in the group and the individual: The case of final stop deletion. In William Labov (ed.), *Locating language in time and space*, 1–36. New York: Academic Press.

Hancock, Ian. 1994. Componentiality and the Creole matrix: The Southwest English contribution. In Michael Montgomery (ed.), *The crucible of Carolina: Essays in the development of Gullah language and culture*, 95–114. Athens: University of Georgia Press.

Hernández-Campoy, Juan & José Jiménez-Cano. 2003. Broadcasting standardisation: An analysis of the linguistic normalisation process in Murcian Spanish. *Journal of Sociolinguistics* 7(3). 321–347.

Hewitt, Roger. 1986. *White talk Black talk. Inter-racial friendship and communication amongst adolescents.* Cambridge: Cambridge University Press.

Ho, Mian-Lian & John Platt. 1993. *Dynamics of a contact continuum: Singaporean English.* Oxford: Oxford University Press.

Holm, John. 1988. *Pidgins and creoles: Volume 1, theory and structure.* Cambridge: Cambridge University Press.

Holmes, Janet. 1997. Setting new standards: Sound changes and gender in New Zealand English. *English World-Wide* 18(1). 107–142.

Horvath, Barbara & David Sankoff. 1987. Delimiting the Sydney speech community. *Language in Society* 16. 179–204.

Hudson, Richard. 1980. *Sociolinguistics.* Cambridge: Cambridge University Press.

Hymes, Dell. 1974. *Foundations in sociolinguistics: An ethnographic approach.* Philadelphia: University of Pennsylvania Press.

Irvine, Alison. 1988. *A study of the linguistic markers of social differentiation in two jamaican communities.* M. Phil. dissertation, University of York.

Irvine, Alison. 1994. Dialect variation in Jamaican English: A study of the phonology of social group marking. *English World Wide* 15(1). 55–78.

Irvine, Judith & Susan Gal. 2000. Language ideology and linguistic differentiation. In Paul Kroskrity (ed.), *Regimes of language*, 35–83. New Mexico: School of American Research Press.

Jamaica Tourist Board. 2001. *Jamaica: Visitor guide.*

JAMPRO. 1992. *Invest Jamaica.*

JAMPRO. 1993. *Choose Jamaica.*

JAMPRO. 1994. *Jamaica: The investment capital of the Caribbean.*

JAMPRO. 1996. *Jamaica: The investment capital of the Caribbean.*

JAMPRO. 1997a. *Business traveller's guide to Kingston.* Volume 1. 1–10.

JAMPRO. 1997b. *Travel agent reference guide.*

Janda, Richard & Julie Auger. 1992. Quantitative evidence, qualitative hypercorrection, sociolinguistic variables – and French speakers' 'eadhaches with english /h/. *Language and Communication* 12. 195–236.

Jenkins, R. 1985. Black workers in the labour market: The price of recession. In Ruth Finnegan Bryan Roberts & Duncan Gallie (eds.), *New approaches to economic life*, 169–183. Manchester: Manchester University Press.

JIDC. 1957. *New opportunities for industrial development.*

JIDC. 1961. *Opportunities for industrial investment.*

Judd, Karen. 1998. The name of the people: Populist ideology and expatriate power in Belize. In Howard Johnson & Karl Watson (eds.), *The White minority in the Caribbean*, 133–158. Kingston: Ian Randle.

Kachru, Braj. 1982. Models for non-native Englishes. In Braj Kachru (ed.), *The other tongue: English across cultures*, 31–57. Urbana: University of Illinois Press.

Kirwin, William. 2001. Newfoundland English. In John Algeo (ed.), *The Cambridge history of the English language, vol. VI, English in North America*, 441–455. Cambridge: Cambridge University Press.

Krapp, George Philip. 1925. *The English language in America: Volume 11.* New York: The Century Company.

Kroskrity, Paul. 2000. Regimenting languages: Language ideological perspectives. In Paul Kroskrity (ed.), *Regimes of language*, 1–34. New Mexico: School of American Research Press.

Kulick, Don. 1998. Age, gender, language shift and the politics of revelation in a Papua New Guinea village. In Bambi Schieffelin, Kathryn Woolard & Paul Kroskrity (eds.), *Language ideologies*, 87–102. Oxford: Oxford University Press.

Labov, William. 1966. *The social stratification of English in New York City*. Washington: Center for Applied Linguistics.

Labov, William. 1968. The reflection of social processes in linguistic structures. In Joshua Fishman (ed.), *Readings in the sociology of language*, 240 251. The Hague: Mouton.

Labov, William. 1972. *Sociolinguistic patterns*. Philadelphia: University of Pennsylvania Press.

Labov, William. 1980. The social origins of sound change. In William Labov (ed.), *Locating language in time and space*, 251–265. New York: Academic Press.

Labov, William. 2001. The anatomy of style-shifting. In Penny Eckert & John Rickford (eds.), *Style and sociolinguistic variation*, 85–108. Cambridge: Cambridge University Press.

LaCharité, Darlene. 1996. The segmental status of [st]: Evidence from basilectal and mesolectal Jamaican Creole. In Päivi Koskinen (ed.), *Proceedings of the 1995 annual conference of the Canadian Linguistic Association*. Toronto: Toronto Working Papers in Linguistics.

Lalla, Barbara & Jean D'Costa. 1989. *Voices in exile. Jamaican texts of the 18th and 19th centuries*. Tuscaloosa: The University of Alabama Press.

Lalla, Barbara & Jean D'Costa. 1990. *Language in exile: Three hundred years of Jamaican Creole*. Tuscaloosa: The University of Alabama Press.

Le Page, Robert. 1960. Jamaican Creole. In Robert Le Page (ed.), *Creole language studies* 1. Cambridge: Cambridge University Press.

Le Page, Robert. 1968. Problems to be faced in the use of English as the medium of education in four West Indian territories. In Joshua Fishman (ed.), *Language problems of developing nations*, 431–442. London: John Wiley & Sons.

Le Page, Robert. 1980. Projection, focussing, diffusion, or steps towards a sociolinguistic theory of language. *York Papers in Linguistics* 9.

Le Page, Robert. 1988. Some premises concerning the standardization of languages, with special reference to Caribbean Creole English. *International Journal of the Sociology of Language* 71. 25–36.

Le Page, Robert & Andrée Tabouret-Keller. 1985. *Acts of identity*. Cambridge: Cambridge University Press.

Lehmann, Winfred. 1973. *Historical linguistics*. New York: Holt, Rinehart & Winston.

Lewis, Gordon. 1968. *The growth of the modern West Indies*. New York: Monthly Review Press.

Lippi-Green, Rosina. 1997. *English with an accent*. London: Routledge.

Long, Edward. 1774. *The history of Jamaica*. London: T. Lowndes.

Marshall, Hayden. 1983. *Unpublished BA Caribbean study.* University of the West Indies (Mona).

McArthur, Tom. 1992. *The BBC and spoken English.* Tom McArthur (ed.). Oxford: Oxford University Press.

McArthur, Tom. 1998. *The English languages.* Cambridge: Cambridge University Press.

Meade, Rocky R. 2001. *Acquisition of Jamaican phonology.* LOT: Netherlands Graduate School of Linguistics.

Miller, Errol. 1989. Educational development in independent Jamaica. In Rex Nettleford (ed.), *Jamaica in independence*, 205–227. Kingston: Heinemann Publishers.

Miller, Errol. 1991. *Men at risk.* Kingston: Jamaica Publishing House Ltd.

Miller, Faye. 1987. *Acrolectal Jamaican speech: A descriptive analysis of its phonology and morpho-syntax.* University of the West Indies (Mona) M.Phil. thesis.

Milroy, James. 1999. The consequences of standardisation in descriptive linguistics. In Tony Bex & Richard Watts (eds.), *Standard English: The widening debate*, 16–39. London: Routledge.

Milroy, James & Lesley Milroy. 1985. *Authority in language.* London: Routledge.

Milroy, Lesley. 1980. *Language and social networks.* Oxford: Basil Blackwell.

Milroy, Lesley. 2002. Introduction: Mobility, contact and language change – working with contemporary speech communities. *Journal of Sociolinguistics* 6,1 1. 3–15.

Milroy, Lesley & Matthew Gordon. 2003. *Sociolinguistics: Method and interpretation.* Oxford: Blackwell Publishing.

Ministry of Education and Culture, Jamaica. 1999. *Revised primary curriculum.* Government of Jamaica/Inter-American Development Bank, Primary Education Improvement Programme.

Moag, Rodney. 1982. The life cycle of non-native Englishes: A case study. In Braj Kachru (ed.), *The other tongue: English across cultures*, 270–288. Urbana: University of Illinois Press.

Mufwene, Salikoko. 1996. The founder principle in Creole genesis. *Diachronica* 13. 83–134.

Mufwene, Salikoko. 2001. *The ecology of language evolution.* Cambridge: Cambridge University Press.

Mugglestone, Lynda. 1995. *'Talking proper': The rise of accent as social symbol.* Oxford: Clarendon Press.

Mühleisen, Susanne. 2002. *Creole discourse* (Creole Language Library 24). Amsterdam: John Benjamins Publishing Company.

Nair-Venugopal, Shanta. 2001. The sociolinguistics of choice in Malaysian business settings. *International Journal of the Sociology of Language* 152. 21–52.

Nettleford, Rex. 1970. *Mirror, mirror.* Jamaica: William Collins & Sangster's Ltd.

Nettleford, Rex. 1972. *Identity, race and protest in Jamaica.* New York: William Morrow & Company.

Neu, Helene. 1980. Ranking of constraints on /t,d/ deletion in American English: A statistical analysis. In William Labov (ed.), *Locating language in time and space*, 37–54. New York: Academic Press.

Nichols, Patricia. 1983. Linguistic options and choices for Black women in the rural South. In Barrie Thorne, Cheris Kramarae & Nancy Henley (eds.), *Language, gender and society.* Rowley, MA: Newbury House.

Paolillo, John. 1997. Sinhala diglossia: Discrete or continuous variation? *Language in Society* 26. 269–296.

Patrick, Peter. 1997. Style and register in Jamaican Patwa. In Edgar Schneider (ed.), *Englishes around the world 2.* 41–55. Amsterdam: John Benjamins Publishing Company.

Patrick, Peter. 1999. *Urban Jamaican Creole.* Philadelphia: John Benjamins Publishing Company.

Patrick, Peter. 2000. Social status and mobility in urban Jamaican Patwa. In *Proceedings of the 13th biennial conference of the Society for Caribbean Linguistics.* Kingston, Jamaica: University of the West Indies.

Patrick, Peter. 2002. Caribbean Creoles and the speech community. *Society for Caribbean Linguistics Occasional Papers* 30.

Patterson, Orlando. 1973. *The sociology of slavery.* London: Associated University Press.

Pegge, Samuel. 1814. *Anecdotes of the English language: Chiefly regarding the local dialect of London and its environs.* London: Nichols, son, & Bentley.

Planning Institute of Jamaica (PIOJ). 2000. *Jamaica: Human development report 2000.* Kingston: PIOJ.

Pollard, Velma. 1998. The lexicon of dread talk in standard Jamaican English. In Velma Pollard Pauline Christie Barbara Lalla & Lawrence Carrington (eds.), *Studies in Caribbean language II.* 178–196. St. Augustine: Society for Caribbean Linguistics.

Preston, Dennis. 1989. *Sociolinguistics and second language acquisition.* Oxford: Blackwell.

Pyles, Thomas & John Algeo. 1993. *The origins and development of the English language.* Fort Worth: Harcourt Brace Jovanovich.

Rickford, John. 1987. *Dimensions of a Creole continuum.* Stanford: Stanford University Press.

References

Rickford, John & Faye McNair-Knox. 1994. Addressee- and topic- influenced styleshift: A quantitative sociolinguistic study. In Douglas Biber & Edward Finegan (eds.), *Sociolinguistic perspectives on register*, 235–276. Oxford: Oxford University Press.

Roberts, Peter. 1988. *West Indians & their language*. Cambridge: Cambridge University Press.

Romaine, Suzanne. 2001. Contact with other languages. In John Algeo (ed.), *The Cambridge history of the English language, vol. VI, English in North America*, 59–85. Cambridge: Cambridge University Press.

Sahgal, Anju & Rama Kant Agnihotri. 1985. Syntax: The common bond. Acceptability of syntactic deviances in Indian English. *English World-Wide* 6(1). 117–129.

Santa Ana, Otto. 1991. *Phonetic simplification processes in the English of the Barrio: A cross-generational sociolinguistic study of the Chicanos of Los Angeles*. University of Pennsylvania dissertation.

Schneider, Edgar. 1998. Negation patterns and the cline of Creoleness in English-oriented varieties in the Caribbean. In Velma Pollard Pauline Christie Barbara Lalla & Lawrence Carrington (eds.), *Studies in Caribbean language II*. 204–227. St. Augustine: Society for Caribbean Linguistics.

Scollon, Ron. 1997. Handbills, tissues and condoms: A site of engagement for the construction of identity in public discourse. *Journal of Sociolinguistics* 1(1). 39–61.

Sealey, Alison & Bob Carter. 2001. Social categories and sociolinguistics: Applying a realist approach. *International Journal of the Sociology of Language* 152. 1–19.

Sharwood-Smith, Michael. 1999. British shibboleths. In Eddie Ronowicz & Colin Yallop (eds.), *English: One language, different cultures*, 46–82. London: Cassell.

Sherlock, Philip & Hazel Bennett. 1998. *The story of the Jamaican people*. Kingston: Ian Randle Publishers.

Shields-Brodber, Kathryn. 1996. Old skeleton, new skin: The relationship between open syllable structure and consonant clusters in Standard Jamaican English. In Pauline Christie (ed.), *Caribbean language issues, old and new*, 4–11. Kingston: Caribbean University Press.

Shields-Brodber, Kathryn. 1997. Requiem for English in an "English-speaking" community: The case of Jamaica. In Edgar Schneider (ed.), *Englishes around the world 2*, 57–67. Amsterdam: John Benjamins Publishing Company.

Shields-Brodber, Kathryn. 1998. Hens can crow too: The female voice of authority on air in Jamaica. In Pauline Christie, Barbara Lalla, Velma Pollard & Lawrence

Carrington (eds.), *Studies in Caribbean language II*, 187–203. St. Augustine: Society for Caribbean Linguistics.

Shields, Kathryn. 1984. *The significance of word-final t/d consonant clusters for syllable structuring in Standard Jamaican English*. Paper presented at the 5th biennial meeting for the Society for Caribbean Linguistics, 1984, Kingston, University of the West Indies (Mona), August 29–September 1.

Shields, Kathryn. 1987. *Language variation in the classroom* dissertation. D. Phil. Dissertation, University of the West Indies (Mona).

Silverstein, Michael. 1996. Monoglot "standard" in America: Standardization and metaphors of linguistic hegemony. In Donald Brenneis & Ronald Macauley (eds.), *The matrix of language: Contemporary linguistic anthropology*, 284–306. Boulder: Westview Press.

Silverstein, Michael. 1998. Contemporary transformations of local linguistic communities. *Annual Reviews of Anthropology* 27. 401–426.

Silverstein, Michael. 2000. Whorfianism and the linguistic imagination of nationality. In Paul Kroskrity (ed.), *Regimes of language*, 85–138. New Mexico: School of American Research Press.

STATIN. 1991. *Population census*. Vol. 1. Kingston: Statistical Institute of Jamaica.

Stewart, Michele. 2002. *The emergence of basilectal varieties in kingston*. Manuscript, Department of Language, Linguistics & Philosophy, University of the West Indies (Mona).

Stewart, William A. 1965. Urban Negro speech: Sociolinguistic factors affecting English teaching. In Roger Shuy, Alva Davis & Robert Hogan (eds.), *Social dialects and language learning: Proceedings of the Bloomington, Indiana conference 1964*, 10–19. National Council of Teachers of English.

Stone, Carl. 1980. *Democracy and clientelism*. New Jersey: Transactions Inc.

Strevens, Peter. 1982. The localized forms of English. In Braj Kachru (ed.), *The other tongue: English across cultures*, 23–30. Urbana: University of Illinois Press.

Taylor, Frank. 1971. *The foundation of the Jamaica tourist industry (up to 1914)*. University of the West Indies (Mona) MA thesis.

Taylor, Frank. 1993. *To hell with paradise: A history of the Jamaica tourist industry*. Pittsburgh: University of Pittsburgh Press.

Thakerar, Jitendra & Howard Giles. 1981. They are – so they speak: Noncontent speech stereotypes. *Language and Communication* 1. 251–256.

Thakerar, Jitendra, Howard Giles & Jenny Cheshire. 1982. Psychological and linguistic parameters of speech accommodation theory. In Colin Fraser & Klaus Scherer (eds.), *Advances in the social psychology of language*, 205–255. Cambridge: Cambridge University Press.

References

Thaxter, Kenneth. 1977. *Language variation in a Jamaican training college.* University of the West Indies (Mona) MA thesis.

Trudgill, Peter. 1972. Sex, covert prestige and linguistic change in the urban British English of Norwich. *Language in Society* 1. 179–195.

Trudgill, Peter. 1978. *Sociolinguistic patterns in British English.* London: Edward Arnold.

Trudgill, Peter. 1986. *Dialects in contact.* Oxford: Blackwell.

Trudgill, Peter. 1999. Standard English: What it isn't. In Tony Bex & Richard Watts (eds.), *Standard English: The widening debate*, 117–128. London: Routledge.

Trudgill, Peter. 2002. *Sociolinguistic variation and change.* Washington DC: Georgetown University Press.

Trudgill, Peter & Jean Hannah. 1994. *International English.* London: Edward Arnold.

Walker, John. 1781. *A rhetorical grammar.* London.

Walters, Keith. 1996. Gender, identity and the political economy of language use: Anglophone wives in Tunisia. *Language in Society* 25. 515–555.

Watt, Dominic. 2000. Phonetic parallels between the close-mid vowels of Tyneside English: Are they internally or externally motivated? *Language Variation and Change* 12(1). 69–101.

Wells, John C. 1973. *Jamaican pronunciation in London.* Oxford: Basil Blackwell.

Wells, John C. 1982a. *Accents of English 1: An introduction.* Cambridge: Cambridge University Press.

Wells, John C. 1982b. *Accents of English 2: The British Isles.* Cambridge: Cambridge University Press.

Wells, John C. 1982c. *Accents of English 3: Beyond the British Isles.* Cambridge: Cambridge University Press.

Williams, Eric. 1970. *From Columbus to Castro. The history of the Caribbean 1492–1969.* New York: Vintage Books.

Wilmot, Swithin. 2002. From bondage to political office: Blacks and vestry politics in two Jamaican parishes, Kingston and St. David, 1831–1865. In Kathleen Monteith & Glen Richards (eds.), *Jamaica in slavery and freedom: History, heritage and culture*, 307–323. Kingston: University of the West Indies Press.

Winford, Donald. 1985. The concept of "diglossia" in Caribbean Creole situations. *Language in Society* 14. 345–356.

Winford, Donald. 1991. The Caribbean. In Jenny Cheshire (ed.), *English around the world*, 565–584. Cambridge: Cambridge University Press.

Winford, Donald. 1997. Re-examining Caribbean English Creole continua. *World Englishes 16* 2. 233–279.

Witter, Michael & George Beckford. 1980. *Small garden, bitter weed.* Morant Bay: Maroon Publishing House.

Wolfram, Walt & Natalie Schilling-Estes. 1998. *American English.* Oxford: Basil Blackwell.

Wolfson, Nessa. 1976. Speech events and natural speech: Some implications for sociolinguistic methodology. *Language in Society* 5. 189–209.

Wright, Philip (ed.). 2002. *Lady Nugent's journal of her residence in Jamaica from 1801 to 1805.* Kingston: The University of the West Indies Press.

Yallop, Colin. 1999. English around the world. In Eddie Ronowicz & Colin Yallop (eds.), *English: One language, different cultures,* 26–45. London: Cassell.

Young, Colville. 1973. *Belize creole: A study of the creolized English spoken in the city of Belize, in its cultural and social setting.* University of York D.Phil. dissertation.

Name index

Agnihotri, Rama Kant, 30
Akers, Glen, 3–5, 34, 35, 39, 41, 43, 45, 52, 55
Algeo, John, 39
Alleyne, Mervyn C., 1, 34, 43, 110
Allsopp, Richard, 2, 13, 39, 60, 111
Alvesson, Mats, 139
Auger, Julie, 109
Austin, Diane, 126, 148

Bailey, Beryl, 1, 3–5
Barrow, Steve, 129
Baugh, Albert, 40
Beal, Joan, 37, 41, 42, 51, 53
Beckford, George, 139
Beckford-Wassink, Alicia, 13, 17, 22, 27, 32, 34, 41, 43, 46, 52, 53, 81, 84, 96, 157
Beckles, Hilary, 38
Bell, Allan, 26, 27
Bennett, Hazel, 38
Bickerton, Derek, 1, 3, 6
Bobda, Augustin Simo, 109
Bourdieu, Pierre, 13, 21
Brereton, Bridget, 10
Brodber, Kathryn, 47, 49, 97
Bryan, Patrick, 10, 11, 93
Busby, Margaret, 10

Cable, Thomas, 40
Campbell, Carl, 51
Carmichael, A.C., 10

Carpenter, Joseph E., 48
Carter, Bob, 121
Cassidy, Frederic, 34, 35, 37, 39, 43, 45, 46, 110
Chaudenson, Robert, 1, 2
Cheshire, Jenny, 5, 15, 20
Christie, Pauline, 21, 43, 48, 103, 111, 122
Coye, Dale, 52
Craig, Dennis, 21
Crompton, Rosemary, 92

D'Costa, Jean, 7, 9, 10, 38, 42
Dalton, Peter, 129
DeCamp, David, 1, 3
Deuchar, Margaret, 80
Devonish, Hubert, 1, 4, 34, 35, 41, 43, 56, 60, 117, 118
Dubois, Sylvie, 117
Dyer, Judy, 17, 22, 27, 46, 157

Ervin-Tripp, Susan, 117
Escure, Genevieve, 3, 5–8, 117

Fisher, John H, 11, 51
Freeborn, Dennis, 41, 43, 51

Gal, Susan, 4
Gbedemah, G., 19
Giegerich, Heinz, 48
Giles, Howard, 22, 86
Gimson, A. C., 40
Gordon, Derek, 78

Gordon, Matthew, 26, 27
Graff, David, 27
Green, Lisa, 117
Gupta, Anthea, 15, 31
Guy, Gregory, 54

Hancock, Ian, 51
Hannah, Jean, 40, 48
Harry, Otelemate, 4, 117, 118
Hewitt, Roger, 31
Ho, Mian-Lian, 15
Holm, John, 110
Holmes, Janet, 86
Horvath, Barbara, 117, 138
Hudson, Richard, 30
Hymes, Dell, 14

Irvine, Alison, 17, 45, 53, 75, 81, 139
Irvine, Judith, 4

Janda, Richard, 109
Jenkins, R, 137
Judd, Karen, 9

Kachru, Braj, 11, 13
Kirwin, William, 38
Krapp, George Philip, 38
Kroskrity, Paul, 4
Kulick, Don, 146

Labov, William, 14, 31, 33, 54, 56, 58, 70, 80, 100, 109, 117
Lalla, Barbara, 7, 9, 10, 38, 42
Le Page, Robert, 1, 2, 12, 14, 19, 34, 35, 37, 39, 43, 45, 46, 56, 81, 87, 129
Lehmann, Winfred, 51
Lewis, Gordon, 139
Lippi-Green, Rosina, 13, 20, 30
Long, Edward, 10

McArthur, Tom, 2, 14, 20
McNair-Knox, Faye, 26
Meade, Rocky R., 5, 34, 35, 39, 41, 43, 55
Miller, Errol, 12, 63, 78, 102
Miller, Faye, 13, 39, 45, 53, 81, 96
Milroy, James, 4, 15, 97
Milroy, Lesley, 15, 26, 27, 31, 80, 97
Moag, Rodney, 11
Mufwene, Salikoko, 1, 4, 11, 38, 74
Mugglestone, Lynda, 31, 37, 41, 45, 47, 56, 59, 96

Nair-Venugopal, Shanta, 31
Nettleford, Rex, 93, 139
Neu, Helene, 54, 58, 90
Nichols, Patricia, 80

Paolillo, John, 117
Patrick, Peter, 4, 6, 36, 41, 45, 54, 55, 90, 97, 103, 158
Patterson, Orlando, 11
Pegge, Samuel, 56
Platt, John, 15
Pollard, Velma, 13
Powesland, Peter, 86
Preston, Dennis, 109
Pyles, Thomas, 39

Rickford, John, 12, 14, 15, 26, 31
Roberts, Peter, 37
Romaine, Suzanne, 9

Sahgal, Anju, 30
Sankoff, David, 138
Santa Ana, Otto, 54
Schilling-Estes, Natalie, 158
Schneider, Edgar, 5
Sealey, Alison, 121
Seiler, Walter, 34, 35, 41, 43

Sharwood-Smith, Michael, 20
Sherlock, Philip, 38
Shields, Kathryn, 18, 51, 55
Shields-Brodber, Kathryn, 21, 48, 86,
        106
Silverstein, Michael, 20, 21, 31, 75,
        109, 118, 124, 159
Stewart, Michele, 10
Stewart, William A., 2
Stone, Carl, 93
Strevens, Peter, 11

Taylor, Frank, 122, 123
Thakerar, Jitendra, 22, 63
Thaxter, Kenneth, 13, 31, 39
Trudgill, Peter, 15, 31, 40, 48, 51, 63,
        80, 86, 109

Walker, John, 45
Walters, Keith, 80
Watt, Dominic, 118
Wells, John C., 4, 33–35, 37, 39, 41, 43,
        45, 47, 52, 53
Williams, Eric, 102
Wilmot, Swithin, 12
Winford, Donald, 1, 4, 12, 17, 58, 152
Witter, Michael, 139
Wolfram, Walt, 158
Wolfson, Nessa, 14, 26
Wright, Philip, 42

Yallop, Colin, 60
Young, Colville, 9, 26, 39

Subject index

accent, 15, 22, 31, 34, 47, 60, 125, 128

acrolect, 2–9, 11–14, 16–18, 24, 29, 32–34, 39, 41, 52, 54, 55[11], 60, 63, 81, 84, 118, 148, 149, 152, 153, 157, 158, 160

adoptive, 47–49

affricate, 49–52, 59, 73, 74, 74[7], 89, 99, 110, 112, 113, 143, 152, 154

age, 16, 70, 101–106, 109, 114, 117, 137, 140, 154–156

   see also age cohorts

age cohorts, 105–109

AJE, 13, 16, 39, 45

alveolar stop, 39, 41, 49, 52

alveopalatal affricate, 33, 110

   see also culture type word

American English, 20, 53[10], 117

architecture, 115

back diphthong, 68, 105, 118, 141, 146, 154

   see also front diphthong

Barbados, 1

basilect, 2–6, 12, 18, 34, 41, 52, 55[11], 84, 160

   see also linguistic continuum

basilectalization, 1

BBC, 8, 20, 130

   see also mid vowel

Belize, 1, 7–9, 11[5], 21, 26[8]

Belizean, 8, 39

butter type words, 88

Canadian, 5, 34, 38, 128, 129

careful speech, 43, 44, 48, 57, 117

cluster simplification, 47, 56, 57, 92, 116

   see also word-final clusters

colonial period, 12, 40, 106

   see also frontline staff,

   see also senior management

Creole, 1–7, 10, 10[3], 10[4], 16–19, 21–23, 23[7], 24, 31, 38, 39, 41–43, 45–47, 49–51, 51[9], 52, 55, 56, 59, 68–74, 74[7], 75, 76[8], 78, 82, 84–86, 88, 95, 96, 98, 100, 101, 103, 105, 106, 108, 111–116, 124, 129–131, 140–142, 146, 150, 152, 155, 157–160

data collection, 24, 79, 136

decreolization, 1, 7, 12, 15, 149, 160

diglossia, 117, 155

diphthong use, 105, 142

education level, 76, 88, 104

   see also education type

endonormative approach, 32, 113, 146, 149

female speech, 16, 45, 84, 85, 88, 89, 99, 113, 148, 157
    see also gender
formal speech, 13, 26, 27, 33, 40, 45, 50, 58, 70, 81, 87[10], 97, 117
    see also careful speech
front diphthong, 47, 104, 105, 142, 154
    see also front vowel,
    see also mid vowel
front vowel, 44, 84, 111, 116
frontline staff, 67, 132, 133, 135, 136, 139, 140, 142–144, 146, 148, 153, 159

gender, 11, 16, 26, 43, 54, 60, 69, 78, 79, 79[9], 80, 82, 84, 87–90, 92, 95–99, 101, 105, 108, 112, 114, 117, 134, 140, 143, 146, 154–157, 162
General American, 9, 20, 48, 123, 149
glottal fricative, 32, 35, 110, 114, 153
    see also h-drop
good English, 50, 75, 80, 103, 113, 140, 144, 146, 158, 159
    see also local standard
group affiliation, 117, 154
Guyana, 1, 11[5], 15, 97[12]
Guyanese, 12, 14, 15, 31

h-drop, 37, 38, 66, 69, 70, 95, 118, 144, 146, 147, 159
    see also hypercorrection
hypercorrection, 38, 39, 41, 47[7], 58, 74, 109–114, 152, 160
    see also qualitative hypercorrection

IAE, 13, 21, 36, 42, 117
idiolect, 108

implicational scale, 5, 52
implicational scales, 13
interdental fricative, 5, 39, 74, 82, 117

Jamaican continuum, 5, 18, 33, 34, 52, 96
Jamaican Creole, 18, 35, 38, 41, 51, 51[9], 52, 60, 76[8], 129, 156, 160
Jamaican social context, 14, 24, 127, 155, 158, 160
Jamaican speech community, 24, 42, 112, 149, 153
JAMPRO, 23, 24, 26–34, 38, 39, 42, 44, 47–50, 53, 58, 64, 65, 65[4], 66[5], 69, 78, 79, 86, 89, 90, 99, 101–105, 109, 110, 119, 121, 122, 126–129, 131, 132, 134–137, 139, 140, 144, 146, 148, 150, 152, 155, 157, 159, 161, 162
JE, 24, 33–36, 42, 44–51, 51[9], 52–54, 55[11], 56, 58, 59, 61, 69–73, 75, 82, 88–90, 92, 94–99, 101, 103, 105, 106, 109–119, 132, 139–144, 146, 149, 150, 152, 154, 155, 157–160
JIDC, 126, 126[3], 128, 129, 162
JNEC, 126, 126[3], 162
JNIP, 126, 126[3], 162
JSA, 162
JTB, 122, 123, 125, 129

Kingston, 10, 12, 16, 17, 19, 22, 24, 36, 38, 78, 84, 130

Lady Nugent, 9, 42
language acquisition, 3, 34, 159
language contact, 1, 3, 9, 11[5], 39
linguistic continuum, 1, 149, 155, 157, 158

literary standard, 15, 31, 34
load-bearing, 115
load-bearing variable, 155, 156
local standard, 3, 4, 18, 34, 81, 149, 152, 158
long vowel, 45, 46, 58, 85, 116
low back vowel, 68
low central vowel, 32, 41, 45, 53, 114, 153
    see also low back vowel
low vowel, 41, 59, 69, 95, 103, 112, 140

Malaysia, 31
mesolect, 1, 34, 55, 55[11]
metropolitan norm, 59, 73
    see also MSE
Ministry of Education, 18, 63
morphophonemic cluster, 114, 153
    see also phonological cluster
MSE, 4–10, 13, 16–19, 21, 21[6], 24, 43, 45, 49–51, 59, 72, 73, 81, 103, 142, 146, 149, 152, 153, 158

native speaker, 8, 9
    see also non-native English
NBC, 20
Niger-Congo, 1
non-native English, 8, 11

occupation, 92
official language, 9, 125, 129, 130
orthography, 37, 47, 50

palatal glide, 45, 46, 96[11], 97
parent's background, 53, 150, 152
patois, 123, 125, 129–131, 158
phonological cluster, 54, 89
PJS, 34, 68, 74, 85, 86, 88

    see also implicational scales
prestige form, 85, 90, 101, 109, 112, 113
    see also acrolect
prestige norm, 52, 106, 107
    see also local standard
prestige variety, 6, 74, 80, 81

qualitative hypercorrection, 109, 116, 144
quantitative hypercorrection, 70, 75, 109
    see also prestige variety

race, 63[1], 134, 138, 139
    see also skin colour
retroflexion, 12, 48, 86, 88
rhoticity, 17, 32, 33, 47, 48, 52, 53, 53[10], 59, 74, 75, 78, 89, 92, 98, 100, 107–109, 111, 112, 114, 115, 117, 118, 143, 153, 154
    see also post-vocalic rhoticity
RP, 10, 12, 15, 18, 20, 31, 47, 48[7], 51, 109, 129, 130, 149
    see also British Standard English

senior management, 29, 30, 66, 79, 126, 128, 132, 133, 136, 140, 157, 161
Sinhala, 117
SJE, 6, 13, 14, 18, 19, 21, 23, 24, 26, 27, 30, 34, 55, 56, 60, 61, 63, 64, 97, 108, 114, 117, 148–150, 152–160
skin colour, 63[1], 134, 139, 140
socio-economic class, 13, 16, 81
    see also some other term also of interest

speaky-spoky, 36, 41

spelling pronunciation, 47, 48, 50, 52

spirantization, 50

Standard English, 2, 4, 7, 8, 13–15, 21, 24, 26[8], 28, 29, 34, 80, 81, 130, 131, 146, 148, 149, 159

standard variety, 8, 47[6], 63, 80, 131

style shift, 80, 117, 154

tense marking, 32, 54, 55, 58, 90
    see also interdental fricative

Trinidad, 1, 51, 58, 97[12]

Trinidadian, 32

velar stop, 32, 35, 46, 74, 114, 116, 118, 141, 153

vernacular, 3, 7, 9, 10, 17, 24, 33, 47, 74, 97, 109, 112

voiced interdental fricative, 27

voiceless interdental fricative, 32, 114, 116, 118, 153
    see also hypercorrection,
    see also th stopping

vowel inventory, 34

word-final clusters, 54

www.ingramcontent.com/pod-product-compliance
Lightning Source LLC
Chambersburg PA
CBHW080914100426

42812CB00007B/2270